SCHAUM'S OUTLINE OF

THEORY AND PROBLEMS

OF

BOOKKEEPING·
and
ACCOUNTING
Second Edition

•

BY

JOEL J. LERNER, M.S., P.D.
Chairman, Faculty of Business
Sullivan County Community College

•

SCHAUM'S OUTLINE SERIES
McGRAW-HILL BOOK COMPANY

New York St. Louis San Francisco Auckland Bogotá Hamburg London
Madrid Mexico Milan Montreal New Delhi Panama Paris
São Paulo Singapore Sydney Tokyo Toronto

JOEL J. LERNER is Professor and Chairman of the Business Division at Sullivan County Community College, Loch Sheldrake, New York. He received his B.S. from New York University and his M.S. and P.D. from Columbia University. Professor Lerner has published a booklet for *The New York Times* on teaching college business courses and has acted as editor for both *Readings in Business Organization and Management* and *Introduction to Business: A Contemporary Reader*. He has coauthored the Schaum's Outlines of *Accounting I*, *Accounting II*, *Intermediate Accounting I*, and *Business Mathematics* and is the sole author of *Introduction to Business Organization and Management*. He is the president of MASTCA Publishing Corp. and is the editor of ''The Middle/Fixed Income Letter,'' a monthly financial publication.

Schaum's Outline of Theory and Problems of
BOOKKEEPING AND ACCOUNTING

1 2 3 4 5 6 7 8 9 10 11 12 13 14 15 16 17 18 19 20 SHP SHP 8 9 2 1 0 9 8 7

ISBN 0-07-037231-4

Sponsoring Editor, John Aliano
Production Supervisor, Joe Campanella
Editing Supervisor, Marthe Grice

Library of Congress Cataloging-in-Publication Data

Lerner, Joel J.
  Schaum's outline of theory and problems of
bookkeeping and accounting.

  (Schaum's outline series)
  Rev. ed. of: Schaum's outline of theory and
problems of bookkeeping and accounting. © 1978.
  Includes index.
  1. Bookkeeping—Problems, exercises, etc.
2. Accounting—Problems, exercises, etc. I. Lerner,
Joel J. Schaum's outline of theory and problems of
bookkeeping and accounting. II. Title.
HF5661.L46 1987   657'.076   87-3800
ISBN 0-07-037231-4

Preface

This volume brings to the study of bookkeeping and accounting the same solved-problems approach that has proved so successful in the disciplines of engineering, mathematics, and accounting. In contrast to previous supplementary materials, which have been little more than summary textbooks, this book is organized around the practical application of basic bookkeeping and accounting concepts. By providing

1. Concise definitions and explanations, in easily understood terms,

2. Fully worked-out solutions to a large range of problems (against which students can check their own solutions),

3. Review questions,

4. Sample examinations typical of those used by high schools and 2- and 4-year colleges,

this book develops the student's ability to understand and solve bookkeeping and accounting problems.

I am grateful to Carl Klein for his assistance with certain sections of the manuscript and for the patience of my wife Anita, and my three children, Marc, Steven, and Caren.

JOEL J. LERNER

Contents

CONTENTS

CONTENTS

CONTENTS

Chapter 1

Assets, Liabilities, and Capital

1.1 NATURE OF BOOKKEEPING AND ACCOUNTING

An understanding of the principles of bookkeeping and accounting is essential for anyone who is interested in a successful career in business. The purpose of bookkeeping and accounting is to provide information concerning the financial affairs of a business. This information is needed by owners, managers, creditors, and governmental agencies.

An individual who earns a living by recording the financial activities of a business is known as a bookkeeper, while the process of classifying and summarizing business transactions and interpreting their effects is accomplished by the accountant. The bookkeeper is concerned with techniques involving the recording of transactions, and the accountant's objective is the use of data for interpretation. Bookkeeping and accounting techniques both will be discussed.

1.2 BASIC ELEMENTS OF FINANCIAL POSITION:
THE ACCOUNTING EQUATION

The financial condition or position of a business enterprise is represented by the relationship of assets to liabilities and capital.

Assets. Properties that are owned and have money value; for instance, cash, inventory, buildings, equipment.

Liabilities. Amounts owed to outsiders, such as notes payable, accounts payable, bonds payable. Liabilities may also include certain deferred items, such as income taxes to be allocated.

Capital. The interest of the owners in an enterprise. Also known as owners' equity.

These three basic elements are connected by a fundamental relationship called *the accounting equation.* This equation expresses the equality of the assets on one side with the claims of the creditors and owners on the other side:

$$\text{Assets} = \text{Liabilities} + \text{Capital}$$

According to the accounting equation, a firm is assumed to possess its assets subject to the rights of the creditors and owners.

EXAMPLE 1

Assume that a business owned assets of $100,000, owed creditors $80,000, and owed the owner $20,000. The accounting equation would be:

Assets	=	Liabilities	+	Capital
$100,000	=	$80,000	+	$20,000

Suppose that $6,000 was used to reduce liabilities and the balance remained in assets. The equation would then be:

Assets	=	Liabilities	+	Capital
$94,000	=	$74,000	+	$20,000

We shall call any business event that alters the amount of assets, liabilities, or capital a *transaction*. In Example 1, the net changes in asset groups were discussed; in Example 2, we show how the accountant

1

makes a meaningful record of a series of transactions, reconciling them step by step with the accounting equation.

EXAMPLE 2

During the month of January, Ted Drew, Lawyer,

(1) Invested $4,000 to open his practice.

(2) Bought supplies (stationery, forms, pencils, and so on) for cash, $300.

(3) Bought office furniture from Robinson Furniture Company on account, $2,000.

(4) Received $2,500 in fees earned during the month.

(5) Paid office rent for January, $500.

(6) Paid salary for part-time help, $200.

(7) Paid $1,200 to Robinson Furniture Company on account.

(8) After taking an inventory at the end of the month, Drew found that he had used $200 worth of supplies.

(9) Withdrew $400 for personal use.

These transactions might be analyzed and recorded as follows:

Transaction (1). Mr. Drew invested $4,000 to open his practice. There are two accounts that are affected: the asset Cash is increased, and the capital of the firm is increased by the same amount.

Assets	=	Liabilities	+	Capital
Cash				T. Drew, Capital
(1) +$4,000	=		+	+$4,000

Transaction (2). Bought supplies for cash, $300. In this case, Mr. Drew is substituting one asset for another; he is receiving (+) the asset Supplies and paying out (−) the asset Cash. Note that the capital of $4,000 remains unchanged.

Assets			=	Liabilities	+	Capital
Cash	+	Supplies				T. Drew, Capital
$4,000						$4,000
(2) −300		+$300				
$3,700	+	$300	=		+	$4,000

Transaction (3). Bought office furniture from Robinson Furniture Company on account, $2,000. Mr. Drew is receiving the asset Furniture but is not paying for it with the asset Cash. Instead, he will owe the money to the Robinson Furniture Company. Therefore, he is liable for this amount in the future, thus creating the liability Accounts Payable.

Assets					=	Liabilities	+	Capital
Cash	+	Supplies	+	Furniture		Accounts Payable		T. Drew, Capital
$3,700		$300						$4,000
(3)				+$2,000		+$2,000		
$3,700	+	$300	+	$2,000	=	$2,000	+	$4,000

Transaction (4). Received $2,500 in fees earned during the month. Because Mr. Drew received $2,500, the asset Cash increased, and also his capital increased. It is important to note that he labels the $2,500 *fees income* to show its origin.

Assets					=	Liabilities	+	Capital
Cash	+	Supplies	+	Furniture		Accounts Payable		T. Drew, Capital
$3,700		$300		$2,000		$2,000		$4,000
(4) +2,500								+2,500 Fees Income
$6,200	+	$300	=	$2,000	=	$2,000	+	$6,500

Transaction (5). Paid office rent for January, $500. When the word "paid" is stated, you know it means a deduction from Cash, since Mr. Drew is paying out his asset Cash. Payment of expense is a reduction of capital. It is termed *rent expense*.

	Assets			=	Liabilities	+	Capital
	Cash	+ Supplies	+ Furniture		Accounts Payable		T. Drew, Capital
	$6,200	$300	$2,000		$2,000		$6,500
(5)	−500						−500 Rent Expense
	$5,700	+ $300	+ $2,000	=	$2,000	+	$6,000

Transaction (6). Paid salary for part-time help, $200. Again the word "paid" means a deduction of cash and a reduction in capital. This time it refers to *salaries expense*.

	Assets			=	Liabilities	+	Capital
	Cash	+ Supplies	+ Furniture		Accounts Payable		T. Drew, Capital
	$5,700	$300	$2,000		$2,000		$6,000
(6)	−200						−200 Salaries Expense
	$5,500	+ $300	+ $2,000	=	$2,000	+	$5,800

Transaction (7). Paid $1,200 to Robinson Furniture Company on account. Here Mr. Drew is reducing the asset Cash because he is paying $1,200, and he is also reducing the liability Accounts Payable. He will now owe $1,200 less.

	Assets			=	Liabilities	+	Capital
	Cash	+ Supplies	+ Furniture		Accounts Payable		T. Drew, Capital
	$5,500	$300	$2,000		$2,000		$5,800
(7)	−1,200				−1,200		
	$4,300	+ $300	+ $2,000	=	$ 800	+	$5,800

Transaction (8). After taking an inventory at the end of the month, Mr. Drew found that he had used $200 worth of supplies. The original amount of supplies purchased has been reduced to the amount that was found to be left at the end of the month. Therefore, the difference was the amount used ($300 − $100 = $200). This reduces the asset Supplies by $200 and reduces capital by the same amount. It is termed *supplies expense*.

	Assets			=	Liabilities	+	Capital
	Cash	+ Supplies	+ Furniture		Accounts Payable		T. Drew, Capital
	$4,300	$300	$2,000		$800		$5,800
(8)		−200					−200 Supplies Expense
	$4,300	+ $100	+ $2,000	=	$800	+	$5,600

Transaction (9). Withdrew $400 for personal use. The withdrawal of cash is a reduction not only in Mr. Drew's cash position but also in his capital. This is *not an expense* but a personal withdrawal, a reduction of the amount invested.

	Assets			=	Liabilities	+	Capital
	Cash	+ Supplies	+ Furniture		Accounts Payable		T. Drew, Capital
	$4,300	$100	$2,000		$800		$5,600
(9)	−400						−400 Drawing
	$3,900	+ $100	+ $2,000	=	$800	+	$5,200

T. Drew, Attorney
Month of January 198X

	Cash	+	Supplies	+	Furniture	=	Accounts Payable	+	T. Drew, Capital
	Assets					**=**	**Liabilities**	**+**	**Capital**
(1)	$4,000								$4,000
(2)	−300	+	$300						
	$3,700	+	$300			=			$4,000
(3)					$2,000		$2,000		
	$3,700	+	$300	+	$2,000	=	$2,000	+	$4,000
(4)	+2,500								+2,500 Fees Income
	$6,200	+	$300	+	$2,000	=	$2,000	+	$6,500
(5)	−500								−500 Rent Expense
	$5,700	+	$300	+	$2,000	=	$2,000	+	$6,000
(6)	−200								−200 Salaries Expense
	$5,500	+	$300	+	$2,000	=	$2,000	+	$5,800
(7)	−1,200						−1,200		
	$4,300	+	$300	+	$2,000	=	$800	+	$5,800
(8)			−200						−200 Supplies Expense
	$4,300	+	$100	+	$2,000	=	$800	+	$5,600
(9)	−400								−400 Drawing
	$3,900	+	$100	+	$2,000	=	$800	+	$5,200

Summary

1. The accounting equation is _____ = _____ + _____ .

2. Items owned by a business that have money value are known as _____ .

3. _____ is the interest of the owners in a business.

4. Money owed to an outsider is a _____ .

5. The difference between assets and liabilities is _____ .

6. An investment in the business increases _____ and _____ .

7. To purchase ''on account'' is to create a _____ .

8. When the word "paid" occurs, it means a deduction of _____.

9. Income increases net assets and also _____.

10. A withdrawal of cash reduces cash and _____.

Answers: 1. assets, liabilities, capital; 2. assets; 3. Capital; 4. liability; 5. capital; 6. assets and capital; 7. liability; 8. cash; 9. capital; 10. capital

Solved Problems

1.1 Given any two known elements, the third can easily be computed. Determine the missing amount in each of the accounting equations below.

	Assets	=	Liabilities	+	Capital
(a)	$ 7,200	=	$2,800	+	?
(b)	7,200	=	?	+	$4,400
(c)	?	=	2,800	+	4,400
(d)	20,000	=	5,600	+	?
(e)	18,000	=	?	+	6,000
(f)	?	=	4,280	+	8,420

SOLUTION

	Assets	=	Liabilities	+	Capital
(a)	$ 7,200	=	$2,800	+	$4,400
(b)	7,200	=	2,800	+	4,400
(c)	7,200	=	2,800	+	4,400
(d)	20,000	=	5,600	+	14,400
(e)	18,000	=	12,000	+	6,000
(f)	12,700	=	4,280	+	8,420

1.2 Classify each of the following as elements of the accounting equation using the following abbreviations: A = Assets; L = Liabilities; C = Capital.

(a) Cash

(b) Accounts Payable

(c) Owners' Investment

(d) Accounts Receivable

(e) Supplies

(f) Notes Payable

(g) Land

(h) Equipment

SOLUTION

(a)	A	(c)	C	(e)	A	(g)	A
(b)	L	(d)	A	(f)	L	(h)	A

1.3 Determine the effect of the following transactions on capital.

(*a*) Bought machinery on account.

(*b*) Paid the above bill.

(*c*) Withdrew money for personal use.

(*d*) Received fees for services rendered.

(*e*) Bought supplies for cash.

(*f*) Inventory of supplies decreased by the end of the month.

SOLUTION

(*a*) No effect—only the asset (machinery) and liability are affected (accounts payable).

(*b*) No effect—same reason.

(*c*) Decrease in capital—capital is withdrawn.

(*d*) Increase in capital—fees are income that increases capital.

(*e*) No effect—the asset cash is decreased while the asset supplies is increased.

(*f*) Decrease in capital—supplies that are used represent an expense (reduction in capital).

1.4 Determine the net effect of the transactions listed below, using I = increase; D = decrease; NE = no effect.

(*a*) Invested cash in a business.

(*b*) Purchased equipment for cash.

(*c*) Purchased supplies on account.

(*d*) Paid creditors.

(*e*) Borrowed $5,000 from bank.

(*f*) Received fees.

(*g*) Withdrew money for personal use.

	Assets	**=**	**Liabilities**	**+**	**Capital**
(*a*)	_____		_____		_____
(*b*)	_____		_____		_____
(*c*)	_____		_____		_____
(*d*)	_____		_____		_____
(*e*)	_____		_____		_____
(*f*)	_____		_____		_____
(*g*)	_____		_____		_____

SOLUTION

	Assets	**=**	**Liabilities**	**+**	**Capital**
(*a*)	I		NE		I
(*b*)	NE		NE		NE
(*c*)	I		I		NE
(*d*)	D		D		NE
(*e*)	I		I		NE
(*f*)	I		NE		I
(*g*)	D		NE		D

1.5 T. Drew invests in his new firm $8,600 cash, $4,000 worth of supplies, equipment, and machinery valued at $12,000, and a $5,000 note payable based on the equipment and machinery. What is the capital of the firm?

SOLUTION

Assets	=	Liabilities	+	Capital
$ 8,600				
4,000				
12,000				
$24,600	=	$5,000	+	$19,600

1.6 Record the following entry: Bought an automobile for $9,800, paying $3,000 cash and giving a note for the balance.

	Assets	=	Liabilities	+	Capital
	Cash and Equipment		Notes Payable		
Balance	$15,000				$15,000
Entry (?)	3000		_____		_____
Balance (?)	12,00 + 9,8a > 6,8				

SOLUTION

	Assets	=	Liabilities	+	Capital
	Cash and Equipment		Notes Payable		
Balance	$15,000				$15,000
Entry	−3,000 + $9,800		$6,800*		_____
Balance	$12,000 + $9,800		$6,800	+	$15,000

*Total value of auto	$9,800
Less cash deposit	3,000
Amount owed	$6,800

1.7 Record the following entry: The inventory of supplies at the end of the year is valued at $2,200.

	Assets	=	Liabilities	+	Capital
	Supplies				
Balance (Beginning of month)	$6,400	=		+	$6,400
Entry (?)	+2,200				_____
Balance (?) (End of month)	4,260				

SOLUTION

	Assets	=	Liabilities	+	Capital
	Supplies				
Balance					
(Beginning of month)	$6,400			+	$6,400
Entry	−4,200				−4,200 Supplies Expense
Balance	$2,200				$2,200
(End of month)					

Supplies is an asset. Supplies expense ($4,200) represents the amount that has been used. This amount is applied as a reduction in capital.

1.8 The summary data of the Ellery's laundry are presented below. Describe each transaction.

	Assets			=	Liabilities	+	Capital	
	Cash	+ Supplies	+ Machinery	=	Accounts Payable			
(1)	$8,000 +	$4,000 +	$ 5,000			+	$17,000	
(2)	−3,000 +	3,000						
(3)	−2,000 +		9,000		+7,000			
(4)	+9,000					+	9,000	Laundry Income
(5)	−1,200						−1,200	Salaries Expense
(6)		−2,000					−2,000	Supplies Expense
(7)	−7,000				−7,000			
(8)	−1,000						−1,000	Withdrawal
	$2,800	$5,000	$14,000			+	$21,800	

SOLUTION

(1) Invested cash, supplies, and machinery into the firm.

(2) Bought additional supplies for cash.

(3) Bought a $9,000 machine, paying $2,000 down and owing the balance.

(4) Income for the period.

(5) Paid salary expenses.

(6) Supplies inventory was determined.

(7) Paid in full amount owed (see transaction 3).

(8) Owner withdrew cash for personal use.

1.9 Summary financial data of the Rag Time Band Co. for October are presented below in transaction form.

(1) Began operations by depositing $22,000 in a business bank account.

(2) Purchased musical equipment for $10,000, paying $4,000 in cash with the balance on account.

(3) Purchased supplies for cash, $500.

(4) Cash income received for musical engagement, $3,000.

(5) Paid salaries for the month, $1,200.

(6) Paid general expenses, $600.

(7) Paid $1,000 on account.

(8) The inventory of supplies on hand at the end of the month was $200.

Record the transactions and running balances below.

	Assets			=	Liabilities	+	Capital
	Cash	+ Supplies	+ Equipment		Accounts Payable		Rag Time Band Co.
(1)							22,000
(2)	22000						4000
Balance	– 4000						
(3)	18,000		10,000		6,0006		22,000
Balance	500						300
(4)	17500 + 500		10,000		60000		22,000
Balance	300						3000
(5)	20,500 500		10,000		6000		25,000
Balance	1200						1200
(6)	19 300 500		10,000		6000		23800
Balance	600						600
(7)	18,700 500		10,000				1000
Balance	1000						
(8)	17,700 500		10,000		5000		23,200
Balance							300
	200		10,000				22,900

27,900 = 27,900   28,500

SOLUTION

	Assets			=	Liabilities	+	Capital	
	Cash	+ Supplies	+ Equipment		Accounts Payable		Rag Time Band Co.	
(1)	$22,000						$22,000	
(2)	−4,000		+$10,000		+$6,000			
Balance	$18,000		$10,000	=	$6,000	+	$22,000	
(3)	−500	+$500		=				
Balance	$17,500 +	$500	+ $10,000	=	$6,000	+	$22,000	
(4)	+3,000						3,000	Fees Income
Balance	$20,500 +	$500	+ $10,000	=	$6,000	+	$25,000	
(5)	−1,200						−1,200	Salaries Expense
Balance	$19,300 +	$500	+ $10,000	=	$6,000	+	$23,800	
(6)	−600						−600	General Expense
Balance	$18,700 +	$500	+ $10,000	=	$6,000	+	$23,200	
(7)	−1,000					−1,000		
Balance	$17,700 +	$500	+ $10,000	=	$5,000	+	$23,200	
(8)		−300					−300	Supplies Expense
Balance	$17,700 +	$200	+ $10,000	=	$5,000	+	$22,900	

1.10 Robert Lawn has just passed the law exam and started practicing. Below are his first month's transactions.

Jan. 1 Began business by investing $5,000 cash and land with a value of $4,500.
  4 Purchased $750 worth of supplies on account.
  9 Paid rent for the month, $300.
  15 Received $1,100 for legal fees.

Jan. 17 Paid salaries for month, $900.
   21 Purchased printing equipment for $1,000 cash.
   24 Paid $500 on account.
   27 Withdrew $500 for personal expenses.
   29 Made improvements to land, paying $1,500 cash.
   31 Supplies on hand, $400.

Record the transactions and running balances in the form below.

					Liabilities	
Cash	**+ Supplies**	**+ Equipment**	**+ Land**	**=**	**Accounts Payable**	**+ R. Lawn, Capital**
Jan. 1	5000	4500		4500 =		9500
4		750			750	
Balance	5000	750		4500	750	9500
Jan. 9	-300					-300
Balance	4700	750		4500	750	9200
Jan. 15	1100					+1100
Balance	45800	750		4500	750	10300
Jan. 17	-900					-900
Balance	4900	750		4500	750	9400
Jan. 21	1000		1000			
Balance	3900	750	1000	4500	750	9400
Jan. 24	-500				-500	9400
Balance	2400	750	1000	4500	250	9400
Jan. 27	-500					-500
Balance	2900	750	1000	4500	250	8900
Jan. 29	-1500			+1500		
Balance	1400	750	1000	6000	250	8900
Jan. 31	1400	-350				-350
1/31 balance	1400	400	1000	6000 =	250	8850

SOLUTION

					Liabilities	
Cash	**+ Supplies**	**+ Equipment**	**+ Land**	**=**	**Accounts Payable**	**+ R. Lawn, Capital**
Jan. 1	$5,000			$4,500		$9,500
4		+$750			+$750	
Balance	$5,000	$750		$4,500	$750	$9,500
Jan. 9	-300					-300 Rent Expense
Balance	$4,700	$750		$4,500	$750	$9,200
Jan. 15	+1,100					+1,100 Fees Earned
Balance	$5,800	$750		$4,500	$750	$10,300
Jan. 17	-900					-900 Salaries Expense
Balance	$4,900	$750		$4,500	$750	$9,400
Jan. 21	-1,000		+1,000			

	Cash	+ Supplies	+ Equipment	+ Land	Liabilities = Accounts Payable	+ R. Lawn, Capital
Balance	$3,900	$750	$1,000	$4,500	$750	$9,400
Jan. 24	−500				−500	
Balance	$3,400	$750	$1,000	$4,500	$250	$9,400
Jan. 27	−500					−500 Drawing
Balance	$2,900	$750	$1,000	$4,500	$250	$8,900
Jan. 29	−1,500			+1,500		
Balance	$1,400	$750	$1,000	$6,000	$250	$8,900
Jan. 31		−350				−350 Supplies Expense
1/31 balance	$1,400	$400	$1,000	$6,000	$250	$8,550

1.11 Financial information of B. Glatt, Carpenter, for December is presented below.

(1) Began business by investing $14,000 cash and $6,000 equipment in the business.

(2) Bought additional equipment for $2,000 on account.

(3) Purchased supplies, $600, for cash.

(4) Paid $500 to creditor on account.

(5) Received $2,400 in fees earned during the month.

(6) Paid salary of part-time assistant, $300.

(7) Paid general expenses, $400.

(8) Paid balance due on equipment.

(9) Withdrew $700 for personal use.

(10) Cost of supplies used during month, $450.

Enter each transaction in the form below.

	Assets			= Liabilities	+ Capital
	Cash	+ Supplies	+ Equipment	Accounts Payable	B. Glatt, Capital
(1)	14000		6000		20,000
(2)			+ 2000	2000	20,000
Balance	14,000		8000		
(3)	− 600	+ 600	8000	2000	20,00
Balance	13,400	600		500	
(4)	−500			1500	20,000
Balance	12,900	600	8000		2400
(5)	+2400			1500	22400
Balance	15300	600	8000		−300
(6)	−300			1500	28100
Balance	15000	600	8000		−400
(7)	−400			1500	21700
Balance	14600	600	8000	1500	
(8)	−1500			0	21700
	13100	600	8000		21700

8600
13100
21700

	Assets			=	Liabilities	+	Capital
	Cash	+ Supplies	+ Equipment		Accounts Payable		B. Glatt, Capital
Balance	13100	600	8000				21700
(9)	-700						-700
Balance	12400	5600	8000				21000
(10)		-450					-450
Balance	12400	150	8000	✓			20550

SOLUTION

	Assets			=	Liabilities	+	Capital	
	Cash +	Supplies +	Equipment		Accounts Payable		B. Glatt, Capital	
(1)	$14,000		$6,000				$20,000	
(2)			+2,000	=	+$2,000			
Balance	$14,000 +		+ $8,000	=	$2,000	+	$20,000	
(3)	−600	+$600						
Balance	$13,400 +	$600	+ $8,000	=	$2,000	+	$20,000	
(4)	−500				−500			
Balance	$12,900 +	$600	+ $8,000	=	$1,500	+	$20,000	
(5)	+2,400						+2,400	Fees Income
Balance	$15,300 +	$600	+ $8,000	=	$1,500	+	$22,400	
(6)	−300						−300	Salaries Expense
Balance	$15,000 +	$600	+ $8,000	=	$1,500	+	$22,100	
(7)	−400						−400	General Expense
Balance	$14,600 +	$600	+ $8,000	=	$1,500	+	$21,700	
(8)	−1,500				−1,500			
Balance	$13,100 +	$600	+ $8,000	=	—	+	$21,700	
(9)	−700						−700	Drawing
Balance	$12,400 +	$600	+ $8,000	=	—	+	$21,000	
(10)		−450					−450	Supplies Expense
Balance	$12,400 +	$150	+ $8,000	=			$20,550	

1.12 M. Boyd operates a taxi company known as the Boyd Taxi Co. The balances of his accounts as of July 1 of the current year are as follows: cash, $6,400; supplies, $800; automobile, $4,500; accounts payable, $2,000; capital, $9.700. The transactions of the firm during the month of July appear below.

(1) Paid the balance owed to the creditor.

(2) Income (cash) for the month, $8,200.

(3) Paid wages for the month, $1,900.

(4) Paid for advertising, $200.

(5) Purchased an additional used taxi for $5,000, terms half in cash and the balance on account.

(6) Paid $425 for maintenance of automobiles.

(7) Sold $100 of our supplies at cost as an accommodation.

(8) Withdrew $800 for personal use.

(9) Inventory of supplies at the end of the month was $350.

Enter each transaction on the form below.

	Assets					=	Liabilities	+	Capital
	Cash	+	Supplies	+	Automobiles		Accounts Payable		Capital
Balance	$ 6,400		$800		$4,500		$2,000		$ 9,700
(1)						=		+	
Balance									
(2)						=		+	
Balance									
(3)						=		+	
Balance									
(4)						=		+	
Balance									
(5)						=		+	
Balance									
(6)						=		+	
Balance									
(7)						=		+	
Balance									
(8)						=		+	
Balance									
(9)						=		+	
Balance									

SOLUTION

	Assets					=	Liabilities	+	Capital	
	Cash	+	Supplies	+	Automobiles		Accounts Payable		Capital	
Balance	$ 6,400	+	$800	+	$4,500	=	$2,000	+	$ 9,700	
(1)	−2,000						−2,000			
Balance	$ 4,400	+	$800	+	$4,500	=	$ —	+	$ 9,700	
(2)	−8,200								8,200	Fee Income
Balance	$12,600	+	$800	+	$4,500	=	$ —	+	$17,900	
(3)	−1,900								1,900	Wage Expense
Balance	$10,700	+	$800	+	$4,500	=	$ —	+	$16,000	
(4)	−200								−200	Advertising Expense
Balance	$10,500	+	$800	+	$4,500	=	$ —	+	$15,800	
(5)	−2,500				+5,000		+$2,500			
Balance	$ 8,000	+	$800	+	$9,500	=	$2,500	+	$15,800	
(6)	−425								−425	Maintenance Expense
Balance	$ 7,575	+	$800	+	$9,500	=	$2,500	+	$15,375	
(7)	+100		−100							
Balance	$ 7,675	+	$700	+	$9,500	=	$2,500	+	$15,375	
(8)	−800								−800	Drawing
Balance	$ 6,875	+	$700	+	$9,500	=	$2,500	+	$14,575	
(9)			−350						−350	Supplies Expense
Balance	$ 6,875	+	$350	+	$9,500	=	$2,500	+	$14,255	

Chapter 2

Debits and Credits: The Double-Entry System

2.1 INTRODUCTION

Preparing a new equation $A = L + C$ after each transaction would be cumbersome and costly, especially when there are a great many transactions in an accounting period. Also, information for a specific item such as cash would be lost as successive transactions were recorded. This information could be obtained by going back and summarizing the transactions, but that would be very time-consuming.

A much more efficient way is to classify the transactions according to items on the balance sheet and income statement. The increases and decreases are then recorded according to type of item by means of a summary called an *account*.

2.2 THE ACCOUNT

An account may be defined as *a record of the increases, decreases, and balances in an individual item of asset, liability, capital, revenue, or expense.*

The simplest form of the account is known as the "T" account because it resembles the letter "T". The account has three parts (1) the name of the account and the account number, (2) the debit side (left side), and (3) the credit side (right side). The increases are entered on one side, the decreases on the other. The balance (the excess of the total of one side over the total of the other) is inserted near the last figure on the side with the larger account.

Date	Item	Ref.	Debit	Date	Item	Ref.	Credit

Account Title — 1

Account Number — 1

2   3

2.3 DEBITS AND CREDITS

When an amount is entered on the left side of an account, it is a debit, and the account is said to be *debited*. When an amount is entered on the right side, it is a credit, and the account is said to be *credited*. The abbreviations for debit and credit are *Dr.* and *Cr.*, respectively.

Whether an increase in a given item is credited or debited depends on the category of the item. By convention, asset and expense increases are recorded as debits, whereas liability, capital, and income increases are recorded as credits. Asset and expense decreases are recorded as credits, whereas liability, capital, and income decreases are recorded as debits. The following tables summarize the rule.

Assets and Expenses			Liabilities, Capital, and Income	
Dr.	Cr.		Dr.	Cr.
+	−		−	+
(Increases)	(Decreases)		(Decreases)	(Increases)

EXAMPLE 1

Let us reexamine the transactions that occurred in T. Drew's practice during the first month of operation. These are the same as in Chapter 1, except that accounts are now used to record the transactions.

Transaction (1). **Mr. Drew opened his law practice, investing $4,000 in cash.** The two accounts affected are Cash and Capital. Remember that an increase in an asset (cash) is debited, whereas an increase in capital is credited.

	Cash				Capital	
	Dr.	Cr.			Dr.	Cr.
	+	−			−	+
(1)	4,000					4,000	(1)

Transaction (2). **Bought supplies for cash, $300.** Here we are substituting one asset (cash) for another asset (supplies). We debit Supplies because we are receiving more supplies. We credit Cash because we are paying out cash.

	Cash					Supplies	
	Dr.	Cr.				Dr.	Cr.
	+	−				+	−
	4,000	300	(2)	(2)		300	

Transaction (3). **Bought furniture from Robinson Furniture Company on account, $2,000.** We are receiving an asset (equipment) and, therefore, debit Furniture to show the increase. We are not paying cash but creating a new liability, thereby increasing the liability account (Accounts Payable).

	Furniture				Accounts Payable	
	Dr.	Cr.			Dr.	Cr.
	+	−			−	+
(3)	2,000					2,000	(3)

Transaction (4). **Received $2,500 in fees earned during the month.** In this case, we are increasing the asset account Cash, since we have received $2,500. Therefore, we debit it. We are increasing the capital, yet we do not credit Capital. It is better temporarily to separate the income from the owners' equity (capital) and create a new account, Fees Income.

	Cash				Fees Income	
	Dr.	Cr.			Dr.	Cr.
	+	−			−	+
	4,000	300				2,500	(4)
(4)	2,500						

Transaction (5). **Paid office rent for January, $500.** We must decrease the asset account Cash because we are paying out money. Therefore, we credit it. It is preferable to keep expenses separated from the owners' equity. Therefore, we open a new account for the expense involved, Rent Expense. The $500 is entered on the left side, since expense decreases capital.

	Cash				Rent Expense	
	Dr.	Cr.			Dr.	Cr.
	+	−			+	−
	4,000	300		(5)	500	
	2,500	500	(5)			

Transaction (6).   **Paid salary for part-time help, $200.** Again, we must reduce our asset account (Cash) because we are paying out money. Therefore, we credit the account. Drew's capital was reduced by an expense, and we open another account, Salaries Expense. A debit to this account shows the decrease in capital.

Cash				Salaries Expense	
Dr.	Cr.			Dr.	Cr.
+	−			+	−
4,000	300		(6)	200	
2,500	500				
	200	(6)			

Transaction (7).   **Paid $1,200 to Robinson Furniture Company on account.** This transaction reduced our asset account (Cash) since we are paying out money. We therefore credit Cash. We also reduce our liability account (Accounts Payable) by $1,200; we now owe that much less. Thus, we debit Accounts Payable.

Cash				Accounts Payable	
Dr.	Cr.			Dr.	Cr.
+	−			−	+
4,000	300		(7)	1,200	2,000
2,500	500				
	200				
	1,200	(7)			

Transaction (8).   **After taking inventory at the end of the month, Mr. Drew found that he had used $200 worth of supplies.** We must reduce the asset account Supplies by crediting it for $200. Supplies Expense is debited for the decrease in capital. This is computed as follows: Beginning inventory of $300, less supplies on hand at the end of the month $100, indicates that $200 must have been used during the month.

Supplies				Supplies Expense	
Dr.	Cr.			Dr.	Cr.
+	−			+	−
300	200	(8)	(8)	200	

Transaction (9).   **Withdrew $400 for personal use.** The withdrawal of cash means that there is a reduction in the asset account Cash. Therefore, it is credited. The amount invested by the owner is also $400 less. We must open the account Drawing, which is debited to show the decrease in capital.

Cash				Drawing	
Dr.	Cr.			Dr.	Cr.
+	−			+	−
4,000	300		(9)	400	
2,500	500				
	200				
	1,200				
	400	(9)			

An account has a debit balance when the sum of its debits exceeds the sum of its credits; it has a credit balance when the sum of the credits is the greater. In double-entry accounting, which is in almost universal use, there are equal debit and credit entries for every transaction. Where there are only two accounts affected, the debit and credit amounts are equal. If more than two accounts are affected, the total of the debit entries must equal the total of the credit entries.

2.4   THE LEDGER

The complete set of accounts for a business entry is called a *ledger*. It is the "reference book" of the accounting system and is used to classify and summarize transactions and to prepare data for financial statements. It is also a valuable source of information for managerial purposes, giving, for example, the amount of sales for the period or the cash balance at the end of the period.

2.5   THE CHART OF ACCOUNTS

It is desirable to establish a systematic method of identifying and locating each account in the ledger. The *chart of accounts*, sometimes called the *code of accounts*, is a listing of the accounts by title and numerical designation. In some companies, the chart of accounts may run to hundreds of items.

In designing a numbering structure for the accounts, it is important to provide adequate flexibility to permit expansion without having to revise the basic system. Generally, blocks of numbers are assigned to various groups of accounts, such as assets, liabilities, and so on. There are various systems of coding, depending on the needs and desires of the company.

EXAMPLE 2

A simple chart structure is to have the first digit represent the major group in which the account is located. Thus, accounts that have numbers beginning with 1 are assets; 2, liabilities; 3, capital; 4, income; and 5, expenses. The second or third digit designates the position of the account in the group.

In the two-digit system, assets are assigned the block of numbers 11–19, and liabilities 21–29. In larger firms, a three-digit (or higher) system may be used, with assets assigned 101–199 and liabilities 201–299. Following are the numerical designations for the account groups under both methods.

Account Group	Two-Digit	Three-Digit
1. Assets	11–19	101–199
2. Liabilities	21–29	201–299
3. Capital	31–39	301–399
4. Income	41–49	401–499
5. Expenses	51–59	501–599

Thus, Cash may be account 11 under the first system and 101 under the second system. The cash account may be further broken down as: 101, Cash—First National Bank; 102, Cash—Second National Bank; and so on.

2.6   THE TRIAL BALANCE

As every transaction results in an equal amount of debits and credits in the ledger, the total of all debit entries in the ledger ought to equal the total of all credit entries. At the end of the accounting period, we check this equality by preparing a two-column schedule called a *trial balance*, which compares the total of all debit balances with the total of all credit balances. The procedure is as follows:

1. List account titles in numerical order.
2. Record balances of each account, entering debit balances in the left column and credit balances in the right column.

    Note: Asset and expense accounts are debited for increases and would normally have debit balances. Liabilities, capital, and income accounts are credited for increases and would normally have credit balances.

3. Add the columns and record the totals.
4. Compare the totals.

If the totals agree, the trial balance is in balance, indicating that debits and credits are equal for the hundreds or thousands of transactions entered in the ledger. While the trial balance provides arithmetic proof of the accuracy of the records, it does not provide theoretical proof. For example, if the purchase of a machine was incorrectly charged to Expense, the trial balance columns may agree, but theoretically the accounts would be wrong, as Expense would be overstated and Machinery understated. In addition to providing proof of arithmetic accuracy in accounts, the trial balance facilitates the preparation of the periodic financial statements. Generally, the trial balance comprises the first two columns of a worksheet, from which financial statements are prepared. The worksheet procedure is discussed in Chapter 9.

EXAMPLE 3

The summary of the transactions for Mr. Drew (see Example 1), and their effect on the accounts, is shown below. The trial balance is then taken.

Assets

Cash — 11

	Dr.		Cr.	
(1)	4,000	300	(2)
(4)	2,500	500	(5)
		200	(6)
		1,200	(7)
		400	(9)

Supplies — 12

(2)	300	200	(8)

Furniture — 13

(3)	2,000		

Liabilities

Accounts Payable — 21

(7)	1,200	2,000	(3)

Capital

Capital — 31

		4,000	(1)

Drawing — 32

(9)	400	

Fees Income — 41

		2,500	(4)

Rent Expense — 51

(5)	500	

Salaries Expense — 52

(6)	200	

Supplies Expense — 53

(8)	200	

T. Drew
Trial Balance
January 31, 198X

	Dr.	Cr.
Cash	$3,900	
Supplies	100	
Furniture	2,000	
Accounts Payable		$ 800
T. Drew, Capital		4,000
Drawing	400	
Fees Income		2,500
Rent Expense	500	
Salaries Expense	200	
Supplies Expense	200	
	$7,300	$7,300

Summary

1. To classify and summarize a single item of an account group, we use a form called an
    ___Account___ .

2. The accounts make up a record called a ___ledger___ .

3. The left side of the account is known as the ___debit___ , while the right side is the
    ___credit___ .

4. Increases in all asset accounts are ___debit___ .

5. Increases in all liability accounts are ___credit___ .

6. Increases in all capital accounts are ___credit___ .

7. Increases in all income accounts are ~~debit~~ *Cred?* .

8. Increases in all expense accounts are ___debit___ .

9. Expenses are debited because they decrease ___capital___ .

10. The schedule showing the balance of each account at the end of the period is known as the
    ___trial balance___

Asset + Expense

Debit | Credit
+   -

Liab, Capital, Income
Debit | Cred
* -   +*

Answers: 1. account; 2. ledger; 3. debit side, credit side; 4. debited; 5. credited; 6. credited; 7. credited;
             8. debited; 9. capital; 10. trial balance

Solved Problems

2.1   In each of the following types of T accounts, enter an increase (by writing +) and a decrease (by
          writing −).

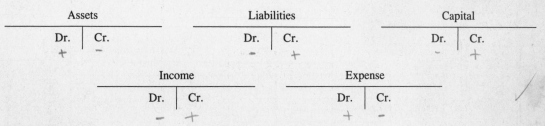

SOLUTION

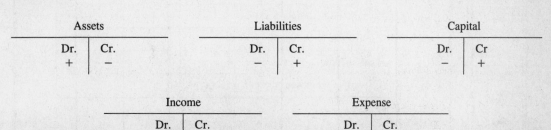

2.2   Below are a list of accounts. Rearrange them as they would appear in the ledger and assign a numerical
designation for each one from these numbers: 17, 22, 32, 59, 12, 51, 41, 11, 21, 31.

Accounts

Accounts Payable

Accounts Receivable

Capital

Cash

Drawing

Equipment

Fees Income

Miscellaneous Expense

Notes Payable

Rent Expense

SOLUTION

	Designated Number
Cash	11
Accounts Receivable	12
Equipment	17
Accounts Payable	21
Notes Payable	22
Capital	31
Drawing	32
Fees Income	41
Rent Expense	51
Miscellaneous Expense	59

2.3   Indicate in the columns below the increases and decreases in each account by placing a check mark
in the appropriate column.

		Debit	Credit
(a)	Capital is increased		✓
(b)	Cash is decreased		✓
(c)	Accounts Payable is increased		✓
(d)	Rent Expense is increased	✓	
(e)	Equipment is increased	✓	
(f)	Fees Income is increased		✓
(g)	Capital is decreased (through drawing)	✓	

SOLUTION

(a) Cr. (b) Cr. (c) Cr. (d) Dr. (e) Dr. (f) Cr. (g) Dr.

2.4 For each transaction in the table below, indicate the account to be debited and the account to be credited by placing the letter representing the account in the appropriate column.

Name of Account		Transaction	Dr.	Cr.
(a)	Accounts Payable	1. Invested cash in the firm	C	B
(b)	Capital	2. Paid rent for month	H	C
(c)	Cash	3. Received cash fees for services	C	F
(d)	Drawing	4. Paid salaries		
(e)	Equipment	5. Bought equipment on account		
(f)	Fees Income	6. Paid balance on equipment		
(g)	Notes Payable	7. Bought supplies on account		
(h)	Rent Expense	8. Borrowed money from bank, giving a note in exchange		
(i)	Salaries Expense	9. Supplies inventory showed one-third used during the month		
(j)	Supplies	10. Withdrew cash for personal use		
(k)	Supplies Expense			

$A \rightarrow E$ Inc, Capital, Liab.
+ | −   − | +
debit CR   DR | CR

SOLUTION

	Dr.	Cr.
1.	(c)	(b)
2.	(h)	(c)
3.	(c)	(f)
4.	(i)	(c)
5.	(e)	(a)
6.	(a)	(c)
7.	(j)	(a)
8.	(c)	(g)
9.	(k)	(j)
10.	(d)	(c)

2.5 Record each *separate transaction* in the accompanying accounts.

(a) Bought supplies on account for $600.

(b) Bought equipment for $2,700, paying one-third down and owing the balance.

(c) Gave a note in settlement of transaction (b).

(d) Received $500 in plumbing fees.

(a)   Supplies   Cash   Accounts Payable

Bal. 2,000

(b)
Equipment		Cash		Accounts Payable	
		Bal. 1,000			

(c)
Accounts Payable		Notes Payable	
	1,800 Bal.		

(d)
Cash		Fees Income	

SOLUTION

(a)
Supplies		Cash		Accounts Payable	
600		Bal. 2,000			600

(b)
Equipment		Cash		Accounts Payable	
2,700		Bal. 1,000	900		1,800

(c)
Accounts Payable		Notes Payable	
1,800	1,800 Bal.		1,800

(d)
Cash		Fees Income	
500			500

2.6 The ten accounts that follow summarize the first week's transactions of the Charles Taxi Company appear below.

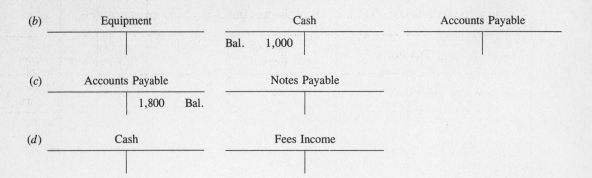

Cash			
(a)	14,000	10,000	(b)
(e)	1,000	200	(d)
		300	(f)
		500	(g)
		100	(h)
		2,000	(i)
		300	(j)

Supplies		
(d)	200	

Equipment		
(b)	10,000	
(c)	6,000	

Accounts Payable			
(i)	2,000	6,000	(c)

Capital		
	14,000	(a)

Drawing		
(h)	100	

Fees Income		
	1,000	(e)

Salaries Expense		
(f)	300	

Rent Expense		
(g)	500	

Gasoline Expense		
(j)	300	

Complete the form below. (The analysis of the first transaction is given as a sample.)

	Transaction	Account Debited	Effect of Debit	Account Credited	Effect of Credit
(a)	Invested $14,000 in firm	Cash	Increased asset	Capital	Increased capital
(b)					
(c)					
(d)					
(e)					
(f)					
(g)					
(h)					
(i)					
(j)					

SOLUTION

	Transaction	Account Debited	Effect of Debit	Account Credited	Effect of Credit
(a)	Invested $14,000 in firm	Cash	Increased asset	Capital	Increased capital
(b)	Bought $10,000 of equipment for cash	Equipment	Increased asset	Cash	Decreased asset
(c)	Bought $6,000 of additional equipment on account	Equipment	Increased asset	Accounts Payable	Increased liability
(d)	Paid $200 for supplies	Supplies	Increased asset	Cash	Decreased asset
(e)	Received $1,000 in fees	Cash	Increased asset	Fees Income	Increased income
(f)	Paid $300 for salaries	Salaries Expense	Increased expense	Cash	Decreased asset
(g)	Paid $500 for rent	Rent Expense	Increased expense	Cash	Decreased asset
(h)	Withdrew $100 for personal use	Drawing	Decreased capital	Cash	Decreased asset

Transaction	Account Debited	Effect of Debit	Account Credited	Effect of Credit
(i) Paid $2,000 on account	Accounts Payable	Decreased liability	Cash	Decreased asset
(j) Paid $300 for gasoline	Gasoline Expense	Increased expense	Cash	Decreased asset

2.7   Rearrange the following alphabetical list of the accounts and produce a trial balance.

Accounts Payable	$ 9,000
Accounts Receivable	14,000
Capital, P. Henry	32,000
Cash	20,000
Drawing, P. Henry	4,000
Equipment	18,000
Fees Income	26,000
General Expense	1,000
Notes Payable	11,000
Rent Expense	5,000
Salaries Expense	8,000
Supplies	6,000
Supplies Expense	2,000

SOLUTION

	Dr.	Cr.
Cash	$20,000	
Accounts Receivable	14,000	
Supplies	6,000	
Equipment	18,000	
Accounts Payable		$ 9,000
Notes Payable		11,000
P. Henry, Capital		32,000
P. Henry, Drawing	4,000	
Fees Income		26,000
Salaries Expense	8,000	
Rent Expense	5,000	
Supplies Expense	2,000	
General Expense	1,000	
	$78,000	$78,000

2.8   The M. Ramirez Company's trial balance appears below. Certain accounts have been recorded improperly from the ledger to the trial balance causing it not to balance. Present a corrected trial balance based on normal balances of each account.

M. Ramirez
Trial Balance
January 31, 198X

	Dr.	Cr.
Cash	$29,000	
Accounts Receivable	4,000	$ 4,000
Accounts Payable	3,000	
Capital		12,500
Drawing	500	500
Fees Income		22,000
Rent Income	11,000	11,000
Rent Expense	1,000	
Salaries Expense	10,000	
General Expense	4000	4,000
	$54,000	$43,000

SOLUTION

M. Ramirez
Trial Balance
January 31, 198X

	Dr.	Cr.
Cash	$29,000	
Accounts Receivable	4,000	
Accounts Payable		$ 3,000
Capital		12,500
Drawing	500	
Fees Income		22,000
Rent Income		11,000
Rent Expense	1,000	
Salaries Expense	10,000	
General Expense	4,000	
	$48,500	$48,500

2.9 The trial balance of P. Johnson presented below does not balance. In reviewing the ledger, you discover the following:

1. The debits and credits in the cash account total $24,100 and $21,400, respectively.

2. The $400 received in settlement of an account was not posted to the Accounts Receivable account.

3. The balance of the Salaries Expense account should be $200 less.

4. No balance should exist in the Notes Payable account.

5. Each account should have a normal balance.

Prepare a corrected trial balance.

P. Johnson
Trial Balance
December 31, 198X

	Dr.	Cr.
Cash	$ 3,000	
Accounts Receivable	11,800	
Supplies	860	$ 800
Equipment	18,500	
Accounts Payable		1,500
Notes Payable		300
Johnson, Capital		15,400
Johnson, Drawing	500	500
Fees Income		29,000
Salaries Expense	8,200	
Rent Expense	3,000	
Supplies Expense	200	200
General Expense	800	800
	$44,500	$48,500

SOLUTION

P. Johnson
Trial Balance
December 31, 198X

	Dr.	Cr.
Cash	$ 2,700	
Accounts Receivable	11,400	
Supplies	800	
Equipment	18,500	
Accounts Payable		$ 1,500
Notes Payable		
Johnson, Capital		15,400
Johnson, Drawing	500	
Fees Income		29,000
Salaries Expense	8,000	
Rent Expense	3,000	
Supplies Expense	200	
General Expense	800	
	$45,900	$45,900

2.10   Using the information of Problem 1.11, record the entries in the accounts below for B. Glatt, labeling each item by number as in Problem 1.11. Then prepare a trial balance.

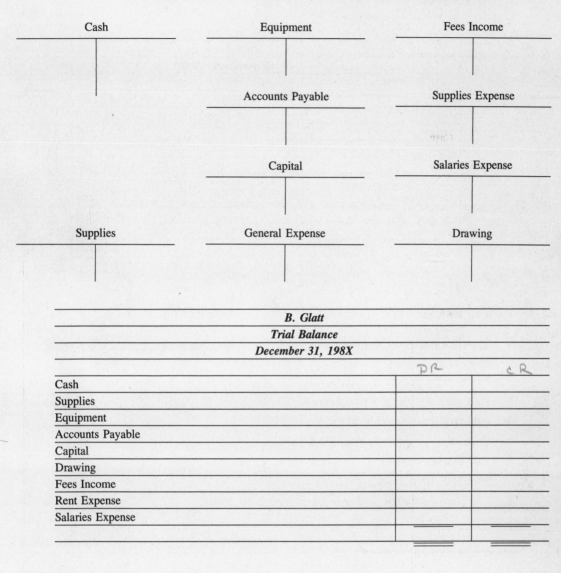

Cash		Equipment		Fees Income	

		Accounts Payable		Supplies Expense	

		Capital		Salaries Expense	

Supplies		General Expense		Drawing	

B. Glatt
Trial Balance
December 31, 198X

		DR	CR
Cash			
Supplies			
Equipment			
Accounts Payable			
Capital			
Drawing			
Fees Income			
Rent Expense			
Salaries Expense			

SOLUTION

Cash

(1)	14,000	600	(3)
(5)	2,400	500	(4)
		300	(6)
		400	(7)
		1,500	(8)
		700	(9)

Equipment

(1)	6,000	
(2)	2,000	

Accounts Payable

(4)	500	2,000	(2)
(8)	1,500		

Capital

	20,000	(1)

Supplies

(3)	600	450	(10)

General Expense

(7)	400	

Fees Income

	2,400	(5)

Supplies Expense

(10)	450	

Salaries Expense

(6)	300	

Drawing

(9)	700	

B. Glatt		
Trial Balance		
December 31, 198X		
Cash	$12,400	
Supplies	150	
Equipment	8,000	
Capital		$20,000
Drawing	700	
Fees Income		2,400
Supplies Expense	450	
Salaries Expense	300	
General Expense	400	
	$22,400	$22,400

2.11 For each transaction below, record the entry in the T accounts furnished.

1. The Nu-Look Dry Cleaning Company opened a business bank account by depositing $12,000 on Nov. 1.
2. Purchased supplies for cash, $220.
3. Purchased dry cleaning equipment for $3,500, paying $1,500 in cash with the balance on account.
4. Paid rent for the month, $425.
5. Cash sales for the month totaled $1,850.
6. Paid salaries of $375.
7. Paid $500 on account.
8. The cost of supplies used was determined to be $60.

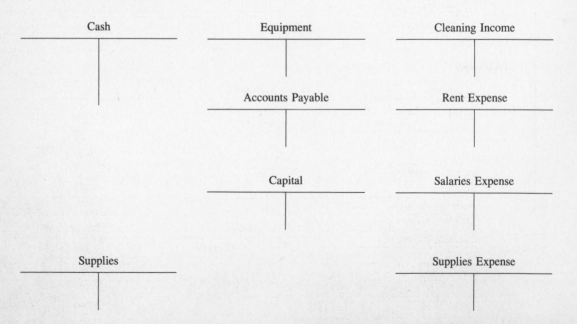

SOLUTION

	Cash				Equipment				Cleaning Income		
(1)	12,000	220	(2)	(3)	3,500				1,850	(5)
(5)	1,850	1,500	(3)								
		425	(4)		Accounts Payable				Rent Expense		
		375	(6)								
		500	(7)	(7)	500	2,000	(3)	(4)	425		

	Supplies				Capital				Salaries Expense		
(2)	220	60	(8)			12,000	(1)	(6)	375		

	Supplies Expense	
(8)	60	

2.12 Prepare a trial balance as of November 30 for the Nu-Look Dry Cleaning Company, using the account balances in Problem 2.11.

<table>
<tr><td colspan="3">Nu-Look Dry Cleaning Company</td></tr>
<tr><td colspan="3">Trial Balance</td></tr>
<tr><td colspan="3">November 30, 198X</td></tr>
<tr><td>Cash</td><td></td><td></td></tr>
<tr><td>Supplies Inventory</td><td></td><td></td></tr>
<tr><td>Equipment</td><td></td><td></td></tr>
<tr><td>Accounts Payable</td><td></td><td></td></tr>
<tr><td>Nu-Look Dry Cleaning Company, Capital</td><td></td><td></td></tr>
<tr><td>Cleaning Income</td><td></td><td></td></tr>
<tr><td>Rent Expense</td><td></td><td></td></tr>
<tr><td>Salaries Expense</td><td></td><td></td></tr>
<tr><td>Supplies Expense</td><td></td><td></td></tr>
</table>

SOLUTION

<table>
<tr><td colspan="3">Nu-Look Dry Cleaning Company</td></tr>
<tr><td colspan="3">Trial Balance</td></tr>
<tr><td colspan="3">November 30, 198X</td></tr>
<tr><td>Cash</td><td>$10,830</td><td></td></tr>
<tr><td>Supplies Inventory</td><td>160</td><td></td></tr>
<tr><td>Equipment</td><td>3,500</td><td></td></tr>
<tr><td>Accounts Payable</td><td></td><td>$ 1,500</td></tr>
<tr><td>Nu-Look Dry Cleaning Company, Capital</td><td></td><td>12,000</td></tr>
<tr><td>Cleaning Income</td><td></td><td>1,850</td></tr>
<tr><td>Rent Expense</td><td>425</td><td></td></tr>
<tr><td>Salaries Expense</td><td>375</td><td></td></tr>
<tr><td>Supplies Expense</td><td>60</td><td></td></tr>
<tr><td></td><td>$15,350</td><td>$15,350</td></tr>
</table>

Chapter 3
Journalizing and Posting Transactions

3.1 INTRODUCTION

In the preceding chapters, we discussed the nature of business transactions and the manner in which they are analyzed and classified. The primary emphasis was the "why" rather than the "how" of accounting operations; we aimed at an understanding of the reason for making the entry in a particular way. We showed the effects of transactions by making entries in T accounts. However, these entries do not provide the necessary data for a particular transaction, nor do they provide a chronological record of transactions. The missing information is furnished by the journal.

3.2 THE JOURNAL

The *journal*, or *day book*, is the book of original entry for accounting data. Afterward, the data is transferred or posted to the ledger, the book of subsequent or secondary entry. The various transactions are evidenced by sales tickets, purchase invoices, check stubs, and so on. On the basis of this evidence, the transactions are entered in chronological order in the journal. The process is called *journalizing*.

There are a number of different journals that may be used in a business. For our purposes, they may be grouped into (1) general journals and (2) specialized journals. The latter type, which are used in businesses with a large number of repetitive transactions, are described in Chapter 5. To illustrate journalizing, we here use the general journal, whose standard form is shown below.

	General Journal			Page
Date (1)	Description (2)	P.R. (3)	Debit (4)	Credit (5)
198X Oct. 7	Cash	11	$10,000	
	Barbara Ledina, Capital	31		$10,000
	(6) Invested cash in the business			

3.3 JOURNALIZING

We describe the entries in the general journal according to the numbering in the table above.

(1) *Date.* The year, month, and day of the first entry are written in the date column. The year and month do not have to be repeated for the additional entries until a new month occurs or a new page is needed.

(2) *Description.* The account title to be debited is entered on the first line, next to the date column. The name of the account to be credited is entered on the line below and indented.

(3) *P.R. (Posting Reference).* Nothing is entered in this column until the particular entry is posted, that is, until the amounts are transferred to the related ledger accounts. The posting process will be described in Section 3.4.

(4) *Debit.* The debit amount for each account is entered in this column. Generally, there is only one item, but there could be two or more separate items.

(5) *Credit.* The credit amount for each account is entered in this column. Here again, there is generally only one account, but there could be two or more accounts involved with different amounts.

(6) *Explanation.* A brief description of the transaction is usually made on the line below the credit. Generally, a blank line is left between the explanation and the next entry.

EXAMPLE 1

To help in understanding the operation of the general journal, let us journalize the transactions previously described for Mr. Drew's law practice (see page 2).

Date	Description	P.R.	Debit	Credit
Transaction (1) 198X Jan. 4	**Invested in business** Cash T. Drew, Capital Investment in law practice		4,000	4,000
Transaction (2) 4	**Bought supplies** Supplies Cash Bought supplies for cash		300	300
Transaction (3) 4	**Bought furniture on account** Furniture Accounts Payable Bought furniture from Robinson Furniture Co.		2,000	2,000
Transaction (4) 15	**Fees earned** Cash Fees Income Received payment for services		2,500	2,500
Transaction (5) 30	**Rent paid** Rent Expense Cash Paid rent for month		500	500
Transaction (6) 30	**Paid salaries** Salaries Expense Cash Paid salaries of part-time help		200	200
Transaction (7) 31	**Payment on account** Accounts Payable Cash Payment on account to Robinson Furniture Co.		1,200	1,200
Transaction (8) 31	**Count of supplies** Supplies Expense Supplies Supplies used during month		200	200
Transaction (9) 31	**Withdrawal for personal use** T. Drew, Drawing Cash Personal withdrawal		400	400

3.4 POSTING

The process of transferring information from the journal to the ledger for the purpose of summarizing is called *posting* and is ordinarily carried out in the following steps:

(1) *Record the Amount and Date.* The date and the amounts of the debits and credits are entered in the appropriate accounts.

General Journal   Page J-1

Date	Description	P.R.	Dr.	Cr.
Jan. 4	Cash		4,000	
	T. Drew, Capital			4,000

Cash	11		T. Drew, Capital	31
Jan. 4 4,000			Jan. 4 4,000	

(2) *Record the Posting Reference in the Account.* The number of the journal page is entered in the account (broken arrows below).

(3) *Record the Posting in the Journal.* For cross-referencing, the code number of the account is now entered in the P.R. column of the journal (solid arrows).

General Journal   Page J-1

Date	Description	P.R.	Dr.	Cr.
Jan. 4	Cash	11	4,000	
	T. Drew, Capital	31		4,000

Cash	11		T. Drew, Capital	31
J-1 4,000			J-1 4,000	

EXAMPLE 2

The results of the posting from the journal appear below.

	Assets			=	Liabilities			+	Capital	

	Cash		11		Accounts Payable		21		T. Drew, Capital	31
(1)	4,000	300	(2)	(7)	1,200	2,000	(3)		4,000	(1)
(4)	2,500	500	(5)							
		200	(6)						T. Drew, Drawing	32
		1,200	(7)					(9)	400	
		400	(9)							

	Supplies		12			Fees Income	41
(2)	300	200	(8)			2,500	(4)

	Furniture		13			Rent Expense	51
(3)	2,000				(5)	500	

		Salaries Expense	52
(6)	200	

		Supplies Expense	53
(8)	200	

T. Drew
Trial Balance
January 31, 198X

	Debit	Credit
Cash	$3,900	
Supplies on Hand	100	
Furniture	2,000	
Accounts Payable		$ 800
T. Drew, Capital		4,000
T. Drew, Drawing	400	
Fees Income		2,500
Rent Expense	500	
Salaries Expense	200	
Supplies Expense	200	
	$7,300	$7,300

Summary

1. The initial book for recording all transactions is known as the _____ .

2. Another name and description of the journal is _____ .

3. The process of transferring information from the journal to the ledger is known as _____ .

4. The list of code numbers that identifies the entries in the journal is called the _____ .

5. Asset account numbers begin with the number _____ , whereas liabilities begin with _____ .

6. All capital account numbers begin with the number _____ .

7. All income account numbers begin with _____ , whereas expense account numbers begin with _____ .

8. The process of recording transactions in the journal is termed _____ .

9. The complete process of accounting is called the _____ .

10. Journals may be grouped into two different classifications. They are _____ and _____ .

Answers: 1. journal; 2. book of original entry; 3. posting; 4. chart of accounts; 5. 1, 2; 6. 3; 7. 4, 5; 8. journalizing; 9. accounting cycle; 10. general, specialized

Solved Problems

3.1 On the line below each entry, write a brief explanation of the transaction that might appear in the general journal.

		Debit	Credit
(a)	Equipment	10,000	
	Cash		2,000
	Accounts Payable, William Smith		8,000
(b)	Accounts Payable, William Smith	8,000	
	Notes Payable		8,000
(c)	Notes Payable	8,000	
	Cash		8,000

SOLUTION

		Debit	Credit
(a)	Equipment	10,000	
	Cash		2,000
	Accounts Payable, William Smith		8,000
	Purchase of equipment, 20% for cash, balance on account		
(b)	Accounts Payable, William Smith	8,000	
	Notes Payable		8,000
	Notes Payable in settlement of accounts payable		
(c)	Notes Payable	8,000	
	Cash		8,000
	Settlement of the notes payable		

3.2 Dr. R. Berg, Dentist, began his practice, investing in the business the following assets:

Cash	$12,000
Supplies	1,400
Equipment	22,600
Furniture	10,000

Record the opening entry in the journal.

	Debit	Credit

SOLUTION

	Debit	Credit
Cash	12,000	
Supplies	1,400	
Equipment	22,600	
Furniture	10,000	
R. Berg, Capital		46,000

3.3 If, in Problem 3.2, Dr. Berg owed a balance of $3,500 on the equipment, what would the opening entry then be?

	Debit	Credit

SOLUTION

	Debit	Credit
Cash	12,000	
Supplies	1,400	
Equipment	22,600	
Furniture	10,000	
Accounts Payable		3,500
R. Berg, Capital		42,500

3.4 Record the following entries in the general journal for the Stephenson Cleaning Company:

(a) Invested $10,000 cash in the business

(b) Paid $2,000 for office furniture

(c) Bought equipment costing $6,000, on account

(d) Received $2,200 in cleaning income

(e) Paid one-fourth of the amount owed on the equipment

		Debit	Credit
(a)			
(b)			
(c)			
(d)			
(e)			

SOLUTION

		Debit	Credit
(a)	Cash	10,000	
	Stephenson, Capital		10,000
(b)	Office Furniture	2,000	
	Cash		2,000
(c)	Equipment	6,000	
	Accounts Payable		6,000
(d)	Cash	2,200	
	Cleaning Income		2,200
(e)	Accounts Payable	1,500	
	Cash		1,500

3.5 Record the following entries in the general journal for the Gavis Medical Group.

(a) Invested $18,000 in cash, $4,800 in supplies, and $12,200 in equipment (of which there is owed $7,000) to begin the Medical Group

(b) Received $2,400 from cash patients for the week

(c) Invested additional cash of $5,000 in the firm

(d) Paid one-half of the amount owed

		Debit	Credit
(a)			
(b)			
(c)			
(d)			

SOLUTION

		Debit	Credit
(a)	Cash	18,000	
	Supplies	4,800	
	Equipment	12,200	
	Accounts Payable		7,000
	Gavis, Capital		28,000
(b)	Cash	2,400	
	Fees Income		2,400

		Debit	Credit
(c)	Cash	5,000	
	Gavis, Capital		5,000
(d)	Accounts Payable	3,500	
	Cash		3,500

3.6   If, in Problem 3.5, the Gavis Medical Group billed patients for the month for $2,400, and a month later received $1,000, present the necessary journal entries to record each transaction.

		Debit	Credit
(a)			
(b)			

SOLUTION

		Debit	Credit
(a)	Accounts Receivable	2,400	
	Fees Income		2,400
	To record services rendered on account		
(b)	Cash	1,000	
	Accounts Receivable		1,000
	Received cash on account		

Note: Fees Income had already been recorded in the previous month, when the service had been rendered. On the accrual basis, income as well as expense is recorded in the period of service or use, not in the period of payment.

3.7   On January 1, 198X, Mr. Ling started a dry cleaning service. Record the following entries for the month of January in general journal form.

Jan. 1 Invested $5,000 cash and equipment valued at $4,100 to start business.
   12 Paid first month's rent, $400.
   13 Purchased supplies on account, $700.
   16 Received $1,700 for cleaning fees.
   19 Purchased supplies paying $550 cash.
   21 Paid creditors $500 from Jan. 13 transaction.
   22 Paid electric bill, $275.
   23 Withdrew $500 for personal use.
   25 Received $1,100 for cleaning fees.
   26 Purchased equipment, paying $900 cash.
   28 Sent bills to customers totaling $500 for cleaning fees.
   30 Received $300 from Jan. 28 transaction.
   30 Paid creditor the balanced owed.

General Journal

Date	Description	Debit	Credit
Jan. 1			
12			
13			
16			
19			
21			
22			
23			
25			
26			
28			
30			
30			

SOLUTION

General Journal

Date	Description	Debit	Credit
Jan. 1	Cash	5,000	
	Equipment	4,100	
	Capital		9,100

Date	Description	Debit	Credit
Jan. 12	Rent Expense	400	
	Cash		400
13	Supplies	700	
	Accounts Payable		700
16	Cash	1,700	
	Cleaning Fees		1,700
19	Supplies	550	
	Cash		550
21	Accounts Payable	500	
	Cash		500
22	Utilities Expense	275	
	Cash		275
23	Drawing	500	
	Cash		500
25	Cash	1,100	
	Cleaning Fees		1,100
26	Equipment	900	
	Cash		900
28	Accounts Receivable	500	
	Cleaning Fees		500
30	Cash	300	
	Accounts Receivable		300
30	Accounts Payable	200	
	Cash		200

3.8   Post the following journal entries for the Charles Taxi Company to the T accounts below. Disregard folio numbers at this time.

		P.R.	Debit	Credit
(a)	Cash		9,000	
	Charles, Capital			9,000
(b)	Equipment		8,000	
	Accounts Payable			4,000
	Cash			4,000

		P.R.	Debit	Credit
(c)	Accounts Payable		3,000	
	Cash			3,000
(d)	Cash		1,500	
	Fares Income			1,500
(e)	Salaries Expense		600	
	Cash			600

Cash	Equipment	Accounts Payable

Charles, Capital	Fares Income	Salaries Expense

SOLUTION

Cash

(a)	9,000	4,000	(b)
(d)	1,500	3,000	(c)
		600	(e)

Equipment

| (b) | 8,000 | |

Accounts Payable

| (c) | 3,000 | 4,000 | (b) |

Charles, Capital

| | 9,000 | (a) |

Fares Income

| | 1,500 | (d) |

Salaries Expense

| (e) | 600 | |

3.9   Use the balances of the T accounts in Problem 3.8 to prepare a trial balance.

Charles Taxi Company

Trial Balance

Cash		
Equipment		
Accounts Payable		
Charles, Capital		
Fares Income		
Salaries Expense		

SOLUTION

Charles Taxi Company

Trial Balance

Cash	$ 2,900	
Equipment	8,000	
Accounts Payable		$ 1,000
Charles, Capital		9,000
Fares Income		1,500
Salaries Expense	600	
	$11,500	$11,500

3.10 From the T accounts below, prepare a trial balance.

Cash		Capital		Drawing	
10,000	1,000		15,500	1,000	
5,000			2,000		
6,000					
500					

Rent Expense		Accounts Payable		Notes Payable	
500		500	500		1,000
			600		500
			1,000		

Equipment		Land		Accounts Receivable	
2,500		5,000		500	500
				5,000	
				200	

Supplies		Sales Income		Wages Expense	
300			7,000	1,450	
150			9,000		

Ace Hardware Store

Trial Balance

December 31, 198X

Cash		
Accounts Receivable		
Supplies		
Land		
Equipment		
Drawing		
Capital		
Accounts Payable		
Notes Payable		
Sales Income		
Rent Expense		
Wages Expense		

SOLUTION

Ace Hardware Store		
Trial Balance		
December 31, 198X		
Cash	$20,500	
Accounts Receivable	5,200	
Supplies	450	
Land	5,000	
Equipment	2,500	
Drawing	1,000	
Capital		$17,500
Accounts Payable		1,600
Notes Payable		1,500
Sales Income		16,000
Rent Expense	500	
Wages Expense	1,450	
	$36,600	$36,600

3.11 Journalize the following transactions: (*a*) Sylvia Ellery opened a dry cleaning store on March 1, 198X, investing $12,000 cash, $6,000 in equipment, and $4,000 worth of supplies; (*b*) bought $2,600 worth of equipment on account from J. Laym, Inc., Invoice 101; (*c*) received $2,800 from cash sales for the month; (*d*) paid rent, $200; (*e*) paid salaries, $600; (*f*) paid $1,600 on account to J. Laym, Inc.; (*g*) withdrew $500 for personal use; (*h*) used $1,000 worth of supplies during the month.

Page J-4

	P.R.	Debit	Credit
(*a*)			
(*b*)			
(*c*)			
(*d*)			
(*e*)			

		P.R.	Debit	Credit
(*f*)				
(*g*)				
(*h*)				

SOLUTION

		P.R.	Debit	Credit
(*a*)	Cash	11	12,000	
	Supplies	12	4,000	
	Equipment	13	6,000	
	Sylvia Ellery, Capital	31		22,000
	Investment in business			
(*b*)	Equipment	13	2,600	
	Accounts Payable	21		2,600
	J. Laym, Inc., Invoice 101			
(*c*)	Cash	11	2,800	
	Cleaning Income	41		2,800
	Sales for month			
(*d*)	Rent Expense	51	200	
	Cash	11		200
	Rent for month			
(*e*)	Salaries Expense	52	600	
	Cash	11		600
	Salaries for month			
(*f*)	Accounts Payable	21	1,600	
	Cash	11		1,600
	Paid J. Lyam, Inc., on account			
(*g*)	Sylvia Ellery, Drawing	32	500	
	Cash	11		500
	Personal withdrawal			
(*h*)	Supplies Expense	53	1,000	
	Supplies	12		1,000
	Supplies used during month			

3.12 Post from the journal in Problem 3.11 to the following accounts:

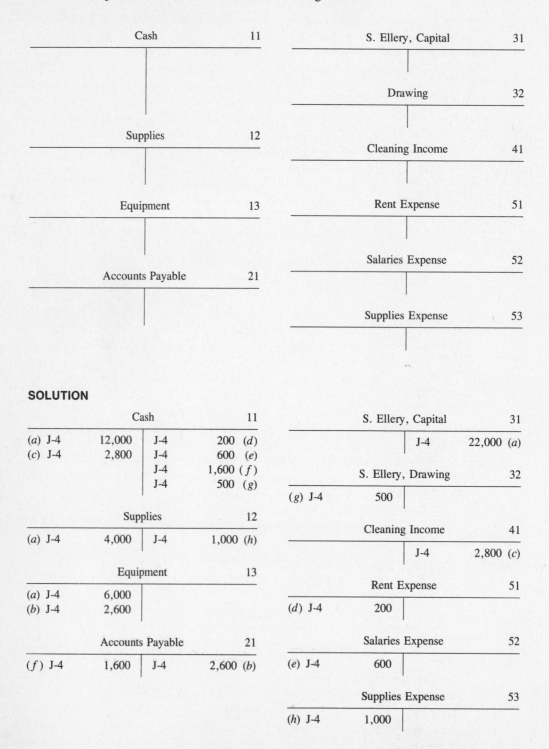

Cash	11

Supplies	12

Equipment	13

Accounts Payable	21

S. Ellery, Capital	31

Drawing	32

Cleaning Income	41

Rent Expense	51

Salaries Expense	52

Supplies Expense	53

SOLUTION

Cash   11

(a) J-4	12,000	J-4	200	(d)
(c) J-4	2,800	J-4	600	(e)
		J-4	1,600	(f)
		J-4	500	(g)

Supplies   12

(a) J-4	4,000	J-4	1,000	(h)

Equipment   13

(a) J-4	6,000		
(b) J-4	2,600		

Accounts Payable   21

(f) J-4	1,600	J-4	2,600	(b)

S. Ellery, Capital   31

	J-4	22,000	(a)

S. Ellery, Drawing   32

(g) J-4	500	

Cleaning Income   41

	J-4	2,800	(c)

Rent Expense   51

(d) J-4	200	

Salaries Expense   52

(e) J-4	600	

Supplies Expense   53

(h) J-4	1,000	

3.13 From the information obtained in Problem 3.12, prepare a trial balance for Sylvia Ellery Dry Cleaning Company.

S. Ellery Dry Cleaning Company Trial Balance		
Cash		
Supplies on Hand		
Equipment		
Accounts Payable		
S. Ellery, Capital		
S. Ellery, Drawing		
Cleaning Income		
Rent Expense		
Salaries Expense		
Supplies Expense		

SOLUTION

S. Ellery Dry Cleaning Company Trial Balance		
Cash	$11,900	
Supplies	3,000	
Equipment	8,600	
Accounts Payable		$ 1,000
S. Ellery, Capital		22,000
S. Ellery, Drawing	500	
Cleaning Income		2,800
Rent Expense	200	
Salaries Expense	600	
Supplies Expense	1,000	
	$25,800	$25,800

3.14 The trial balance for Dampman Playhouse on October 31, 198X, was as follows:

Dampman Playhouse Trial Balance October 31, 198X		
Cash	$ 2,400	
Accounts Receivable	1,500	
Supplies Inventory	350	
Equipment	11,200	
Building	10,000	
Accounts Payable		$ 9,450
Notes Payable		12,000
Dampman Playhouse, Capital		4,000
	$25,450	$25,450

Selected transactions for November were as follows:

(*a*) Nov. 2 Paid $1,000 due on the notes payable.
(*b*)   8 Paid $3,000 on account.
(*c*)   15 Receipts for the 2-week period totaled $8,400.
(*d*)   22 Bought an additional projector at a cost of $15,500 with a cash down payment of
                  $5,000, the balance to be paid within 1 year.
(*e*)   30 Paid salaries of $1,600.

Using this data, transfer the October 31 balances to the ledger accounts below, prepare journal entries
for the month of November, and post to the ledger accounts.

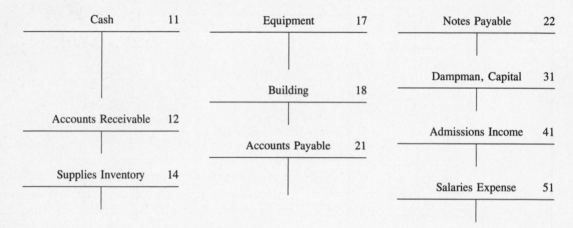

| Cash | 11 | | Equipment | 17 | | Notes Payable | 22 |

| Accounts Receivable | 12 | | Building | 18 | | Dampman, Capital | 31 |

| Supplies Inventory | 14 | | Accounts Payable | 21 | | Admissions Income | 41 |

| | | | | | | Salaries Expense | 51 |

Journal   Page J-6

Date	Description	P.R.	Debit	Credit

SOLUTION

		Journal			Page J-6
	Date	Description	P.R.	Debit	Credit
	198X				
(a)	Nov. 2	Notes Payable	22	1,000	
		Cash	11		1,000
		Payment of installment note			
(b)	8	Accounts Payable	21	3,000	
		Cash	11		3,000
		Payment on outstanding accounts			
(c)	15	Cash	11	8,400	
		Admissions Income	41		8,400
		Receipts for the 2-week period to date			
(d)	22	Equipment	17	15,500	
		Cash	11		5,000
		Accounts Payable	21		10,500
		Purchase of a projector with cash			
		payment, balance due in 1 year			
(e)	30	Salaries Expense	51	1,600	
		Cash	11		1,600
		Salaries paid to employees			

Cash 11	Equipment 17	Notes Payable 22
Bal. 2,400 │ J-6 1,000 (a)	Bal. 11,200 │	(a) J-6 1,000 │ Bal. 12,000
(c) J-6 8,400 │ J-6 3,000 (b)	(d) J-6 15,500 │	
│ J-6 5,000 (d)		
│ J-6 1,600 (e)		Dampman, Capital 31
	Buildings 18	│ Bal. 4,000
	Bal. 10,000 │	
Accounts Receivable 12		Admissions Income 41
Bal. 1,500 │		│ J-6 8,400 (c)
	Accounts Payable 21	
	(b) J-6 3,000 │ Bal. 9,450	
Supplies Inventory 14	│ J-6 10,500 (d)	Salaries Expense 51
Bal. 350 │		(e) J-6 1,600 │

3.15 For Dampman Playhouse (Problem 3.14), prepare a trial balance.

Dampman Playhouse		
Trial Balance		
November 30, 198X		
Cash		
Accounts Receivable		
Supplies Inventory		
Equipment		
Building		
Accounts Payable		
Notes Payable		
Dampman, Capital		
Admissions Income		
Salaries Expense		

SOLUTION

Dampman Playhouse		
Trial Balance		
November 30, 198X		
Cash	$ 200	
Accounts Receivable	1,500	
Supplies Inventory	350	
Equipment	26,700	
Building	10,000	
Accounts Payable		$16,950
Notes Payable		11,000
Dampman, Capital		4,000
Admissions Income		8,400
Salaries Expense	1,600	
	$40,350	$40,350

Chapter 4

Financial Statements

4.1 INTRODUCTION

The two principal questions that the owner of a business asks periodically are:

(1) What is my net income (profit)?

(2) What is my capital?

The simple balance of assets against liabilities and capital provided by the accounting equation is insufficient to give complete answers. For (1) we must know the type and amount of income and the type and amount of each expense for the period in question. For (2) it is necessary to obtain the type and amount of each asset, liability, and capital account at the end of the period. The information to answer (1) is provided by the income statement and to answer (2) by the balance sheet.

4.2 INCOME STATEMENT

The *income statement* may be defined as *a summary of the revenue (income), expenses, and net income of a business entity for a specific period of time*. This may also be called a profit and loss statement, operating statement, or statement of operations. Let us review the meanings of the elements entering into the income statement.

Revenue. The increase in capital resulting from the delivery of goods or rendering of services by the business. In amount, the revenue is equal to the cash and receivables gained in compensation for the goods delivered or services rendered.

Expenses. The decrease in capital caused by the business's revenue-producing operations. In amount, the expense is equal to the value of goods and services used up or consumed in obtaining revenue.

Net income. The increase in capital resulting from profitable operation of a business; it is the excess of revenue over expenses for the accounting period.

It is important to note that a *cash receipt* qualifies as revenue only if it serves to increase capital. Similarly, a *cash payment* is an expense only if it decreases capital. Thus, for instance, borrowing cash from a bank does not contribute to revenue.

EXAMPLE 1

Mr. T. Drew's total January income and the totals for his various expenses can be obtained by analyzing the transactions. The income from fees amounted to $2,500 and the expenses incurred to produce this income were: rent, $500; salaries, $200; and supplies, $200. The formal income statement can now be prepared.

T. Drew
Income Statement
Month of January 198X

Fees Income		$2,500
Operating Expenses		
Rent Expense	$500	
Salaries Expense	200	
Supplies Expense	200	
Total Operating Expenses		900
Net Income		$1,600

In many companies, there are hundreds and perhaps thousands of income and expense transactions in a month. To lump all these transactions under one account would be very cumbersome and would, in addition, make it impossible to show relationships among the various items. For example, we might wish to know the relationship of selling expenses to sales and whether the ratio is higher or lower than in previous periods. To solve this problem, we set up a temporary set of income and expense accounts. The net difference of these accounts, the net profit or net loss, is then transferred as one figure to the capital account.

4.3 ACCRUAL BASIS AND CASH BASIS OF ACCOUNTING

Because an income statement pertains to a definite period of time, it becomes necessary to determine just when an item of revenue or expense is to be accounted for. Under the accrual basis of accounting, revenue is recognized only when earned and expense is recognized only when incurred. This differs significantly from the cash basis of accounting, which recognizes revenue and expense generally with the receipt and payment of cash. Essential to the accrual basis is the matching of expenses with the revenue that they helped produce. Under the accrual system, the accounts are adjusted at the end of the accounting period to properly reflect the revenue earned and the cost and expenses applicable to the period.

Most business firms use the accrual basis, whereas individuals and professional people generally use the cash basis. Ordinarily, the cash basis is not suitable when there are significant amounts of inventories, receivables, and payables.

4.4 BALANCE SHEET

The information needed for the balance sheet items are the net balances at the end of the period, rather than the total for the period as in the income statement. Thus, management wants to know the balance of cash in the bank, the balance of inventory, equipment, and so on, on hand at the end of the period.

The *balance sheet* may then be defined as *a statement showing the assets, liabilities, and capital of a business entity at a specific date*. This statement is also called a statement of financial position or statement of financial condition.

In preparing the balance sheet, it is not necessary to make any further analysis of the data. The needed data—that is, the balances of the asset, liability, and capital accounts—are already available.

EXAMPLE 2

T. Drew
Balance Sheet
January 31, 198X

ASSETS

Cash	$3,900
Supplies	100
Furniture	2,000
Total Assets	$6,000

T. Drew
Balance Sheet, cont.
January 31, 198X

LIABILITIES AND CAPITAL

Liabilities			
Accounts Payable			$ 800
Capital			
Balance, January 1, 198X		$4,000	
Net Income for January	$1,600		
Less: Withdrawals	400		
Increase in Capital		1,200	
Total Capital			5,200
Total Liabilities and Capital			$6,000

The close relationship of the income statement and the balance sheet is apparent. The net income of $1,600 for January, shown as the final figure on the income statement of Example 1, is also shown as a separate figure on the balance sheet of Example 2. The income statement is thus the connecting link between two balance sheets. As discussed earlier, the income and expense items are actually a further analysis of the capital account.

The balance sheet of Example 2 is arranged in report form, with the liabilities and capital sections shown below the asset section. It may also be arranged in account form, with the liabilities and capital sections to the right of, rather than below, the asset section, as shown in Example 3.

EXAMPLE 3

T. Drew
Balance Sheet
January 31, 198X

ASSETS		**LIABILITIES AND CAPITAL**			
Cash	$3,900	Liabilities			
Supplies	100	Accounts Payable			$ 800
Furniture	2,000	Capital			
		Balance, January 31, 198X		$4,000	
		Net Income for January	$1,600		
		Less: Withdrawals	400		
		Increase in Capital		1,200	
		Total Capital			5,200
Total Assets	$6,000	Total Liabilities and Capital			$6,000

Instead of showing the details of the capital account in the balance sheet, we may show the changes in a separate form called the *capital statement*. In that case, we have three interrelated statements, as shown in Example 4.

EXAMPLE 4

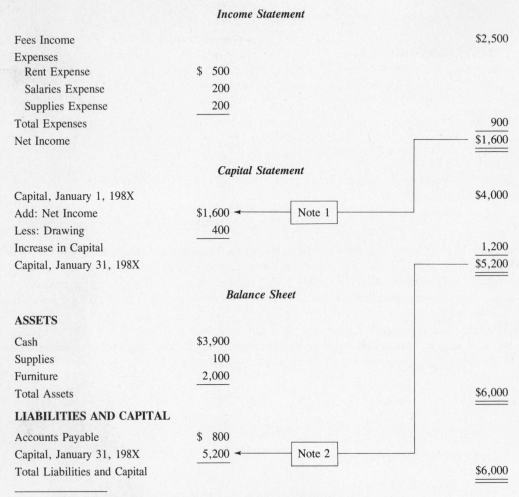

Income Statement

Fees Income		$2,500
Expenses		
Rent Expense	$ 500	
Salaries Expense	200	
Supplies Expense	200	
Total Expenses		900
Net Income		$1,600

Capital Statement

Capital, January 1, 198X		$4,000
Add: Net Income	$1,600 ◄── Note 1	
Less: Drawing	400	
Increase in Capital		1,200
Capital, January 31, 198X		$5,200

Balance Sheet

ASSETS

Cash	$3,900	
Supplies	100	
Furniture	2,000	
Total Assets		$6,000

LIABILITIES AND CAPITAL

Accounts Payable	$ 800	
Capital, January 31, 198X	5,200 ◄── Note 2	
Total Liabilities and Capital		$6,000

Note 1. The net income of the income statement, $1,600, is transferred to the capital statement.

Note 2. The capital is summarized in the capital statement and the final balance included in the balance sheet.

4.5 CLASSIFIED FINANCIAL STATEMENTS

Financial statements become more useful when the individual items are classified into significant groups for comparison and financial analysis. The classifications relating to the primary statements, the income statement and the balance sheet, will be discussed in this section.

The Income Statement

The classified *income statement* sets out the amount of each function and enables management, stockholders, analysts, and others to study the changes in function costs over successive accounting periods. There are four functional classifications of the income state.

(a) **Revenue.** Revenue includes gross income from the sale of products or services. It may be designated as sales, income from fees, and so on, to indicate gross income. The gross amount is reduced by sales returns and by sales discounts to arrive at net sales.

(b) **Cost of goods sold.** Cost of goods sold includes the costs related to the products or services sold. It is relatively simple to compute for a firm that retails furniture; it is more complex for a manufacturing firm that changes raw materials into finished products.

(c) **Operating expenses.** Operating expenses includes all expenses or resources consumed in obtaining revenue. Operating expenses are further divided into two groups. Selling expenses are those related to the promotion and sale of the company's product or service. Generally, one individual is held accountable for this function, and his or her performance is measured by the results in increasing sales and maintaining selling expenses at an established level. General and administrative expenses are those related to the overall activities of the business, such as the salaries of the president and other officers. When preparing income statements, list expenses from highest to lowest except Miscellaneous, which is always last no matter how large.

(d) **Other expenses (net).** Other expenses includes nonoperating and incidental expenses such as interest expense. Often any incidental income, such as interest income, is offset against the expense and a net amount shown.

EXAMPLE 5

F. Saltzmann
Classified Income Statement

(a)	Gross Sales			
	Sales Income		$25,000	
	Less: Sales Returns	$1,250		
	Sales Discounts	750	2,000	
	Net Sales			$23,000
(b)	Cost of Goods Sold			
	Inventory, January 1		$ 2,500	
	Purchases		16,500	
			$19,000	
	Inventory, December 31		3,000	
	Cost of Goods Sold			16,000
	Gross Profit			$ 7,000
(c)	Operating Expenses			
	Selling Expenses			
	Sales Salaries	$1,200		
	Travel Expense	600		
	Advertising	200	$ 2,000	
	General Expenses			
	Office Salaries	$1,000		
	Insurance	600	1,600	
	Total Operating Expenses			3,600
	Net Income from Operations			$ 3,400
(d)	Other Expenses (net)			
	Interest Expense		$ 500	
	Less: Interest Income		100	
	Other Expenses (net)			400
	Net Income			$ 3,000

The Balance Sheet

The balance sheet becomes a more useful statement for comparison and financial analysis if the asset and liability groups are classified. For example, an important index of the financial state of a business, derivable from the classified balance sheet, is the ratio of current assets to current liabilities. This current ratio ought, generally, to be at least 2:1. That is, current assets should be twice current liabilities. For our purposes, we will designate the following classifications:

Assets

Current assets
Property, plant, and equipment
Other assets

Liabilities

Current liabilities
Long-term liabilities

Current assets.   Assets reasonably expected to be converted into cash or used in the current operation of the business. (The current period is generally taken as 1 year.) Examples are cash, notes receivable, accounts receivable, inventory, and prepaid expenses (prepaid insurance, prepaid rent, and so on). List these current assets in the order of liquidity.

Property, plant, and equipment.   Long-lived assets used in the production of goods or services. These assets, sometimes called *fixed assets* or *plant assets*, are used in the operation of the business rather than being held for sale, as are inventory items.

Other assets.   Various assets other than current assets, fixed assets, or assets to which specific captions are given. For instance, the caption "Investments" would be used if significant sums were invested. Often, companies show a caption for intangible assets such as patents or goodwill. In other cases, there may be a separate caption for deferred charges. If, however, the amounts are not large in relation to total assets, the various items may be grouped under one caption, "Other Assets."

Current liabilities.   Debts that must be satisfied from current assets within the next operating period, usually 1 year. Examples are accounts payable, notes payable, the current portion of long-term debt, and various accrued items such as salaries payable and taxes payable.

Long-term liabilities.   Liabilities that are payable beyond the next year. The most common examples are bonds payable and mortgages payable. Example 6, which follows, shows a classified balance sheet of typical form.

EXAMPLE 6

F. Saltzmann
Classified Balance Sheet

ASSETS

Current Assets		
Cash	$5,400	
Accounts Receivable	1,600	
Supplies	500	
Total Current Assets		$ 7,500
Fixed Assets		
Land	$4,000	
Building	8,000	
Equipment	2,000	
Total Fixed Assets		14,000
Total Assets		$21,500

F. Saltzmann
Classified Balance Sheet, cont.

LIABILITIES AND CAPITAL

Current Liabilities		
Accounts Payable	$2,000	
Notes Payable	1,750	
Total Current Liabilities		$ 3,750
Long-Term Liabilities		
Mortgage Payable		12,000
Total Liabilities		$15,750
Capital		
F. Saltzmann, Capital, January 1	$4,750	
Net Income for the Year	$3,000	
Less: Withdrawals	2,000	
Increase in Capital	1,000	
F. Saltzmann, Capital, December 31		5,750
Total Liabilities and Capital		$21,500

Summary

1. Another term for an accounting report is an _____ .

2. The statement that shows net income for the period is known as the _____ statement.

3. The statement that shows net loss for the period is known as the _____ statement.

4. Two groups of items making up the income statement are _____ and _____ .

5. The difference between income and expense is known as _____ .

6. Withdrawal of money by the owner is not an expense but a reduction of _____ .

7. To show the change in capital of a business, the _____ statement is used.

8. The balance sheet contains _____ , _____ , and _____ .

9. Assets must equal _____ .

10. Expense and income must be matched in the same _____ .

Answers: 1. accounting statement; 2. income; 3. income; 4. income, expense; 5. net income; 6. capital; 7. capital; 8. assets, liabilities, capital; 9. liabilities and capital; 10. year or period

Solved Problems

4.1 Place a check mark in the appropriate box below to indicate the name of the account group in which each account belongs.

	Income Statement		Balance Sheet		
	Income	Expense	Assets	Liability	Capital
Accounts Payable					
Accounts Receivable					
Building					
Capital					
Cash					
Drawing					
Equipment					
Fees Income					
General Expense					
Interest Expense					
Interest Income					
Land					
Notes Payable					
Other Income					
Rent Expense					
Rent Income					
Salaries Expense					
Supplies					
Supplies Expense					
Tax Expense					

SOLUTION

	Income Statement		Balance Sheet		
	Income	Expense	Assets	Liability	Capital
Accounts Payable				✔	
Accounts Receivable			✔		
Building			✔		
Capital					✔
Cash			✔		
Drawing					✔
Equipment			✔		
Fees Income	✔				
General Expense		✔			
Interest Expense		✔			
Interest Income	✔				
Land			✔		
Notes Payable				✔	
Other Income	✔				
Rent Expense		✔			
Rent Income	✔				
Salaries Expense		✔			
Supplies			✔		
Supplies Expense		✔			
Tax Expense		✔			

4.2   Below is an income statement with some of the information missing. Fill in the information needed to complete the income statement.

Sales Income		(b)
Operating Expenses:		
Wages Expense	$16,910	
Rent Expense	(a)	
Utilities Expense	3,150	
Total Operating Expenses		32,150
Net Income		$41,300

SOLUTION

(*a*) 12,090; (*b*) $73,450

4.3   Based on the following information, determine the capital as of December 31, 198X. Net Income for period, $18,000; Drawing, $6,000; Capital (January 1, 198X), $20,000.

SOLUTION

Capital, January 1, 198X		$20,000
Net Income	$18,000	
Less: Drawing	6,000	
Increase in Capital		12,000
Capital, December 31, 198X		$32,000

4.4   The following information was taken from an income statement:

Fees Income	$14,000
Rent Expense	2,000
Salaries Expense	5,000
Miscellaneous Expense	1,000

If the owner withdrew $2,000 from the firm, what is the increase or decrease in capital?

SOLUTION

There are two steps to solving this problem:

1. Prepare an income statement.
2. Increases or decreases in capital are determined by subtracting the drawing (withdrawal) from the net income.

Fees Income		$14,000
Expenses		
Rent Expense	$2,000	
Salaries Expense	5,000	
Miscellaneous Expense	1,000	
Total Expenses		8,000
Net Income		$ 6,000
Net Income	6,000	
Drawing	2,000	
Increase in Capital	$4,000	

4.5 Based on the information in Problem 4.4, if the withdrawal were $9,000 instead of $2,000, what would the increase (decrease) become?

SOLUTION

If the withdrawal is larger than the net income, a decrease in capital will result.

Net Income	$6,000
Drawing	9,000
Decrease in Capital	$3,000

4.6 If the capital account has a balance of $32,000 on January 1, what will be the balance by December 31 (*a*) based on Problem 4.4? (*b*) based on Problem 4.5?

(*a*)

(*b*)

SOLUTION

(*a*)

Capital, January 1		$32,000
Net Income	$6,000	
Drawing	2,000	
Increase in Capital		4,000
Capital, December 31		$36,000

(*b*)

Capital, January 1		$32,000
Net Income	6,000	
Drawing	9,000	
Decrease in Capital		3,000
Capital, December 31		$29,000

4.7   Eccleston Company had a capital balance as of January 1, 198X, of $43,000. During its first year of operation, it had produced a net loss of $13,000 and drawings of $6,000. What is the capital balance of the company as of December 31, 198X?

SOLUTION

Capital, January 1, 198X		$43,000
Net loss	$13,000	
Drawing	6,000	
Decrease in Capital		19,000
Capital, December 31, 198X		$24,000

Note: Net loss and drawing are *added* together and then subtracted from capital because both reduce the capital of the firm.

4.8   Based on the following information, determine the capital on December 31.

Cash	$6,000
Supplies	400
Equipment	8,000
Accounts Payable	4,500
Notes Payable	2,500

SOLUTION

ASSETS

Cash	$ 6,000
Supplies	400
Equipment	8,000
	$14,400

LIABILITIES AND CAPITAL

Accounts Payable	$4,500	
Notes Payable	2,500	
Total Liabilities		7,000
Capital		7,400*
Total Liabilities and Capital		$14,400

*$14,400	Assets
−7,000	Liabilities
$ 7,400	Capital

4.9   Prepare a balance sheet as of December 31, 198X, from the data below:

Accounts Payable	$ 3,000
Cash	4,000
Equipment	16,000
Notes Payable	12,000
Supplies	200
Net Income	11,400
Drawing	10,200
Capital, January 1, 198X	4,000

ASSETS		
Cash		
Equipment		
Supplies		
Total Assets		
LIABILITIES AND CAPITAL		
Accounts Payable		
Notes Payable		
Total Liabilities		
Capital, December 31, 198X		
Total Liabilities and Capital		
CAPITAL STATEMENT		

SOLUTION

ASSETS		
Cash		$ 4,000
Equipment		16,000
Supplies		200
Total Assets		$20,200
LIABILITIES AND CAPITAL		
Accounts Payable	$ 3,000	
Notes Payable	12,000	
Total Liabilities		$15,000
Capital, December 31, 198X		5,200
Total Liabilities and Capital		$20,200
CAPITAL STATEMENT		
Capital, January 1, 198X		$ 4,000
Net Income	$11,400	
Drawing	10,200	
Increase in Capital		1,200
Capital, December 31, 198X		$ 5,200

4.10 Classify the following accounts by placing a check mark in the appropriate column.

		Current Asset	Fixed Asset	Current Liability	Long-Term Liability
(a)	Accounts Receivable				
(b)	Accounts Payable				
(c)	Notes Payable				
(d)	Mortgage Payable				
(e)	Cash				
(f)	Supplies Inventory				
(g)	Salaries Payable				
(h)	Bonds Payable				
(i)	Equipment				
(j)	Land				

SOLUTION

		Current Asset	Fixed Asset	Current Liability	Long-Term Liability
(a)	Accounts Receivable	✔			
(b)	Accounts Payable			✔	
(c)	Notes Payable			✔	
(d)	Mortgage Payable				✔
(e)	Cash	✔			
(f)	Supplies Inventory	✔			
(g)	Salaries Payable			✔	
(h)	Bonds Payable				✔
(i)	Equipment		✔		
(j)	Land		✔		

4.11 From the information that follows, prepare a classified balance sheet as of December 31.

Cash	$ 6,000	Accounts Payable	$ 2,500
Accounts Receivable	3,000	Notes Payable	1,500
Supplies Inventory	1,000	Mortgage Payable	12,000
Equipment	14,000	Capital, December 31	8,000

ASSETS		
Current Assets		
Total Current Assets		
Fixed Assets		
Total Assets		
LIABILITIES AND CAPITAL		
Current Liabilities		
Total Current Liabilities		
Long-Term Liabilities		
Total Liabilities		
Capital		
Total Liabilities and Capital		

SOLUTION

ASSETS		
Current Assets		
Cash	$6,000	
Accounts Receivable	3,000	
Supplies Inventory	1,000	
Total Current Assets		$10,000
Fixed Assets		
Equipment		14,000
Total Assets		$24,000
LIABILITIES AND CAPITAL		
Current Liabilities		
Accounts Payable	$2,500	
Notes Payable	1,500	
Total Current Liabilities		$ 4,000
Long-Term Liabilities		
Mortgage Payable		12,000
Total Liabilities		$16,000
Capital		8,000
Total Liabilities and Capital		$24,000

4.12 Below are account balances as of December 31, 198X of R. Dames, owner of a movie theatre.

Accounts Payable	$11,400	Film Rental Expense	$ 6,000
Admissions Income	34,200	Miscellaneous Expense	4,000
Capital, January 1, 198X	16,000	Notes Payable	1,000
Cash	7,500	Rent Expense	10,000
Drawing	5,400	Salaries Expense	7,000
Equipment	18,500	Supplies Inventory	4,200

Prepare (*a*) an income statement, (*b*) a capital statement, (*c*) a balance sheet.

(a)

R. Dames		
Income Statement		
Year Ended December 31, 198X		

(b)

R. Dames		
Capital Statement		
Year Ended December 31, 198X		

(c)

R. Dames		
Balance Sheet		
December 31, 198X		

SOLUTION

(a)

R. Dames		
Income Statement		
Year Ended December 31, 198X		
Admissions Income		$34,200
Expenses		
Film Rental Expense	$ 6,000	
Rent Expense	10,000	
Salaries Expense	7,000	
Miscellaneous Expense	4,000	
Total Expenses		27,000
Net Income		$ 7,200

(b)   The capital statement is needed to show the capital balance at the end of the year. Mr. Dames' capital balance above is at the beginning. Net income increases capital, and drawing reduces capital.

R. Dames		
Capital Statement		
Year Ended December 31, 198X		
Capital, January 1, 198X		$16,000
Add: Net Income	$7,200	
Less: Drawing	5,400	
Increase in Capital		1,800
Capital, December 31, 198X		$17,800

(c)

R. Dames		
Balance Sheet		
December 31, 198X		
ASSETS		
Cash	$ 7,500	
Supplies Inventory	4,200	
Equipment	18,500	
Total Assets		$30,200
LIABILITIES AND CAPITAL		
Accounts Payable	$11,400	
Notes Payable	1,000	
Total Liabilities		$12,400
Capital		17,800
Total Liabilities and Capital		$30,200

4.13   Wilbur Wright owns and operates an airplane repair shop. Listed below are the year-end balances. Prepare an income statement, capital statement, and balance sheet in good report form.

Cash	$12,200
Supplies	5,150
Accounts Receivable	3,100
Prepaid Insurance	1,150
Equipment	15,920
Accounts Payable	3,200
Wages Payable	2,600
W. Wright, Capital (Jan.)	26,575
W. Wright, Drawing	9,500
Repair Shop Income	98,800
Wages Expense	41,500
Rent Expense	28,200
Utilities Expense	10,100
Supplies Expense	3,980
Miscellaneous Expense	375

Wilbur Wright Repair Shop
Income Statement
Year Ended December 31, 198X

Wilbur Wright Repair Shop
Capital Statement
Year Ended December 31, 198X

Wilbur Wright Repair Shop
Balance Sheet
December 31, 198X

ASSETS

LIABILITIES

CAPITAL

SOLUTION

Wilbur Wright Repair Shop		
Income Statement		
Year Ended December 31, 198X		
Repair Shop Income		$98,800
Operating Expenses:		
Wages Expense	$41,500	
Rent Expense	28,200	
Utilities Expense	10,100	
Supplies Expense	3,980	
Miscellaneous Expense	375	
Total Operating Expenses		84,155
Net Income		$14,645

Wilbur Wright Repair Shop		
Capital Statement		
Year Ended December 31, 198X		
Capital, January 1, 198X		$26,575
Net Income for Year	$14,645	
Less Drawing	9,500	
Increase in Capital		5,145
Capital, December 31, 198X		$31,720

Wilbur Wright Repair Shop		
Balance Sheet		
December 31, 198X		
ASSETS		
Current Assets		
Cash	$12,200	
Accounts Receivable	3,100	
Supplies	5,150	
Prepaid Insurance	1,150	
Total Current Assets		$21,600
Plant Assets		
Equipment		15,920
Total Assets		$37,520
LIABILITIES		
Current Liabilities		
Accounts Payable	$ 3,200	
Wages Payable	2,600	
Total Liabilities		$ 5,800
CAPITAL		
Wilbur Wright, Capital		31,720
Total Liabilities and Capital		$37,520

4.14 From the information from the preceding problem, if revenues were only $84,000 and drawing was $10,200, and Wright's beginning capital balance was $42,075, what affect would this have on the financial statements? Prepare new financial statements with these changes.

Wilbur Wright Repair Shop		
Income Statement		
Year Ended December 31, 198X		

Wilbur Wright Repair Shop		
Capital Statement		
Year Ended December 31, 198X		

Wilbur Wright Repair Shop		
Balance Sheet		
December 31, 198X		
ASSETS		
LIABILITIES		

Wilbur Wright Repair Shop		
Balance Sheet, cont.		
Year Ended December 31, 198X		
CAPITAL		

SOLUTION

Wilbur Wright Repair Shop		
Income Statement		
Year Ended December 31, 198X		
Repair Shop Income		$84,000
Operating Expenses		
Wages Expense	$41,500	
Rent Expense	28,200	
Utilities Expense	10,100	
Supplies Expense	3,980	
Miscellaneous Expense	375	
Total Operating Expenses		84,155
Net Loss		$ (155)

Wilbur Wright Repair Shop		
Capital Statement		
Year Ended December 31, 198X		
Capital, January 1, 198X		$ 42,075
Net Loss	$ (155)	
Less: Drawing	(10,200)	
Decrease in Capital		(10,355)
Capital, December 31, 198X		$ 31,720

Wilbur Wright Repair Shop		
Balance Sheet		
December 31, 198X		
ASSETS		
Current Assets		
Cash	$12,200	
Accounts Receivable	3,100	
Supplies	5,150	
Prepaid Insurance	1,150	
Total Current Assets		$21,600
Plant Assets		
Equipment		15,920
Total Assets		$37,520

Wilbur Wright Repair Shop		
Balance Sheet, cont.		
Year Ended December 31, 198X		
LIABILITIES		
Current Liabilities		
Accounts Payable	$ 3,200	
Wages Payable	2,600	
Total Liabilities		$ 5,800
CAPITAL		
Wilbur Wright, Capital		31,720
Total Liabilities and Capital		$37,520

4.15 Jim Brown owns a store that sells leather goods. The name of the store is The Bean Bag. Listed below are the year-end balances needed for an income statement. From this information, prepare a classified income statement for the year ending December 31, 198X.

Sales Returns	$ 1,500	Sales Salaries Expense	$27,200
Sales Discounts	1,375	Advertising Expense	8,100
Sales Income	197,000	Commissions on Sales (expense)	2,500
Beginning Inventory	17,500	Office Salaries Expense	21,400
Purchases	82,000	Insurance Expense	5,200
Ending Inventory	19,800	Interest Income	900

The Bean Bag			
Income Statement			
Year Ended December 31, 198X			

SOLUTION

	The Bean Bag		
	Income Statement		
	Year Ended December 31, 198X		
Sales		$197,000	
Less: Sales Returns	$ 1,500		
Sales Discounts	1,375	2,875	
Net Sales			$194,125
Cost of Goods Sold			
Beginning Inventory	$17,500		
Purchases	82,000		
Goods Available for Sale		$ 99,500	
Less Ending Inventory		19,800	
Cost of Goods Sold			79,700
Gross Profit from Sales			$114,425
Operating Expenses			
Selling Expense			
Sales Salaries Expense	$27,200		
Advertising Expense	8,100		
Commission on Sales	2,500	$ 37,800	
General Expenses			
Office Salary Expense	$21,400		
Insurance Expense	5,200	26,600	
Total Operating Expenses			64,400
Net Income from Operations			$ 50,025
Other Incomes and Expenses			
Interest Income			900
Net Income			$ 50,925

4.16 The balances of the accounts of Dr. C. Moss, Psychologist, appear as follows:

Accounts Payable	$ 2,800
Accounts Receivable	3,600
Building	12,000
Capital, January 1, 198X	19,000
Cash	12,200
Fees Income	38,000
Drawing	6,000
Equipment	15,000
Furniture	3,000
Mortgage Payable	10,000
Miscellaneous Expense	2,000
Notes Payable	2,000
Supplies Inventory	6,000
Salaries Expense	8,000
Supplies Expense	4,000

Using the forms provided below, prepare (*a*) an income statement, (*b*) a capital statement, and (*c*) a classified balance sheet.

(a)

Dr. C. Moss		
Income Statement		
Year Ended December 31, 198X		
Fees Income		
Expenses		
Total Expenses		
Net Income		

(b)

Dr. C. Moss		
Capital Statement		
Year Ended December 31, 198X		
Capital, January 1, 198X		
Add: Net Income		
Less: Drawing		
Increase in Capital		
Capital, December 31, 198X		

(c)

Dr. C. Moss		
Balance Sheet		
December 31, 198X		
ASSETS		
Current Assets		
Total Current Assets		
Fixed Assets		
Total Fixed Assets		
Total Assets		
LIABILITIES AND CAPITAL		
Current Liabilities		
Total Current Liabilities		
Long-Term Liabilities		
Total Liabilities		
Capital		
Total Liabilities and Capital		

SOLUTION

(a)

Dr. C. Moss		
Income Statement		
Year Ended December 31, 198X		
Fees Income		$38,000
Expenses		
Salaries Expense	$8,000	
Supplies Expense	4,000	
Miscellaneous Expense	2,000	
Total Expenses		14,000
Net Income		$24,000

(b)

Dr. C. Moss		
Capital Statement		
Year Ended December 31, 198X		
Capital, January 1, 198X		$19,000
Add: Net Income	$24,000	
Less: Drawing	6,000	
Increase in Capital		18,000
Capital, December 31, 198X		$37,000

(c)

Dr. C. Moss		
Balance Sheet		
December 31, 198X		
ASSETS		
Current Assets		
Cash	$12,200	
Accounts Receivable	3,600	
Supplies Inventory	6,000	
Total Current Assets		$21,800
Fixed Assets		
Building	$12,000	
Equipment	15,000	
Furniture	3,000	
Total Fixed Assets		30,000
Total Assets		$51,800
LIABILITIES AND CAPITAL		
Current Liabilities		
Accounts Payable	$ 2,800	
Notes Payable	2,000	
Total Current Liabilities		4,800
Long-Term Liabilities		
Mortgage Payable		10,000
Total Liabilities		$14,800
Capital (see Capital Statement)		37,000
Total Liabilities and Capital		$51,800

Chapter 5

Adjusting and Closing Procedures

5.1 INTRODUCTION: THE ACCRUAL BASIS OF ACCOUNTING

Accounting records are kept on an accrual basis, except in the case of very small businesses. *To accrue* means *to collect or accumulate.* This means that revenue is recognized when earned, regardless of when cash is actually collected, and expense is matched to the revenue, regardless of when cash is paid out. Most revenue is earned when goods or services are delivered. At this time, title to the goods or services is transferred, and there is created a legal obligation to pay for such goods or services. Some revenue, such as rental income, is recognized on a time basis and is earned when the specified period of time has passed. The accrual concept demands that expenses be kept in step with revenue, so that each month sees only that month's expenses applied against the revenue for that month. The necessary matching is brought about through a type of journal entry. In this chapter, we shall discuss these adjusting entries and also the closing entries through which the adjusted balances are ultimately transferred to balance sheet accounts at the end of the fiscal year.

5.2 ADJUSTING ENTRIES COVERING RECORDED DATA

To adjust expense or income items that have already been recorded, only a reclassification is required; that is, amounts have only to be transferred from one account (for example, Prepaid Insurance) to another (Insurance Expense). The following examples will show how adjusting entries are made for the principal types of recorded expenses.

EXAMPLE 1   Prepaid Insurance

Assume that a business paid a $1,200 premium on April 1 for 1 year's insurance in advance. This represents an increase in one asset (prepaid expense) and a decrease in another asset (cash). Thus, the entry would be:

Prepaid Insurance	1,200	
Cash		1,200

At the end of April, one-twelfth of the $1,200 or $100 had expired or been used up. Therefore, an adjustment has to be made, decreasing or crediting Prepaid Insurance and increasing or debiting Insurance Expense. The entry would be:

Insurance Expense	100	
Prepaid Insurance		100

Thus, $100 would be shown as Insurance Expense in the income statement for April, and the balance of $1,100 would be shown as Prepaid Insurance in the balance sheet.

EXAMPLE 2   Prepaid Rent

Assume that on March 1 a business paid $1,500 to cover rent for the balance of the year. The full amount would have been recorded as a debit to prepaid expense in March. Since there is a 10-month period involved, the rent expense each month is $150. The balance of Prepaid Rent would be $1,350 at the beginning of April. The adjusting entry for April would be:

Rent Expense	150	
Prepaid Rent		150

At the end of April, the balance in the prepaid rent account would be $1,200.

EXAMPLE 3　Supplies on Hand

A type of prepayment that is somewhat different from those previously described is the payment for office or factory supplies. Assume that $400 worth of supplies were purchased on April 1. At the end of April, when expense and revenue are to be matched and statements prepared, a count of the amount on hand will be made. Assume that the inventory count shows that $250 of supplies are still on hand. Then the amount consumed during April was $150 ($400 − $250). The two entries would be as follows:

Apr. 1	Supplies	400	
	Cash		400
30	Supplies Expense	150	
	Supplies		150

Supplies Expense of $150 will be included in the April income statement; Supplies on Hand of $250 will be included as an asset on the balance sheet of April 30.

In each of the above examples, the net effect of the adjusting entry is to credit the same account as was originally debited. The following examples illustrate what are called valuation or offset accounts.

EXAMPLE 4　Allowance for Uncollectible Accounts

A business with many accounts receivable will reasonably expect to have some losses from uncollectible accounts. It will not be known which specific accounts will not be collected, but past experience furnishes an estimate of the total uncollectible amount.

Assume that a company estimates that 1 percent of sales on account will be uncollectible. Then, if such sales are $10,000 for April, it is estimated that $100 will be uncollectible. The actual loss may not definitely be determined for a year or more, but the loss attributed to April sales would call for an adjusting entry:

Uncollectible Accounts Expense	100	
Allowance for Uncollectible Accounts		100

If the balance in Accounts Receivable at April 30 was $9,500 and the previous month's balance in Allowance for Uncollectible Accounts was $300, the balance sheet at April 30 would show the following:

Accounts Receivable	$9,500	
Less: Allowance for Uncollectible Accounts	400	$9,100

EXAMPLE 5　Accumulated Depreciation

Accumulated Depreciation is also a valuation or offset account, which means that the balance is offset against the related asset account. In the case of property, plant, and equipment, it is desirable to know the original cost as well as the value after depreciation. Assume that machinery costing $15,000 was purchased on February 1 of the current year and was expected to last 10 years. With the straight-line method of accounting (that is, equal charges each period), the depreciation would be $1,500 a year, or $125 a month. The adjusting entry would be as follows:

Depreciation Expense	125	
Accumulated Depreciation		125

At the end of April, Accumulated Depreciation would have a balance of $375, representing 3 months' accumulated depreciation. The account would be shown in the balance sheet as follows:

Machinery	$15,000	
Less: Accumulated Depreciation	375	$14,625

5.3　ADJUSTING ENTRIES COVERING UNRECORDED DATA

In the previous section, we discussed various kinds of adjustments to accounts to which entries had already been made. Now we consider those instances in which an expense has been incurred or an income earned but the applicable amount has not been recorded during the month. For example, if salaries are paid on a weekly basis, the last week of the month may apply to 2 months. If April ends on a Tuesday, then the first 2 days of the week will apply to April and be an April expense, while the last 3 days will be a May expense. To arrive at the proper total for salaries for the month of April, we must include along with the April payrolls that were paid in April the 2 days' salary that was not paid until May. Thus, we make an entry to accrue the 2 days' salary. As mentioned earlier, to accrue means to collect or accumulate.

The following example shows an adjusting entry for the most common type of unrecorded expenses (accrued expenses).

EXAMPLE 6   Accrued Salaries

Assume that April 30 falls on Tuesday for the last weekly payroll period. Then, 2 days of that week will apply to April, 3 days to May. The payroll for the week amounted to $2,500, of which $1,000 applied to April and $1,500 to May. The entries would be as follows:

Apr. 30	Salaries Expense	1,000	
	Salaries Payable		1,000

When the payment of the payroll is made—say, on May 3—the entry would be as follows:

May 3	Salaries Expense	1,500	
	Salaries Payable	1,000	
	Cash		2,500

As can be seen above, $1,000 was charged to expense in April and $1,500 in May. The debit to Salaries Payable of $1,000 in May merely canceled the credit entry made in April, when the liability was set up for the April salaries expense.

5.4   CLOSING ENTRIES

After the income statement and balance sheet have been prepared, a summary account—variously known as Expense and Income Summary, Profit and Loss Summary, and so on—is set up. Then, by means of closing entries, each expense account is credited so as to produce a zero balance, and the total amount for the closed-out accounts is debited to Expense and Income Summary. Similarly, the individual revenue accounts are closed out by debiting, and the total amount is credited to the summary account. Thus, the new fiscal year starts with zero balances in the income and expense accounts, whereas the Expense and Income Summary balance gives the net income or the net loss for the old year.

EXAMPLE 7

To illustrate closing procedure, we refer to the accounts of T. Drew (see Chapter 1).

T. Drew
Trial Balance
January 31, 198X

Cash	$3,900	
Supplies on Hand	100	
Furniture	2,000	
Accounts Payable		$ 800
T. Drew, Capital		4,000
T. Drew, Drawing	400	
Fees Income		2,500
Rent Expense	500	
Salaries Expense	200	
Supplies Expense	200	
	$7,300	$7,300

The closing entries are as follows.

(1) **Close out income accounts.** Debit the individual income accounts and credit the total to Expense and Income Summary. Here, there is only one income account.

Jan. 31	Fees Income	2,500	
	Expense and Income Summary		2,500

(2) **Close out expense accounts.** Credit the individual expense accounts and debit the total to Expense and Income Summary.

Jan. 31	Expense and Income Summary	900	
	Rent Expense		500
	Salaries Expense		200
	Supplies Expense		200

(3) **Close out the Expense and Income Summary account.** If there is a profit, the credit made for total income in (1) above will exceed the debit made for total expense in (2) above. Therefore, to close out the balance to zero, a debit entry will be made to Expense and Income Summary. A credit will be made to the capital account to transfer the net income for the period. If expenses exceed income, then a loss has been sustained, and a credit would be made to Expense and Income Summary and a debit to the capital account. Based on the information given, the entry is:

Jan. 31	Expense and Income Summary	1,600	
	T. Drew, Capital		1,600

(4) **Close out the Drawing account.** The drawing account would be credited for the total amount of the drawings for the period and the capital account debited for that amount. The difference between net income and drawing for the period represents the net change in the capital account for the period. The net income of $1,600, less drawings of $400, results in a net increase of $1,200 in the capital account. The closing entry for the drawing account is:

Jan. 31	T. Drew, Capital	400	
	T. Drew, Drawing		400

In summary, the procedure is as follows:

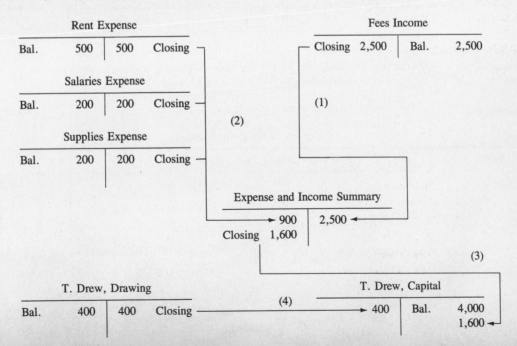

After the closing entries (1) through (4) are made, the various accounts will appear as below. The income and expense accounts and the drawing account are ruled off or closed out, thus showing no balance. The net profit for the period and the drawing account balance were transferred to T. Drew, Capital, a balance sheet account.

Cash		Furniture		T. Drew, Capital	
Bal. 3,900		Bal. 2,000		(4) 400	Bal. 4,000
					1,600 (3)

Supplies on Hand		Accounts Payable		T. Drew, Drawing	
Bal. 100			Bal. 800	Bal. 400	400 (4)

Fees Income		Salaries Expense		Expense and Income Summary	
(1) 2,500	Bal. 2,500	Bal. 200	200 (2)	(2) 900	2,500 (1)
				(3) 1,600	
				2,500	2,500

Rent Expense		Supplies Expense	
Bal. 500	500 (2)	Bal. 200	200 (2)

5.5 RULING ACCOUNTS

After the posting of the closing entries, all revenue and expense accounts and the summary accounts are to be closed. When ruling an account where only one debit and one credit exist, a double rule is drawn below the entry across the debit and credit money columns. The date and reference columns also have a double rule in order to separate the transactions from the period just ended and the entry to be made in the subsequent period.

EXAMPLE 8

Salaries Expense

Date	Item	P.R.	Debit	Date	Item	P.R.	Credit
Jan. 30		J-1	200	Jan. 31		J-2	200

If more than one entry appears on either side of the account, a single ruled line is drawn below the last entry across the debit and credit money columns. The totals are entered just below the single line, and a double ruling line is drawn below the totals. The date and reference column also will have a double ruling line.

EXAMPLE 9

Expense and Income Summary

Date	Item	P.R.	Debit	Date	Item	P.R.	Credit
Jan. 31		J-2	900	Jan. 31		J-1	2,500
31		J-2	1,600				
			2,500				2,500

The assets, liabilities, and capital accounts will have balances. These open accounts are ruled so that their balances are carried forward to the new fiscal year.

EXAMPLE 10

Cash

Date	Item	P.R.	Debit	Date	Item	P.R.	Credit
Jan. 4			4,000	Jan. 4			300
15			2,500	30			500
				30			200
				31			1,200
				31			400
	→ 3,900		6,500				2,600
					Bal.		3,900
			6,500				6,500
Feb. 1	Bal.		3,900				

Balance of the account. Pencil footing

The balance of the account is entered on the first day of the following month.

Note: When there are several entries on each side, both the debit column and the credit column are pencil-footed. The pencil footing of one side is subtracted from the other side. The difference is written in the "Item" column on the side of the account that has the larger total.

5.6 POST-CLOSING TRIAL BALANCE

After the closing entries are made and the accounts ruled, only balance sheet accounts—assets, liabilities, and capital—remain open. It is desirable to produce another trial balance to ensure that the accounts are in balance. This is known as a post-closing trial balance.

EXAMPLE 11

T. Drew
Post-Closing Trial Balance
January 31, 198X

Cash	$3,900	
Supplies	100	
Furniture	2,000	
Accounts Payable		$ 800
T. Drew, Capital		5,200
	$6,000	$6,000

5.7 BOOKKEEPING AND ACCOUNTING CYCLE

Figure 5-1 illustrates the steps involved in recording transactions of a business.

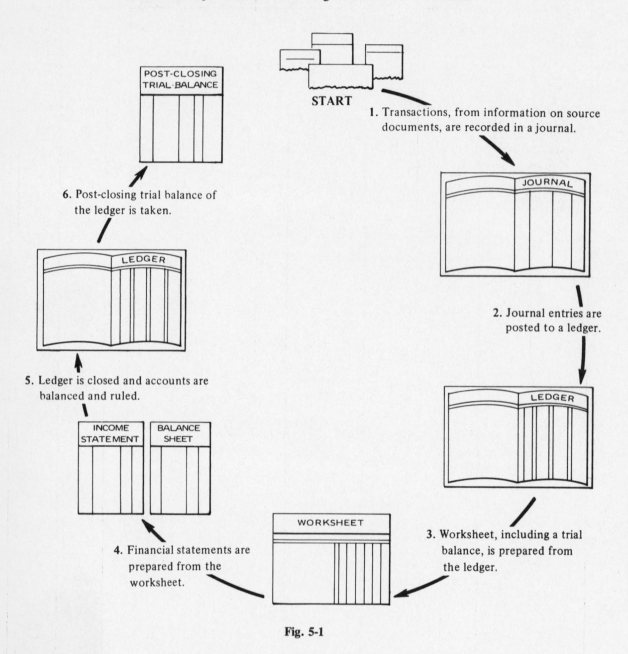

Fig. 5-1

Summary

1.. The basis of accounting that recognizes revenue when earned, regardless of when cash is received, and matches the expenses to the revenue, regardless of when cash is paid out, is known as the _____ .

2. An adjusting entry that records the expired amount of prepaid insurance would create the _____ account.

3. Supplies on hand is classified as an _____ and appears in the _____ , whereas supplies expense is an _____ and appears in the _____ .

4. Accrued salaries is treated in the balance sheet as a _____ , whereas Salaries Expense appears in the income statement as an _____ .

5. Both Allowance for Uncollectible Accounts and Accumulated Depreciation appear in the balance sheet as _____ from their related assets.

6. The related accounts discussed in Question 5 are _____ and _____ .

7. An expense paid in advance is known as a _____ .

8. The revenue and expense accounts are closed out to the summary account known as _____ .

9. Eventually, all income, expense, and drawing accounts, including summaries, will be closed into the _____ account.

10. The post-closing trial balance will involve only _____ , _____ , and _____ accounts.

Answers: 1. accrual basis; 2. insurance expense; 3. asset, balance sheet, expense, income statement; 4. liability account, expense account; 5. deductions; 6. Accounts Receivable, Equipment; 7. Prepaid Expense; 8. Expense and Income Summary; 9. Capital; 10. asset, liability, capital

Solved Problems

5.1 A business pays weekly salaries of $10,000 on Friday for the five-day week. Show the adjusting entry when the fiscal period ends on (*a*) Tuesday; (*b*) Thursday.

(*a*)

(*b*)

SOLUTION

(*a*)	Salaries Expense	4,000	
	Salaries Payable		4,000
(*b*)	Salaries Expense	8,000	
	Salaries Payable		8,000

5.2   An insurance policy covering a 2-year period was purchased on November 1 for $600. The amount was debited to Prepaid Insurance. Show the adjusting entry for the 2-month period ending December 31.

SOLUTION

Insurance Expense	50*	
Prepaid Insurance		50

* $\dfrac{\$600}{2 \text{ years}} \times \dfrac{2}{12} \text{ years} = \$50$

5.3   Office supplies purchases of $900 were debited to Office Supplies on Hand. A count of the supplies at the end of the period showed $500 still on hand. Make the adjusting entry at the end of the period.

SOLUTION

Office Supplies Expense	400	
Office Supplies		400

5.4   Machinery costing $12,000, purchased November 30, is being depreciated at the rate of 10 percent per year. Show the adjusting entry for December 31.

SOLUTION

Depreciation Expense—Machinery	100*	
Accumulated Depreciation—Machinery		100

* $\$12,000 \times 10\% \text{ per year} \times \dfrac{1}{12} \text{ year} = \$100$

5.5   A large tractor costing $60,000 was purchased on September 30, is being depreciated by the straight-line method over 5 years, and has no salvage value. Show the year-end adjusting entry. (The tractor was put into use on October 1.)

SOLUTION

Depreciation	3,000*	
Accumulated Depreciation		3,000

* $\dfrac{\text{Cost} - \text{salvage value}}{\text{Depreciation period}} \times \text{months in use} = \dfrac{\$60,000 - 0}{60 \text{ mo.}} = \$1,000 \times 3 \text{ mo.} = \$3,000$

5.6   Salaries paid to employees are \$500 per day. The weekly payroll ends on Friday, but Tuesday is the last day of the accounting period. Show the necessary adjusting entry (5-day week).

SOLUTION

Salaries Expense	1,000*	
Salaries Payable		1,000

* \$500 × 2 = \$1,000

5.7   On June 1, Dry Lake camps purchased a 3-year fire insurance policy costing \$9,000. This was debited to a Prepaid Insurance account. The camp's year ends on November 30. (*a*) Show the necessary adjusting entry. (*b*) Show the entry if the above insurance policy was debited to an Insurance Expense account.

(*a*)

(*b*)

SOLUTION

(*a*)

Insurance Expense	1,500*	
Prepaid Insurance		1,500

$$* \ \frac{\$9,000}{36 \text{ mo.}} = \$250 \times 6 \text{ mo.} = \$1,500$$

(*b*)

Prepaid Insurance	7,500*	
Insurance Expense		7,500

$$* \ \frac{\$9,000}{36 \text{ mo.}} = \$250 \times 30 \text{ mo.} = \$7,500$$

Note that here we are concerned with how much is left of the policy amount.

5.8   Supplies costing \$2,000 were debited to Supplies. The year-end inventory showed \$1,150 of supplies on hand. (*a*) Show the necessary year-end adjusting entry. (*b*) Show the above adjusting entry if the supplies were debited to a Supplies Expense account when purchased.

(*a*)

(*b*)

SOLUTION

(a)	Supplies Expense	850*	
	Supplies		850

* $2,000 - $1,150 = $850

(b)	Supplies	1,150	
	Supplies Expense		1,150

5.9 (a) The balance in the Prepaid Insurance account, before adjustments, is $1,800, and the amount expired during the year is $1,200. The amount needed for the adjusting entry required is _____.

(b) A business pays weekly salaries (5-day week) of $4,000 on Friday. The amount of the adjusting entry necessary at the end of the fiscal period ending on Wednesday is _____.

(c) On December 31, the end of the fiscal year, the supplies account had a balance before adjustment of $650. The fiscal supply inventory account on December 31 is $170. The amount of the adjusting entry is _____.

(d) The supplies account on December 31 has an inventory of $500. The supplies used during the year is $200. The amount of the adjusting entry to record this information is _____.

SOLUTION

(a) $1,200
(b) $2,400 ($4,000 ÷ 5 days = $800 per day; $800 × 3 days = $2,400)
(c) $480 ($650 − $170)
(d) $200

5.10 Listed below are the T accounts of Little Frank, who owns four hot dog stands at the local ball park. The year-end adjustments necessary to bring the accounts up to date are:

(a) Inventory of supplies at end of year was $395.
(b) Depreciation for the year was $900.
(c) Wages owed but not paid were $725.
(d) Utilities owed but not paid were $215.
(e) Insurance expense for the year was $1,150.
(f) Cash sales not yet posted were $2,175.

Cash		Accounts Receivable		Supplies		L. Frank, Drawing	
7,555		1,750		915		1,250	

Accounts Payable		L. Frank, Capital		Wages Expense	
	975		17,000	20,665	

Prepaid Insurance		Sales Income		Utilities Expense	
1,575			16,450	715	

First, prepare the adjusting journal entries. Then, make the necessary adjustments to the T accounts. (*Hint*: You will have to open new accounts.)

Adjusting Entries

(a)

(b)

(c)

(d)

(e)

(f)

Cash		Accounts Receivable		Supplies		Accounts Payable	
7,555		1,750		915			975

L. Frank, Capital		Wages Expense		Prepaid Insurance		Sales Income	
	17,000	20,665		1,575			16,450

Utilities Expense		Supplies Expense		Depreciation Expense		Accumulated Depreciation	
715							

Wages Payable	Insurance Expense	L. Frank, Drawing

SOLUTION

Adjusting Entries

(a)	Supplies Expense	520	
	Supplies		520
(b)	Depreciation Expense	900	
	Accumulated Depreciation		900
(c)	Wages Expense	725	
	Wages Payable		725
(d)	Utilities Expense	215	
	Accounts Payable		215
(e)	Insurance Expense	1,150	
	Prepaid Insurance		1,150
(f)	Cash	2,175	
	Sales Income		2,175

Cash		Accounts Receivable		Supplies		Accounts Payable	
7,555		1,750		915	520 (a)		975
(f) 2,175		1,750					215 (d)
9,730				395			1,190

L. Frank, Capital		Wages Expense		Prepaid Insurance		Sales Income	
	17,000	20,665		1,575	1,150 (e)		26,450
	17,000	(c) 725					2,175 (f)
		21,390		425			28,625

Utilities Expense		Supplies Expense		Depreciation Expense		Accumulated Depreciation	
715		(a) 520		(b) 900			900 (b)
(d) 215		520		900			900
930							

Wages Payable		Insurance Expense		L. Frank, Drawing	
	725 (c)	(e) 1,150		1,250	
	725	1,150			

5.11 From the preceding problem about Little Frank's Hot Dog stand, prepare the closing entries from the T accounts after you made the necessary adjustments.

Closing Entries

(1)			
(2)			
(3)			
(4)			

SOLUTION

Closing Entries

(1)	Sales Income	28,625	
	Expense and Income Summary		28,625
(2)	Expense and Income Summary	24,890	
	Wages Expense		21,390
	Insurance Expense		1,150
	Depreciation Expense		900
	Supplies Expense		520
	Utilities Expense		930
(3)	Expense and Income Summary	3,735	
	L. Frank, Capital		3,735
(4)	L. Frank, Capital	1,250	
	L. Frank, Drawing		1,250

5.12 Prior to the adjustment on December 31, the Salaries Expense account had a debit of $200,000. Salaries owed, but not yet paid, totaled $5,000. Present the entries required to record the following:

(a) Accrued salary as of December 31

(b) The closing of the salary expense account

(a)			
(b)			

SOLUTION

(a)	Salaries Expense	5,000	
	Salaries Payable		5,000
(b)	Expense and Income Summary	205,000	
	Salaries Expense		205,000

5.13 Selected accounts from the ledger are presented in the T account form below. Journalize the adjusting entries that have been posted to the accounts.

Cash		Salaries Payable	
36,860			4,000

Prepaid Insurance		Capital	
600	200		32,000

Supplies		Expense and Income Summary	
540	240		

Equipment		Fees Income	
6,000			12,000

Accumulated Depreciation		Salaries Expense	
	1,800	4,000	

		Insurance Expense	
		200	

		Depreciation Expense	
		1,800	

		Supplies Expense	
		240	

SOLUTION

Insurance Expense	200	
Prepaid Insurance		200
Supplies Expense	240	
Supplies		240
Depreciation Expense	1,800	
Accumulated Depreciation		1,800
Salaries Expense	4,000	
Salaries Payable		4,000

5.14 From the information in Problem 5.13, present the necessary closing entries.

(a)			
(b)			
(c)			

SOLUTION

(a)	Fees Income	12,000	
	Expense and Income Summary		12,000
(b)	Expense and Income Summary	6,240	
	Salaries Expense		4,000
	Insurance Expense		200
	Depreciation Expense		1,800
	Supplies Expense		240
(c)	Expense and Income Summary	5,760	
	Capital		5,760

5.15 From the information in Problem 5.14, prepare a post-closing trial balance.

Account	Dr.	Cr.

SOLUTION

Account	Dr.	Cr.
Cash	36,860	
Prepaid Insurance	400	
Supplies	300	
Equipment	6,000	
Accumulated Depreciation		1,800
Salaries Payable		4,000
Capital		37,760
	43,560	43,560

5.16 The trial balance before closing shows service income of $10,000 and interest income of $2,000. The expenses are: salaries, $6,000; rent, $2,000; depreciation, $1,500; and interest, $500. Give the closing entries to be made to Expense and Income Summary for (a) income and (b) expenses.

(a)

(b)

SOLUTION

	Account	Dr.	Cr.
(a)	Service Income	10,000	
	Interest Income	2,000	
	Expense and Income Summary		12,000
(b)	Expense and Income Summary	10,000	
	Salaries Expense		6,000
	Rent Expense		2,000
	Depreciation Expense		1,500
	Interest Expense		500

5.17 Using the solution of Problem 5.16 prepare the closing entry for net income, and post the transactions to the Expense and Income Summary and to the capital account, which had a prior balance of $20,000. Finally, close out the applicable account.

Expense and Income Summary				Capital	
(b)	10,000	12,000	(a)	Bal.	20,000
(c)	?				

SOLUTION

Expense and Income Summary	2,000	
Capital		2,000

Expense and Income Summary				Capital	
(b)	10,000	12,000	(a)	Bal.	20,000
(c)	2,000				2,000 (c)
	12,000	12,000			

5.18 After all revenue and expense accounts were closed at the end of the fiscal year, the Expense and Income Summary had a debit total of $100,000 and a credit total of $150,000. The capital account for Laura Anthony had a credit balance of $50,000; and Laura Anthony, Drawing had a debit balance of $35,000. Journalize the closing entries.

SOLUTION

Expense and Income Summary	50,000	
Laura Anthony, Capital		50,000
Laura Anthony, Capital	35,000	
Laura Anthony, Drawing		35,000

5.19 Based on the balances below, prepare entries to close out (*a*) income accounts, (*b*) expense accounts, (*c*) Expense and Income Summary, (*d*) drawing account.

P. Silvergold, Capital		$22,000
P. Silvergold, Drawing	$6,000	
Service Income		12,000
Interest Income		1,500
Wages and Salaries Expense	8,000	
Rent Expense	4,000	
Depreciation Expense	3,000	
Interest Expense	2,000	

(*a*)

(*b*)

(*c*)

(*d*)

SOLUTION

(*a*)	Service Income	12,000	
	Interest Income	1,500	
	Expense and Income Summary		13,500
(*b*)	Expense and Income Summary	17,000	
	Wages and Salaries Expense		8,000
	Rent Expense		4,000
	Depreciation Expense		3,000
	Interest Expense		2,000
(*c*)	P. Silvergold, Capital	3,500*	
	Expense and Income Summary		3,500
(*d*)	P. Silvergold, Capital	6,000	
	P. Silvergold, Drawing		6,000

* $3,500 represents a net loss and is debited to the capital account.

Examination I

Part I: Multiple Choice

1. The statement that presents assets, liabilities, and capital of a business entity as of a specific date is termed the (*a*) balance sheet, (*b*) income statement, (*c*) capital statement, (*d*) funds statement.

2. A business paid creditors on account. The effect of this transaction on the accounting equation was to (*a*) increase one asset, decrease another asset; (*b*) increase an asset, increase a liability; (*c*) decrease an asset, decrease a liability; (*d*) decrease an asset, decrease capital.

3. Which of the following applications of the rules of debit and credit is false?

		Recorded in Account as	Normal Balance of Account
(*a*)	Increase in drawing	Credit	Credit
(*b*)	Increase in salary expense account	Debit	Debit
(*c*)	Increase in supplies account	Debit	Debit
(*d*)	Decrease in accounts payable account	Debit	Credit
(*e*)	Decrease in accounts receivable account	Credit	Debit

4. Which of the following errors, each considered individually, would cause the trial balance totals to be unequal? (*a*) A payment of $600 to a creditor was posted as a debit of $600 to Accounts Payable and a credit of $60 to Cash. (*b*) Cash received from customers on account was posted as a debit of $200 to Cash and a debit of $200 to Accounts Receivable. (*c*) A payment of $285 for equipment was posted as a debit of $285 to Equipment and a credit of $258 to Cash. (*d*) All of the above. (*e*) None of the above.

5. Entries journalized at the end of an accounting period to remove the balances from the temporary accounts so that they will be ready for use in accumulating data for the following accounting period are termed: (*a*) adjusting entries, (*b*) closing entries, (*c*) correcting entries, (*d*) all of the above, (*e*) none of the above.

6. If the effect of the debit portion of an adjusting entry is to increase the balance of an expense account, which of the following describes the effect of the credit portion of the entry? (*a*) decreases the balance of an asset account, (*b*) increases the balance of an asset account, (*c*) decreases the balance of a liability account, (*d*) increases the balance of a revenue account, (*e*) decreases the balance of the capital account.

7. Which of the following accounts should be closed to Expense and Income Summary at the end of the year? (*a*) depreciation expense, (*b*) sales income, (*c*) supplies expense, (*d*) rent income, (*e*) all of the above.

8. The adjusting entry to record depreciation of equipment is: (*a*) debit depreciation expense, credit depreciation payable; (*b*) debit depreciation payable, credit depreciation expense; (*c*) debit depreciation expense, credit accumulated depreciation; (*d*) debit equipment, credit depreciation expense.

9. The difference between the balance of a plant asset account and the related contra-asset account is termed: (*a*) expired cost, (*b*) accrual, (*c*) book value, (*d*) depreciation, (*e*) none of the above.

10. At the end of the preceding fiscal year, the usual adjusting entry for accrued salaries owed to employees was inadvertently omitted. This error was not corrected, but the accrued salaries were included in the

93

first salary payment in the current fiscal year. Which of the following statements is true? (*a*) Salary expense was understated, and net income was overstated for the preceding year. (*b*) Salary expense was overstated, and net income was understated for the current year. (*c*) Salaries payable was understated at the end of the preceding fiscal year. (*d*) All of the above. (*e*) None of the above.

11. If total assets decreased by $5,000 during a period of time and capital increased by $15,000 during the same period, the amount and direction (increase or decrease) of the period's change in total liabilities is: (*a*) $10,000 increase, (*b*) $10,000 decrease, (*c*) $20,000 increase, (*d*) $20,000 decrease.

12. The total assets and total liabilities of a particular business enterprise at the beginning and at the end of the year appear below. During the year, the owner had withdrawn $18,000 for personal use and had made an additional investment in the enterprise of $5,000.

	Assets	Liabilities
Beginning of year	$166,000	$72,000
End of year	177,000	99,000

The amount of net income or net loss for the year was (*a*) net income of $11,000; (*b*) net income of $13,000; (*c*) net loss of $27,000; (*d*) net loss of $3,000.

13. The balance in the prepaid insurance account before adjustment at the end of the year is $1,840, and the amount of insurance expired during the year is $720. The adjusting entry required is: (*a*) debit insurance expense, $720; credit prepaid insurance, $720; (*b*) debit prepaid insurance, $720; credit insurance expense, $720; (*c*) debit insurance expense, $1,120; credit prepaid insurance, $1,120; (*d*) debit prepaid insurance, $1,120; credit insurance expense, $1,120.

14. A business enterprise pays weekly salaries of $5,000 on Friday for a 5-day week ending on that day. The adjusting entry necessary at the end of the fiscal period ending on Tuesday is: (*a*) debit salaries payable, $2,000; credit salary expense, $2,000; (*b*) debit salary expense, $2,000; credit salaries payable, $2,000; (*c*) debit salary expense, $2,000; credit drawings, $2,000; (*d*) debit drawings, $2,000; credit salaries payable, $2,000.

15. Cash of $650 received from a customer on account was recorded as a $560 debit to Accounts Receivable and a credit to Cash. The necessary correcting entry is: (*a*) debit Cash, $90; credit Accounts Receivable, $90; (*b*) debit Accounts Receivable, $90; credit Cash, $90; (*c*) debit Cash, $650; credit Accounts Receivable, $650; (*d*) debit Cash, $1,210; credit Accounts Receivable, $1,210.

Part II: Problems

1. Below are the account balances of the State-Rite Cleaning Company as of December 31, 198X. Prepare (*a*) an income statement, (*b*) a capital statement, (*c*) a balance sheet.

Accounts Payable	$11,600	Miscellaneous Expense	$ 3,000
Cleaning Income	39,500	Notes Payable	2,800
Capital (beginning)	14,300	Rent Expense	12,600
Cash	9,300	Salaries Expense	9,200
Drawing	4,800	Supplies Expense	2,400
Equipment	19,200	Supplies Inventory	5,300
Equipment Repairs Expense	2,400		

2. For each numbered transaction below, indicate the account to be debited and the account to be credited by placing the letter representing the account in the appropriate column. Accounts Payable (*a*); Capital (*b*); Cash (*c*); Drawing (*d*); Equipment (*e*); Fees Income (*f*); Notes Payable (*g*); Rent Expense (*h*); Salaries Expense (*i*); Supplies (*j*); Supplies Expense (*k*).

		Debit	Credit
(1)	Invested cash in the firm.	(*c*)	(*b*)
(2)	Received cash for services rendered.		
(3)	Paid salaries for the week.		
(4)	Bought equipment on account.		
(5)	Bought supplies on account.		
(6)	Gave a note in settlement of the equipment on account.		
(7)	Borrowed money from the bank.		
(8)	Withdrew cash for personal use.		
(9)	A count showed that approximately three-quarters of the supplies inventory had been used during the year.		
(10)	Paid rent for the month.		

3. The balances of the accounts of the Judith Playhouse, as of November 30, were as follows:

Judith Playhouse
Trial Balance
November 30

Cash	$10,000	
Accounts Receivable	2,100	
Supplies	600	
Equipment	12,000	
Building	9,000	
Accounts Payable		$ 6,500
Notes Payable		12,000
Judith Playhouse, Capital		15,200
	$33,700	$33,700

Selected transactions for the month of December were:

(*a*) Dec. 1 Bought new theatrical equipment for $3,000, paying half in cash and giving our note for the balance.
(*b*) 10 Paid $1,000 due on the notes payable.
(*c*) 14 Receipts for the 2-week period (admissions income) totaled $9,600.
(*d*) 20 Paid utilities, $150.
(*e*) 24 Paid $1,000 for 5-year insurance policy on the theatre.
(*f*) 28 Paid monthly salaries, $1,250.

Prepare all necessary entries to record above transactions.

4. Using the following data, prepare journal entries for the month of December.

   (a) Weekly salaries of $8,000 are payable on Friday for a 5-day week. What is the adjusting entry if the fiscal period ends on Wednesday?

   (b) An insurance policy covering a 4-year period was purchased on February 1 for $1,200. What is the adjusting entry on December 31?

   (c) Office supplies of $700 were debited to Office Supplies at the end of the month. The account has $300 worth still on hand. Prepare the adjusting entry.

5. After all income and expense accounts of the Gold Silver Company were closed at the end of the year, the expense and income summary had a debit balance of $125,000 and a credit balance of $190,000. The capital account had a credit balance of $72,000, whereas the drawing account had a debit balance of $12,000. Journalize the closing entries.

6. Selected accounts from a ledger are presented in T account form. (a) Journalize the adjusting entries that have been posted to the account, (b) journalize the closing entries that have been posted to the account.

Prepaid Insurance		Salaries Expense	
240	125	2,700	6,300
175		2,925	
		675	

Accumulated Depreciation		Insurance Expense	
	2,250	125	125
	400		

		Depreciation Expense	
Salaries Payable		400	400
	675		

		Miscellaneous Expense	
Expense and Income Summary		25	290
7,115		100	
		45	
		50	
		70	

7. Journalize the following transactions:

   (a) Ronald Henderson began his dentistry practice by investing $24,000 cash, $12,000 in equipment, and $6,000 in supplies.

   (b) Bought $5,000 worth of equipment, paying $1,000 and owing the balance to Halpern Company.

   (c) Received $4,200 from fees for the month.

   (d) Paid rent of $600.

   (e) Paid salaries of $1,200.

   (f) Paid half of the amount owed to Halpern Company.

   (g) Withdrew $700 for personal use.

   (h) Supplies on hand, $5,000.

8. Post from the journal in Problem 7 and present a trial balance.

9. Based on the information presented in Problem 8, journalize all necessary entries to close the accounts. Then post and rule them.

Answers to Examination I

Part I

1. (*a*); **2.** (*c*); **3.** (*a*); **4.** (*a*); **5.** (*b*); **6.** (*a*); **7.** (*e*); **8.** (*c*); **9.** (*c*); **10.** (*a*); **11.** (*d*); **12.** (*d*); **13.** (*a*); **14.** (*b*); **15.** (*d*)

Part II

1. (*a*)

State-Rite Cleaning Company
Income Statement
For the Period Ending December 31, 198X

Cleaning Income		$39,500
Expenses		
Equipment Repairs Expense	$ 2,400	
Rent Expense	12,600	
Salaries Expense	9,200	
Supplies Expense	2,400	
Miscellaneous Expense	3,000	
Total Expenses		29,600
Net Income		$ 9,900

(*b*)

State-Rite Cleaning Company
Capital Statement
For the Period Ending December 31, 198X

Capital, January 1, 198X		$14,300
Net Income	$ 9,900	
Less: Drawing	4,800	
Increase in Capital		5,100
Capital, December 31, 198X		$19,400

(*c*)

State-Rite Cleaning Company
Balance Sheet
December 31, 198X

ASSETS

Cash	$ 9,300	
Supplies Inventory	5,300	
Equipment	19,200	
Total Assets		$33,800

LIABILITIES AND CAPITAL

Accounts Payable	$11,600	
Notes Payable	2,800	
Total Liabilities		$14,400
Capital, December 31, 198X		19,400
Total Liabilities and Capital		$33,800

2.

	Debit	Credit
(1)	(c)	(b)
(2)	(c)	(f)
(3)	(i)	(c)
(4)	(e)	(a)
(5)	(j)	(a)
(6)	(a)	(g)
(7)	(c)	(g) or (a)
(8)	(d)	(c)
(9)	(k)	(j)
(10)	(h)	(c)

3.

(a)   Equipment   3,000
  Cash   1,500
  Notes Payable   1,500

(b)   Notes Payable   1,000
  Cash   1,000

(c)   Cash   9,600
  Admissions Income   9,600

(d)   Utilities Expense   150
  Cash   150

(e)   Prepaid Insurance   1,000
  Cash   1,000

(f)   Salaries Expense   1,250
  Cash   1,250

4.

(a)   Salaries Expense   4,800
  Salaries Payable   4,800
  [3 × (8,000 ÷ 5) = 4,800]

(b)   Insurance Expense   275
  Prepaid Insurance   275
  (1,200 ÷ 4 = 300;
  $\frac{11}{12} \times 300 = 275$)

(c)   Supplies Expense   400
  Supplies   400

5.

Expense and Income Summary	65,000	
Capital		65,000
Capital	12,000	
Drawing		12,000

6. (*a*)

Insurance Expense	125	
Prepaid Insurance		125
Depreciation Expense	400	
Accumulated Depreciation		400
Salaries Expense	675	
Salaries Payable		675

(*b*)

Income Summary	7,115	
Salaries Expense		6,300
Depreciation Expense		400
Insurance Expense		125
Miscellaneous Expense		290

7. (*a*)

Cash	24,000	
Supplies	6,000	
Equipment	12,000	
Henderson, Capital		42,000

(*b*)

Equipment	5,000	
Cash		1,000
Accounts Payable—Halpern		4,000

(*c*)

Cash	4,200	
Fees Income		4,200

(*d*)

Rent Expense	600	
Cash		600

(*e*)

Salaries Expense	1,200	
Cash		1,200

(*f*)

Accounts Payable	2,000	
Cash		2,000

(*g*)

Drawing	700	
Cash		700

(*h*)

Supplies Expense	1,000	
Supplies		1,000

8.

Cash			
(a)	24,000	1,000	(b)
(c)	4,200	600	(d)
		1,200	(e)
		2,000	(f)
		700	(g)

Accounts Payable			
(f)	2,000	4,000	(b)

Fees Income		
	4,200	(c)

Capital		
	42,000	(a)

Rent Expense		
(d)	600	

Supplies			
(a)	6,000	1,000	(h)

Drawing		
(g)	700	

Salaries Expense		
(e)	1,200	

Equipment		
(a)	12,000	
(b)	5,000	

Supplies Expense		
(h)	1,000	

Trial Balance

Cash	$22,700	
Supplies	5,000	
Equipment	17,000	
Accounts Payable		$ 2,000
Capital		42,000
Drawing	700	
Fees Income		4,200
Rent Expense	600	
Salaries Expense	1,200	
Supplies Expense	1,000	
	$48,200	$48,200

9.

(i)	Fees Income	4,200	
	Expense and Income Summary		4,200
(j)	Expense and Income Summary	2,800	
	Rent Expense		600
	Salaries Expense		1,200
	Supplies Expense		1,000
(k)	Expense and Income Summary	1,400	
	Capital		1,400
(l)	Capital	700	
	Drawing		700

Capital			
(l)	700	42,000	(a)
		1,400	(k)

Fees Income			
(i)	4,200	4,200	(i)

	Drawing		
(g)	700	700	(l)

	Rent Expense		
(d)	600	600	(j)

	Expense and Income Summary		
(j)	2,800	4,200	(i)
(k)	1,400		
	4,200	4,200	

	Salaries Expense		
(e)	1,200	1,200	(j)

	Supplies Expense		
(h)	1,000	1,000	(j)

PART II: Special Journals and Ledgers

Chapter 6

Repetitive Transactions—Sales Journal

6.1 INTRODUCTION

In the previous chapters, each transaction was recorded by first placing an entry in the general journal and then posting the entry to the related accounts in the general ledger. This system, however, is both time-consuming and wasteful. It is much simpler and more efficient to group together those transactions that are repetitive, such as sales, purchases, cash receipts, and cash payments, and place each of them in a special journal.

Many types of transactions may require the use of special journals, for example, receipt or payment of cash and purchase or sale of goods or services.

The number and design of the special journals will vary, depending on the needs of a particular business. The special journals used in a typical firm are as follows:

Name of Special Journal	Abbreviation	Type of Transaction
Cash receipts journal	CR	All cash received
Cash disbursements journal	CD	All cash paid out
Purchases journal	P	All purchases on account
Sales journal	S	All sales on account

In addition to these four special journals, a general journal (J) is used for recording transactions that do not fit into any of the four types above. The general journal is also used for the recording of adjusting and closing entries at the end of the accounting period.

6.2 SALES JOURNAL

Only sales on account are recorded in the sales journal; cash sales are recorded in the cash receipts journal (page 128).

EXAMPLE 1

Sales on account are made during the month as follows: on February 1 to A. Anderson for $200, on February 2 to B. Butler for $350, on February 12 to C. Chase for $125, and on February 24 to D. Davis and Co. for $400. The procedure to record these sales is as follows:

1. Record the sales on account in the sales journal.
2. At the end of the month only, add the amount column and post the total amount, $1,075, to the general ledger by debiting Accounts Receivable (account number 12) and by crediting Sales Income (account number 41) for $1,075 each.
3. Place a posting reference in the sales journal by recording the account number 12 for Accounts Receivable, and the account number 41 for Sales Income, under the total.
4. In the general ledger, place the source of the entry S-1 in each account.

102

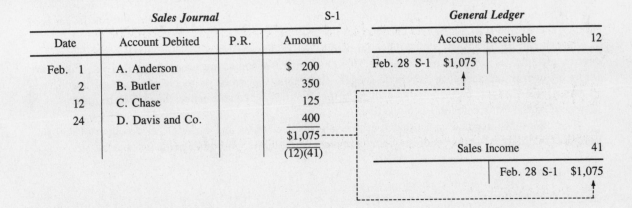

Advantages of Special Journals

1. **Reduces detailed recording.** As demonstrated in the transactions above, each sales transaction is recorded on a single line with all details included on that line: date, customer's name, and amount.

2. **Reduces posting.** There is only *one* posting made to Accounts Receivable and *one* posting to Sales Income, regardless of the number of transactions.

3. **Permits better division of labor.** If there are several journals, it makes it possible for more than one bookkeeper to work on the books at the same time.

6.3 SPECIAL LEDGERS (Subsidiary Ledgers)

Further simplification of the general ledger is brought about by the use of subsidiary ledgers. In particular, for those businesses that sell goods on credit and that find it necessary to maintain a separate account with each customer and with each creditor, the use of a special accounts receivable ledger eliminates the need to make multiple entries in the general ledger.

The advantages of special or subsidiary ledgers are similar to the advantages of special journals. These are:

1. **Reduces ledger detail.** Most of the information will be in the subsidiary ledger, and the general ledger will be reserved chiefly for summary or total figures. Therefore, it will be easier to prepare the financial statements.

2. **Permits better division of labor.** Here again, each special or subsidiary ledger may be handled by a different person. Therefore, one person may work on the general ledger accounts while another person may work simultaneously on the subsidiary ledger.

3. **Permits a different sequence of accounts.** In the general ledger, it is desirable to have the accounts in the same sequence as in the balance sheet and income statement. As a further aid, it is desirable to use numbers to locate and reference the accounts, as explained in Section 2.5. However, in connection with accounts receivable, which involves names of customers or companies, it is preferable to have the accounts in alphabetical sequence.

4. **Permits better internal control.** Better control is maintained if a person other than the person responsible for the general ledger is responsible for the subsidiary ledger. For example, the accounts receivable or customers' ledger trial balance should agree with the balance of the accounts receivable account in the general ledger. The general ledger account acts as a controlling account, and the subsidiary ledger must agree with the control. No unauthorized entry could be made in the subsidiary ledger, as it would immediately put that record out of balance with the control account.

The idea of control accounts introduced above is an important one in accounting. Any group of similar accounts may be removed from the general ledger and a controlling account substituted for it. Not only is another level of error protection thereby provided, but the time needed to prepare the general ledger trial balance and the financial statements becomes further reduced.

In order to be capable of supplying information concerning the business's accounts receivable, a firm needs a separate account for each customer. These customer's accounts are grouped together in a subsidiary ledger known as the accounts receivable ledger. Each time the accounts receivable (control account) is increased or decreased, a customer's account in the accounts receivable ledger must also be increased or decreased by the same amount.

The customers' accounts are usually kept in alphabetical order and include, besides such outstanding balances, information such as address, phone number, credit terms, and other pertinent items.

EXAMPLE 2

The procedure for special ledgers is as follows:

1. After the sale is entered, the amount of the sale is immediately posted as a debit to the customer's account in the subsidiary accounts receivable ledger.

2. In the sales journal, a record of the posting is made in the post reference column by placing a check mark (✔) before the customer's name.

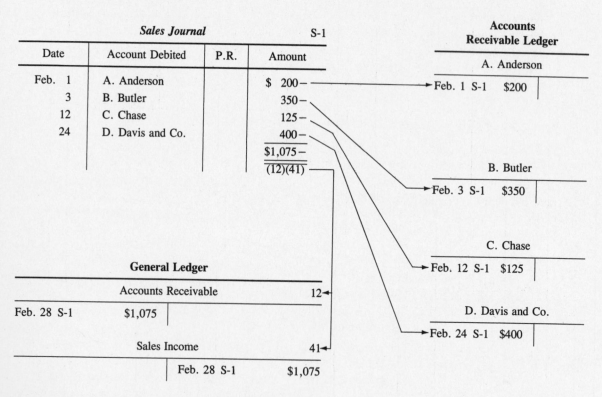

Proving That the Accounts Receivable Subsidiary Ledger Is Equal to the Control

After all individual transactions are posted to the subsidiary ledger and the totals in the sales journal are posted to the general ledger, the bookkeeper is ready to check the accuracy of the work.

EXAMPLE 3

The checking procedure is:

1. At the end of the month, the bookkeeper prepares a list of all open accounts found in the accounts receivable ledger.

2. The total due from customers is compared with the balance in the accounts receivable account in the general ledger. If the schedule and the control account agree, the bookkeeper has proved the accuracy of the recording.

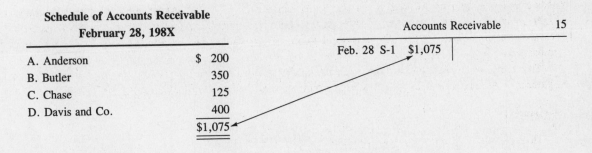

Schedule of Accounts Receivable
February 28, 198X

A. Anderson	$ 200
B. Butler	350
C. Chase	125
D. Davis and Co.	400
	$1,075

Accounts Receivable   15

Feb. 28 S-1 $1,075

6.4 SALES RETURNS

If, during the year, many transactions occur in which customers return goods bought on account, a special journal known as the *sales returns journal* would be used. However, where sales returns are infrequent, the general journal is sufficient.

The entry to record return of sales on account in the general journal would be:

J-1

	P.R.	Debit	Credit
Sales Returns	42	800	
Accounts Receivable, Lawton Company	12		800

The accounts receivable account, which is credited, is posted both in the accounts receivable controlling account and in the accounts receivable ledger.

Accounts Receivable Ledger   **General Ledger**

Lawton Company

Bal.	1,900	J-1	800

Accounts Receivable   12

Bal.	1,900	J-1	800

Sales Returns   42

J-1	800

If the sales returns involve the payment of cash, it would appear in the cash disbursements journal. Sales Returns appears in the income statement as a reduction of Sales Income.

6.5 TYPES OF LEDGER ACCOUNT FORMS

The T account has been used for most illustrations of accounts thus far. The disadvantage of the T account is that it requires totaling the debit and the credit columns in order to find the balance. As it is necessary to have the balance of a customer's or creditor's account available at any given moment, an alternative form of the ledger, *the three-column account*, may be used. The advantage of the form is that an extra column, "Balance," is provided, so that the amount the customer owes is always shown. As each transaction is recorded, the balance is updated. Below is an illustration of an accounts receivable ledger account using this form.

M. Gersten

Date	P.R.	Debit	Credit	Balance
Jan. 2	S-1	650		650
4	S-1	409		1,059
8	J-1		500	559

Summary

1. When transactions that are repetitive in nature are grouped together, they are placed in a _____ journal.

2. The abbreviation for the sales journal is _____ .

3. All sales _____ are recorded in the sales journal.

4. The sales journal helps reduce _____ and _____ .

5. The _____ ledger is used to maintain a separate account with each customer.

6. The account in the general ledger that after postings shows the total amount of dollars owed and agrees with the totals in the subsidiary ledger is termed the _____ account.

7. The extra column in a three-column T account shows the _____ of the account.

8. The list of accounts of individual customers, whose total equals the one figure in the accounts receivable controlling account, is known as the _____ .

9. The account used to show the amount of goods returned is _____ .

10. Infrequent returned sales would be recorded in the _____ journal.

Answers: 1. special; 2. S; 3. on account; 4. detailed recording, posting; 5. accounts receivable; 6. controlling; 7. balance; 8. schedule of accounts receivable; 9. sales returns; 10. general

Solved Problems

6.1   For each of the following transactions, indicate with a check mark the journal in which it should be recorded.

(*a*) Sale of merchandise to B. Orzech on account, $400

(*b*) Sale of merchandise to M. Snyder for cash, $150

(*c*) Cash refunded to M. Snyder for goods returned

(*d*) B. Orzech returned part of the goods sold for credit, $100

	Sales Journal	General Journal	Cash Journal
(a)			
(b)			
(c)			
(d)			

SOLUTION

	Sales Journal	General Journal	Cash Journal
(a)	✔		
(b)			✔
(c)			✔
(d)		✔	

6.2   Which of the transactions in Problem 6.1 should be posted to the subsidiary ledger?

SOLUTION

Transactions (a) and (d), because sales were on account. Transactions (b) and (c) involved cash, thereby creating no accounts receivable.

Accounts Receivable		12	
(a)	400	100	(d)

B. Orzech			
(a)	400	100	(d)

Sales Income		41	
		400	(a)

Sales Returns		42	
(d)	100		

6.3   Record the following transactions in the sales journal:

Jan. 1   Sold merchandise on account to Lombardi Company, $550.
     4   Sold merchandise on account to Gerard Company, $650.
    18   Sold merchandise on account to Harke Company, $300.
    29   Sold additional merchandise to Harke Company, $100.

Sales Journal   S-1

Date	Account Debited	P.R.	Amount

SOLUTION

Sales Journal   S-1

Date	Account Debited	P.R.	Amount
Jan. 1	Lombardi Company	✓	550
4	Gerard Company	✓	650
18	Harke Company	✓	300
29	Harke Company	✓	100
			1,600

6.4 Post the customers' accounts to the accounts receivable subsidiary ledger and prepare a schedule of accounts receivable.

Lombardi Company
_____

Gerard Company
_____

Harke Company
_____

Schedule of Accounts Receivable

Lombardi Company	
Gerard Company	
Harke Company	

SOLUTION

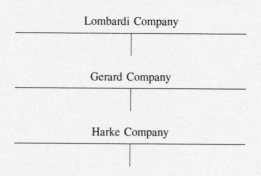

Lombardi Company
Jan. 1 S-1   550

Gerard Company
Jan. 4 S-1   650

Harke Company
Jan. 18 S-1   300
    20 S-1   100

Schedule of Accounts Receivable

Lombardi Company	550
Gerard Company	650
Harke Company	400
	1,600

6.5 For Problem 6.3, make the entries needed to record the sales for the month.

Accounts Receivable   12   Sales Income   41
_____   _____

SOLUTION

Accounts Receivable   12   Sales Income   41
Jan. 31 S-1   1,600   Jan. 31 S-1   1,600

6.6 Based on the following sales journal, post each transaction to its respective accounts receivable account.

Sales Journal   S-4

Date	Account Debited	P.R.	Amount
Jan. 5	J. Gallagher	✓	350
7	R. Glatt	✓	600
9	L. Harmin	✓	450
15	J. Gallagher	✓	250
20	R. Glatt	✓	500
26	R. Glatt	✓	100

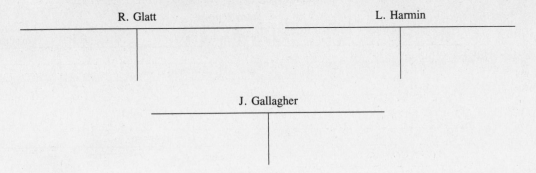

SOLUTION

```
            R. Glatt                              L. Harmin
Jan.  7 S-4    600  |                 Jan. 9 S-4    450  |
     20 S-4    500  |
     26 S-4    100  |

                        J. Gallagher
                 Jan.  5 S-4    350  |
                      15 S-4    250  |
```

6.7 Based on the information in Problem 6.6, post the necessary accounts in the general ledger.

```
       Accounts Receivable     12              Sales Income          41
                    |                                     |
```

SOLUTION

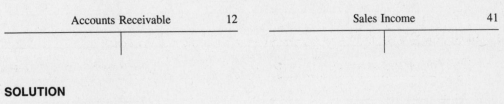

```
       Accounts Receivable     12              Sales Income          41
Jan. 31 S-4    2,250  |                           Jan. 31 S-4    2,250
```

Note: $2,250 is the total of all transactions involving the sale of goods on account.

6.8   Vitman Company was established in December of the current year. Its sales of merchandise on account and related returns and allowances during the remainder of the month are described below.

Dec. 15   Sold merchandise on account to Acme Co., $850.
   19   Sold merchandise on account to Balt Corp., $800.
   20   Sold merchandise on account to Conway, Inc., $1,200.
   22   Issued Credit Memorandum for $40 to Balt Corp. for merchandise returned.
   24   Sold merchandise on account to Davy Company, $1,650.
   25   Sold additional merchandise on account to Balt Corp., $900.
   26   Issued Credit Memorandum for $25 to Acme Co. for merchandise returned.
   27   Sold additional merchandise on account to Conway, Inc., $1,600.

Record the transactions for December in the sales journal and general journal below.

Sales Journal   S-6

Date	Account Debited	P.R.	Amount

General Journal   J-8

Date	Description	P.R.	Dr.	Cr.

SOLUTION

Sales Journal   S-6

Date	Account Debited	P.R.	Amount
Dec. 15	Acme Co.		850
19	Balt Corp.		800
20	Conway, Inc.		1,200
24	Davy Company		1,650
25	Balt Corp.		900
27	Conway, Inc.		1,600
			7,000

General Journal   J-8

Date	Description	P.R.	Dr.	Cr.
Dec. 22	Sales Returns		40	
	Accounts Receivable–Balt Corp.			40
26	Sales Returns		25	
	Accounts Receivable–Acme Co.			25

6.9   Based on the information in Problem 6.8, post to the customers' accounts.

Acme Co.		Conway, Inc.
Balt Corp.		Davy Company

SOLUTION

Acme Co.

Dec. 15 S-6	850	Dec. 26 J-8	25

Conway, Inc.

Dec. 20 S-6	1,200
27 S-6	1,600

Balt Corp.

Dec. 19 S-6	800	Dec. 22 J-8	40
25 S-6	900		

Davy Company

Dec. 24 S-6	1,650

6.10   Prepare a schedule of accounts receivable based on the information in Problem 6.9.

**Schedule of Accounts
Receivable**

Acme Co.	
Balt Corp.	
Conway, Inc.	
Davy Company	

SOLUTION

**Schedule of Accounts
Receivable**

Acme Co.	$ 825
Balt Corp.	1,660
Conway, Inc.	2,800
Davy Company	1,650
	$6,935

6.11   Post the general journal and the sales journal to the three accounts below using the data supplied in Problem 6.8. What is the sum of the balances of the accounts in the subsidiary ledger (Problem 6.10)? What is the balance of the controlling account?

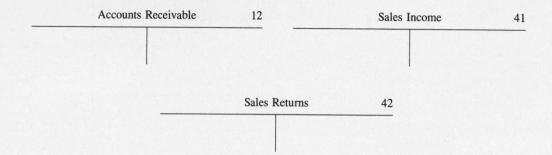

SOLUTION

Accounts Receivable			12
Dec. 31 S-6 7,000	Dec. 21 J-8	40	
	26 J-8	25	

Sales Income		41
	Dec. 31 S-6	7,000

Sales Returns		42
Dec. 22 J-8	40	
26 J-8	25	

The balance in the subsidiary ledger, $6,935, is the same as the balance in the accounts receivable account (control), $6,935.

6.12 Stillman Company was established in March of the current year. Their sales and related accounts for the month of March are listed below:

Mar. 2   Sold 25 lobsters to Conrad Hotel @ $7.50 each on account—total sale $187.50.
      7   Sold 40 pounds of shrimp to Green Hotel @ $11.00 per pound on account—total sale $440.00.
      9   Sold 60 pounds of lox to Winston Hotel @ $9.00 per pound on account—total sale $540.00.
     12   Sold 110 pounds of bluefish to Conrad Hotel @ $4.50 per pound on account—total sale $495.00.
     17   Issued credit memorandum for $25.00 to Conrad Hotel for merchandise returned.
     21   Sold 90 lobsters to Green Hotel @ $7.00 each on account—total sale $630.00.
     25   Issued credit memorandum to Green Hotel for 12 lobsters returned @ $7.00 each ($84.00).
     27   Sold 175 lobsters to Hill Top Hotel @ $7.50 each on account—total sale $1,312.50.

Record the above transactions in the sales journal and general journal below.

Sales Journal   S-10

Date	Account Debited	P.R.	Amount

General Journal   J-4

Date	Description	P.R.	Dr.	Cr.

SOLUTION

Sales Journal   S-10

Date	Account Debited	P.R.	Amount
Mar. 2	Conrad Hotel		187.50
7	Green Hotel		440.00
9	Winston Hotel		540.00
12	Conrad Hotel		495.00
21	Green Hotel		630.00
27	Hill Top Hotel		1,312.50
			3,605.00

General Journal

Date	Description	P.R.	Dr.	Cr.
Mar. 17	Sales Returns		25	
	Accounts Rec./Conrad Hotel			25
25	Sales Returns		84	
	Accounts Rec./Green Hotel			84

From the information above, post to customers' accounts.

6.13   Post the subsidiary accounts, the general journal, and sales journal to the accounts below using the data from Problem 6.12.

Accounts Receivable   Sales Income

Sales Returns

Subsidiary Ledger

Conrad Hotel   Green Hotel

Subsidiary Ledger, cont.

	Winston Hotel		Hill Top Hotel

SOLUTION

Accounts Receivable			
Mar. 31 S-10	3,605	Mar. 17 J-4	25
		Mar. 25 J-4	84

Sales Income	
	Mar. 31 S-10 3,605

Sales Returns	
Mar. 17 J-4	25
25 J-4	84

Conrad Hotel			
Mar. 2 S-10	187.50	Mar. 17 J-4	25.00
12 S-10	495.00		

Green Hotel			
Mar. 7 S-10	440	Mar. 25 J-4	84
21 S-10	630		

Winston Hotel	
Mar. 9 S-10	540

Hill Top Hotel	
Mar. 27 S-10	
1,312.50	

6.14 Prepare a schedule of accounts receivable from the information provided above.

Schedule of Accounts Receivable

Conrad Hotel	
Green Hotel	
Winston Hotel	
Hill Top Hotel	
March Accounts Receivable	

SOLUTION

Schedule of Accounts Receivable

Conrad Hotel	$ 657.50
Green Hotel	986.00
Winston Hotel	540.00
Hill Top Hotel	1,312.50
March Accounts Receivable	$3,496.00

Chapter 7

The Purchases Journal

7.1 PURCHASES AS A COST

Before any firm can sell merchandise (see Sales Journal, Chapter 6), it must purchase goods to be resold. Purchasing goods for resale is synonymous with incurring an expense. Cost accounts are similar to expense accounts, because both decrease the owners' capital and both are temporary. In order to record the cost of all goods bought during an accounting period, a new account, Purchases, must be established. It is important to note that expenses are necessary in order to operate a business, but costs are incurred in order to acquire goods for resale.

7.2 TRADE DISCOUNTS

Manufacturers and wholesalers publish catalogs in order to describe their products and list their retail prices. Usually, they offer deductions from these list prices to dealers who buy in large quantities. These deductions are known as *trade discounts*. By offering these discounts, a business can *adjust* a price at which it is willing to bill its goods without changing the list price in the catalog.

EXAMPLE 1

The Carrie Corporation wants to continue advertising its stereo radio at a list price of $150. However, the radio is offered to dealers at a trade discount of 30 percent, which amounts to $45. Therefore, the dealer pays only $105 for the set.

EXAMPLE 2

Assume that the Carrie Corporation wants to continue advertising its radio at a list price of $150, but because of higher costs, an increase to dealers has to be made. The corporation will issue a new price list on which the trade discount will be reduced from 30 percent to 25 percent, and so they will not have to issue a completely new catalog just to change the price of a few items.

EXAMPLE 3

A trade discount can also be increased so as to offer older goods to dealers at a lower cost. If a new type of stereo radio were to come out at $200, the Carrie Corporation might increase its trade discount to 40 percent on older models in order to encourage dealers to purchase them.

Note that trade discounts are not recorded in the accounting records, as they are used only to determine the *net* purchase price. For accounting purposes, the amount recorded would be the price that must be paid to the seller (retail price minus the trade discount). For example, if the older models were to retail for $150, less a new trade discount of 40 percent, the entry to record the purchase on account would be:

	Dr.	Cr.
Purchases	90	
Accounts Payable		90
($150 − $60 discount)		

7.3 PURCHASE INVOICES

In most businesses, purchases are made regularly and are evidenced by purchase invoices to creditors. A purchase invoice is the source document that supplies the information for recording goods on account.

Such information would include:

1. Seller's name and address
2. Date of purchase and invoice number
3. Method of shipment
4. Terms of the purchase transaction
5. Type and quantity of goods shipped
6. Cost of goods billed

Where there are many transactions for purchases of merchandise for resale, for supplies or equipment, the labor-saving features of a special purchases journal should be utilized.

7.4 PURCHASES JOURNAL

The basic principles that apply to the sales journal (Chapter 6) also apply to the purchases journal. However, a single-column purchases journal is too limited to be practicable, as businesses do not usually restrict their credit purchases only to merchandise bought for resale. Various kinds of goods (office and store supplies, equipment, and so on) are bought on a charge basis. Therefore, the purchases journal can be expanded with special columns to record those accounts frequently affected by credit purchase transactions.

The following illustrative problem demonstrates the use of the purchases journal.

EXAMPLE 4

Jan. 4 Purchased merchandise on account from Agin Corp., $1,000.
    6 Purchased supplies on account from Baker Corp., $500.
    8 Purchased equipment from Connely Company on account, $9,000.
  15 Purchased land from J. Donald on account, $11,000.
  21 Purchased additional supplies from Baker Corp. on account, $200.
  28 Purchased additional merchandise from Agin Corp. on account, $2000.

Purchases Journal   P-1   (1)

Date	Account Credited	P.R.	Acct. Pay. Cr.	Purchases Dr.	Supplies Dr.	Sundry		
						Accounts Dr.	P.R.	Amt.
Jan. 4	(2) Agin Corp.	✓	1,000	1,000				
6	Baker Corp.	✓	500		500			
8	Connely Company	✓	9,000			Equipment	18	9,000
15	Davis Company	✓	11,000			Land	17	11,000
21	Baker Corp.	✓	200		200	(4)		
28	Agin Corp.	✓	2,000	2,000				
			23,700	3,000	700			20,000
			(21)	(51)	(14)			(✓)

(3)

Notes:

(1) P-1 denotes the page number (1) of the purchases journal.

(2) The individual amounts will be posted as credits to their respective accounts in the accounts payable subsidiary ledger. The check marks in the purchases journal indicate such postings.

(3) Accounts Payable, Purchases, and Supplies are posted to the respective accounts in the general ledger as totals only.

(4) The sundry amount of $20,000 is not posted as a total; instead, the individual amounts are posted, as many different accounts may be affected each month.

General Ledger

Supplies	14		Accounts Payable	21
Jan. 31 P-1 700			P-1 Jan. 31 23,700	

Land	17
Jan. 15 P-1 11,000	

Equipment	18		Purchases	51
Jan. 8 P-1 9,000			Jan. 31 P-1 3,000	

7.5 SUBSIDIARY ACCOUNTS PAYABLE LEDGER

In Chapter 6, a new subsidiary ledger, Accounts Receivable, was created for all a company's customers (sales on account): A firm that purchases on account (Accounts Payable) would do the same thing, because the credit balance in accounts payable represents the total amount owed by the company for purchases on account.

Because the account shows only the total liability to all sellers, the need for a subsidiary record for each creditor in a separate ledger is apparent.

Posting to the Subsidiary Ledger

During the month, each individual credit entry is posted from the purchases journal to the creditor's account in the subsidiary ledger. A check mark is placed in the posting reference column in the purchases journal to show that the amount has been posted. The check mark is used because the individual creditors' accounts are not numbered.

1. When a purchase on account is made, the invoice becomes the basis for the credit to the creditor's ledger account.
2. When a payment is made, the account is debited.
3. Any credit balance in a subsidiary account represents an unpaid balance owed to that particular firm.

No postings are made to the general ledger until the end of the month, when all the amounts are accumulated into one total. It is at this time that the total amount of all purchases for the month, as well as other debits, including supplies, equipment, land, and so on, are posted to the respective accounts and then credited to the accounts payable controlling account in the general ledger.

The total of all the credit amounts posted to the accounts payable ledger must equal the total credit to the controlling account in the general ledger. When the postings from the purchases journal are completed for the month, the ledgers should balance.

In order to prove that the subsidiary ledger is in agreement with the controlling account of the general ledger, a schedule of accounts payable is prepared. This schedule is the total of all the balances of each of the credit accounts. Their total must equal that of the controlling accounts payable.

EXAMPLE 5

Using the information in Example 4, the accounts payable ledger after postings would appear as follows:

Accounts Payable Subsidiary Ledger

Agin Corp.		
P-1 Jan. 4	1,000
P-1 28	2,000

Baker Corp.		
P-1 Jan. 6	500
P-1 21	200

Connely Company		
P-1 Jan. 8	9,000

R. Davis Company		
P-1 Jan. 15	11,000

To prove that the accounts payable ledger is in balance, the total owed to the four companies must agree with the balance in the accounts payable control account.

Schedule of Accounts Payable

		Accounts Payable	21
Agin Corp.	$ 3,000		
Baker Corp.	700		
Connely Company	9,000	P-1	23,700
R. Davis Company	11,000		
Total	$23,700		

7.6 RETURN OF MERCHANDISE

Many factors in business will cause a return of merchandise: damaged goods, incorrect size or style, or a price not agreed upon. Returns associated with purchases are recorded as purchase returns, and those associated with sales are recorded as sales returns.

Purchase Returns

If a firm has many purchase returns, a *purchase returns journal* should be used. However, for illustrative purposes, entries for the return of purchases (bought on account) are made here in the general journal:

J-1

	P.R.	Debit	Credit
Accounts Payable, H. Chen	21	420	
Purchase Returns	52		420

The debit portion of the accounts payable is posted to the accounts payable account in the general ledger and also to the accounts payable subsidiary ledger. Because the controlling account and the customer's account are both debited, a diagonal line is needed in the posting reference column to show both postings. For items involving a return for cash, the cash receipts journal is used.

Accounts Payable Ledger

General Ledger

H. Chen				Accounts Payable	21			Purchase Returns	52
J-1	420	Bal.	800	J-1	420	Bal.	800	J-1	420

Purchase Returns appears in the income statement as a reduction of Purchases.

Summary

1. Deductions from list or retail price offered by manufacturers or wholesalers are known as
   _____ .

2. A trade discount of 40 percent on an old model TV retailing at $500 would result in a cost to the
   purchaser of _____ .

3. The evidence of a purchase is accomplished by a _____ .

4. The purchase journal can be expanded with _____ columns to record those accounts frequently affected by credit purchase transactions.

5. The abbreviation and notation for the fifth page of the purchases journal would be _____ .

6. The Sundry amount in the purchases journal is not posted as a _____ . Rather the
   _____ accounts are posted.

7. Postings to the general ledger are made _____ , whereas subsidiary accounts are posted
   _____ .

8. In order to prove the subsidiary ledger in agreement with the controlling account of the general ledger,
   a _____ is prepared.

9. If there are many returns, a special journal termed a _____ journal is implemented.

10. It is common to divide the ledger in a large firm into three separate ledgers, known as the
    _____ , _____ , and _____ ledgers.

Answers: 1. trade discounts; 2. $300; 3. purchase invoice; 4. special; 5. P-5; 6. total, individual; 7. at the end of the
month, immediately; 8. schedule of accounts payable; 9. purchase returns; 10. general, accounts receivable,
accounts payable

Solved Problems

7.1 An appliance with a retail price of $350 is offered at a trade discount of 40 percent. What is the price
a dealer would pay for the item?

SOLUTION

$350		$350	
40%	discount	− 140	
$140	discount	$210	cost to dealer

7.2   What would the entry be to record the above purchase on account? Explain.

	Dr.	Cr.

SOLUTION

	Dr.	Cr.
Purchases	210	
Accounts Payable		210

Trade discounts are not recorded in the accounting records, as they are used only to determine the net purchase price. The amount recorded is the price *paid* to the seller.

7.3   Record the following transactions in the purchases journal:

Apr. 2 Purchased merchandise on account from Kane Company, $450.
  5 Purchased supplies on account from Lane Supply House, $180.
  20 Purchased merchandise on account from Hanson Company, $400.
  24 Purchased additional supplies on account from Lane Supply House, $50.
  29 Purchased equipment on account from Olin Equipment, $1,600.

Purchases Journal   P-1

Date	Account Credited	P.R.	Acct. Pay. Cr.	Purch. Dr.	Supp. Dr.	Sundry Acct. Dr.	P.R.	Amount

SOLUTION

Purchases Journal   P-1

Date	Account Credited	P.R.	Acct. Pay. Cr.	Purch. Dr.	Supp. Dr.	Sundry Acct. Dr.	P.R.	Amount
Apr. 2	Kane Company		450	450				
5	Lane Supply House		180		180			
20	Hanson Company		400	400				
24	Lane Supply House		50		50			
29	Olin Equipment		1,600			Equipment		1,600
			2,680	850	230			1,600

7.4   Post the information from Problem 7.3 into the accounts payable subsidiary ledger and prepare a schedule of accounts payable.

Kane Company

Lane Supply House

Hanson Company

Olin Equipment

Schedule of Accounts Payable

Kane Company	
Lane Supply House	
Hanson Company	
Olin Equipment	

SOLUTION

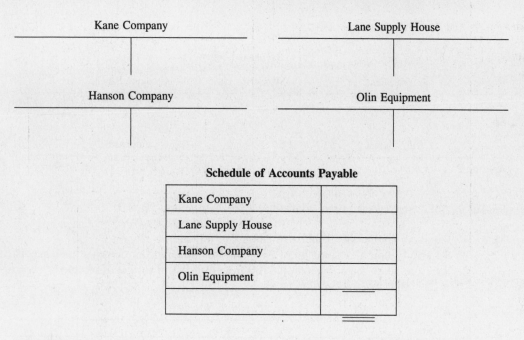

Kane Company

	P-1 Apr. 2	450

Lane Supply House

	P-1 Apr. 5	180
	P-1 24	50

Hanson Company

	P-1 Apr. 20	400

Olin Equipment

	P-1 Apr. 29	1,600

Schedule of Accounts Payable

Kane Company	$ 450
Lane Supply House	230
Hanson Company	400
Olin Equipment	1,600
	$2,680

7.5   Post the purchases journal totals from Problem 7.3 to the accounts in the general ledger.

General Ledger

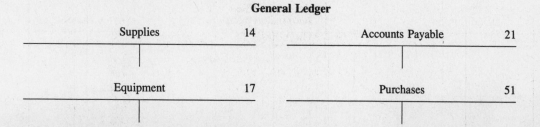

Supplies	14	Accounts Payable	21

Equipment	17	Purchases	51

SOLUTION

General Ledger

Supplies	14		Accounts Payable	21
Apr. 30 P-1 230			P-1 Apr. 30 2,680	

Equipment	17		Purchases	51
Apr. 29 P-1 1,600			Apr. 30 P-1 850	

7.6 Record the following selected transactions in the purchase returns journal:

Mar. 4 Returned $300 in merchandise to Alton Co. for credit.
    8 Received credit memorandum of $150 from Baltic Corp. for defective merchandise.
    12 Received credit memorandum of $180 from Calton Co. for goods returned.

	Purchase Returns		PR-1
Date	Account Dr.	P.R.	Amount

SOLUTION

	Purchase Returns		PR-1
Date	Account Dr.	P.R.	Amount
Mar. 4	Alton Company		300
8	Baltic Corporation		150
12	Calton Company		180
			630

7.7 Based on the information in Problem 7.6, post to the subsidiary ledger accounts and then to the general ledger.

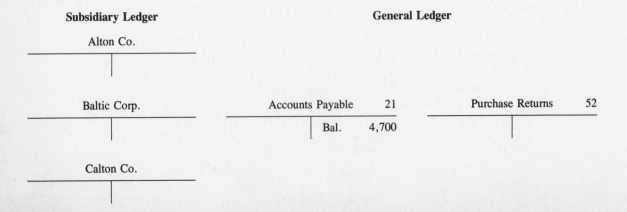

Subsidiary Ledger		General Ledger
Alton Co.		

Baltic Corp.		Accounts Payable 21		Purchase Returns 52
		Bal. 4,700		

Calton Co.

SOLUTION

Subsidiary Ledger   **General Ledger**

Alton Co.

| Mar. 4 PR-1 | 300 | Bal. | 1,200 |

Baltic Corp.   Accounts Payable   21   Purchase Returns   52

| Mar. 8 PR-1 | 150 | Bal. | 1,500 | Mar. 31 PR-1 630 | Bal. 4,700 | PR-1 Mar. 31 630 |

Calton Co.

| Mar. 12 PR-1 | 180 | Bal. | 2,000 |

7.8 Prepare a schedule of accounts payable and compare it to the control account.

Schedule of Accounts Payable   Accounts Payable   21

Alton Co.			Bal.	4,700
Baltic Corp.	
Calton Co.	

SOLUTION

Schedule of Accounts Payable   Accounts Payable   21

| Alton Co. | $ 900 | Mar. 31 PR-1   630 | Bal. | 4,700 |
| Baltic Corp. | 1,350 | --
| Calton Co. | 1,820 | | Bal. | 4,070 |
| | $4,070 |

7.9 Purchases on account and related returns completed by the Dembofsky Book Store appear below:

June 4 Purchased merchandise on account from South Eastern Co., $4,200.
      5 Purchased merchandise on account from Prentice-Foyer, $3,000.
      9 Received a credit memorandum from Prentice-Foyer for $200 for overshipment.
     10 Purchased office supplies from Kristt Supply, $800.
     18 Received a credit memorandum from South Eastern for goods returned, $300.
     24 Purchased office equipment from Robinson Furniture on account, $2,900.
     26 Purchased additional office supplies on account from Kristt Supply, $400.
     29 Received a credit memorandum from Kristt Supply for defective goods, $100.
     30 Purchased store supplies on account from H. Marc, $260.

Record the transactions for June in the purchases and purchase returns journals.

Purchases Journal P-1

Date	Account Credited	P.R.	Acct. Pay. Cr.	Purch. Dr.	Off. Supp. Dr.	Sundry		
						Acct. Dr.	P.R.	Amount

Purchase Returns PR-1

Date	Account Debited	P.R.	Amount

SOLUTION

Purchases Journal P-1

Date	Account Credited	P.R.	Acct. Pay. Cr.	Purch. Dr.	Off. Supp. Dr.	Sundry		
						Acct. Dr.	P.R.	Amt.
June 4	South Eastern Co.		4,200	4,200				
5	Prentice-Foyer		3,000	3,000				
10	Kristt Supply		800		800			
24	Robinson Furniture		2,900			Off. Equip.	18	2,900
26	Kristt Supply		400		400			
30	H. Marc		260			Store Supp.	13	260
			11,560	7,200	1200			3,160
			(21)	(51)	(12)			(✓)

Purchase Returns PR-1

Date	Account Debited	P.R.	Amount
June 9	Prentice-Foyer		200
18	South Eastern		300
29	Kristt Supply		100
			600
			(21/52)

7.10 Post each of the above accounts into the accounts payable subsidiary ledger and prepare a schedule of accounts payable.

Kristt Supply	Prentice-Foyer

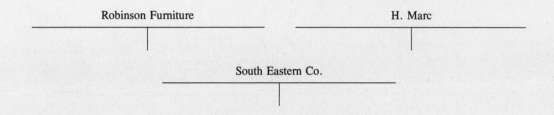

Robinson Furniture	H. Marc

South Eastern Co.

Schedule of Accounts Payable

Kristt Supply	
H. Marc	
Prentice-Foyer	
Robinson Furniture	
South Eastern Co.	

SOLUTION

Kristt Supply

June 29 PR-1	100	P-1 June 10	800
		P-1 26	400

Prentice-Foyer

June 9 PR-1	200	P-1 June 5	3,000

Robinson Furniture

	P-1 June 24	2,900

H. Marc

	P-1 June 30	260

South Eastern Co.

June 18 PR-1	300	P-1 June 4	4,200

Schedule of Accounts Payable

Kristt Supply	$ 1,100
H. Marc	260
Prentice-Foyer	2,800
Robinson Furniture	2,900
South Eastern Co.	3,900
	$10,960

7.11 Post the purchases journal and purchase returns journals from Problem 7.9 to the accounts in the general ledger.

Office Supplies 12	Store Supplies 13

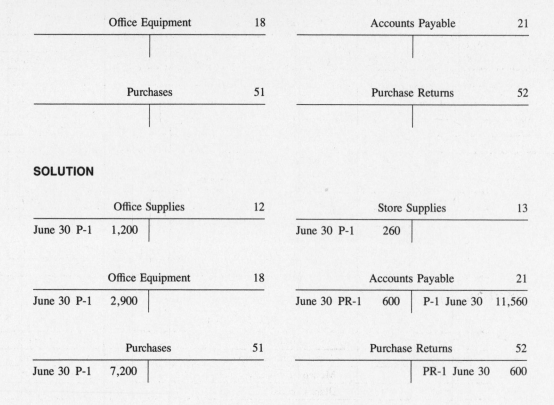

Office Equipment	18		Accounts Payable	21

Purchases	51		Purchase Returns	52

SOLUTION

Office Supplies	12		Store Supplies	13
June 30 P-1 1,200			June 30 P-1 260	

Office Equipment	18		Accounts Payable	21
June 30 P-1 2,900			June 30 PR-1 600	P-1 June 30 11,560

Purchases	51		Purchase Returns	52
June 30 P-1 7,200				PR-1 June 30 600

Note: Balance of Accounts Payable controlling account and total of Schedule of Accounts Payable are the same.

7.12 The Johnston Company transactions involving purchases and sales for the month of January are presented below. All purchases and sales are made on account.

Jan. 3 Sold merchandise to Acme Supply Company, $440.
      5 Purchased merchandise from Balfour Corp., $7,200.
     10 Sold merchandise to Mennon Company, $345.
     10 Sold merchandise to Blant Company, $2,400.
     14 Purchased $750 worth of equipment from Wyde Equipment.
     17 Purchased office supplies from Gold Supply, $850.
     21 Purchased merchandise from Caldon Company, $6,240.
     28 Returned damage merchandise purchased from Balfour Corp., receiving credit of $300.
     30 Issued credit of $60 to Acme Supply Company for defective goods returned to us.

Record the transactions in the sales, purchases, and general journals.

Sales Journal   S-1

Date	Account Debited	P.R.	Amount

Purchases Journal   P-1

Date	Account Cr.	P.R.	Acct. Pay. Cr.	Pur. Dr.	Supp. Dr.	Sundry		
						Acct. Dr.	P.R.	Amount

General Journal   J-1

Date	Description	P.R.	Debit	Credit

SOLUTION

Sales Journal   S-1

Date	Account Debited	P.R.	Amount
Jan. 3	Acme Supply Company	✓	440
10	Mennon Company	✓	345
10	Blant Company	✓	2,400
			3,185

Purchases Journal   P-1

Date	Account Cr.	P.R.	Acct. Pay. Cr.	Pur. Dr.	Supp. Dr.	Sundry		
						Acct. Dr.	P.R.	Amount
Jan. 5	Balfour Corp.	✓	7,200	7,200				
14	Wyde Equipment		750			Equipment		750
17	Gold Supply		850		850			
21	Caldon Company	✓	6,240	6,240				
			15,040	13,440	850			750

General Journal   J-1

Date	Description	P.R.	Debit	Credit
Jan. 28	Accounts Payable, Balfour Corp.		300	
	Purchase Returns			300
30	Sales Returns		60	
	Accounts Receivable, Acme Supply			60
	Company			

Chapter 8

The Cash Journal

8.1 INTRODUCTION

We have observed that the use of the sales journal and the purchases journal enable us to carry out the journalizing and posting processes more efficiently. These special journals save space by permitting the recording of an entry on one line and the posting of *total* columns rather than individual figures. This is also true of the cash receipts journal and the cash disbursements journal.

8.2 CASH RECEIPTS JOURNAL

All receipts (cash and checks) received by a business are recorded daily in either a *cash receipts* or a *combination cash journal*. For control purposes, the cash handling and recording processes are separated. In addition, whenever feasible, receipts are deposited intact (without cash disbursements being made from them) daily. The most common sources of cash receipts are cash sales and collections on account.

The steps for recording and posting the cash receipts journal is described below and illustrated in Example 1.

1. Record the cash receipts in the cash receipts journal, *debiting* Cash for the amount received (Cash column) and *crediting* the appropriate column. Indicate in the Account Credited space provided;

    (a) The customer's name (subsidiary account) for collections on account.

    (b) An explanation (cash sale) for cash sales.

    (c) The title of the item involved in the Sundry account.

2. After recording collections on account, post *by date* to the appropriate subsidiary ledger (customer's) account.

    (a) In the customer's account, record the amount *credited* and indicate the source of the entry (Cr.) in the Posting Reference column.

    (b) Put a (✓) in the Posting Reference column of the journal to indicate that a posting has been completed.

3. At the *end* of the month, total all the columns of the journal and check to be sure that all the columns balance before posting. If they do balance, put a double line under the column totals.

4. Post the column totals (except the Sundry Credit column) to the appropriate general ledger account.

    (a) In the appropriate general ledger account, record the amount *debited* or *credited* and indicate the source of the entry (Cr.) in the Posting Reference column.

    (b) Place the account number of the account posted to *under* the column totals to indicate that a posting has been completed.

    (c) Each item in the Sundry account is posted individually to the general ledger. The total of the Sundry account is not posted.

EXAMPLE 1

Centennial Company had the following receipts in March:

Mar. 2 Received $250 for a return of defective merchandise.
    4 Cash sale of flags for $350.
    9 Collected $50 on account from A. Anderson.

Mar. 14 Collected $350 on account from B. Butler.
    22 Cash sale of Bumper stickers, $200.
    29 Collected $100 on account from C. Chase.

Cash Receipts Journal   CR-1

Date	Account Credited	P.R.	Cash Debit	Sales Discount Debit	Accounts Receivable Credit	Sales Income Credit	Sundry Credit
Mar. 2	Purchase Returns	52	250				250
4	Cash Sales	✔	350			350	
9	A. Anderson	✔	50		50		
14	B. Butler	✔	350		350		
22	Cash Sales	✔	200			200	
29	C. Chase	✔	100		100		
			1,300		500	550	250
			(11)		(14)	(41)	(✔)

General Ledger

Cash	11
Bal. ✔ 10,000	
Mar. 31 CR-1 1,300	

Sales Income	41
	CR-1 Mar. 31 550

Accounts Receivable	14
Bal. 1,075	CR-1 Mar. 31 500

Purchase Returns	52
	CR-1 Mar. 2 250

Accounts Receivable Ledger

A. Anderson	
Bal. ✔ 200	CR-1 Mar. 9 50

C. Chase	
Bal. ✔ 125	CR-1 Mar. 29 100

B. Butler	
Bal. ✔ 350	CR-1 Mar. 14 350

D. Davis	
Bal. ✔ 400	

8.3 CASH DISBURSEMENTS JOURNAL

The cash disbursements journal is used to record all transactions that reduce cash. These transactions may arise from payments to creditors, from cash purchases (of supplies, equipment, or merchandise), from the payment of expenses (salary, rent, insurance, and so on), as well as from personal withdrawals.

The procedure for recording and posting the cash disbursements journal parallels that of the cash receipts journal:

1. A check is written each time a payment is made; the check numbers provide a convenient reference, and they help in controlling cash and in reconciling the bank account.

2. The cash credit column is posted in total to the general ledger at the end of the month.

3. Debits to Accounts Payable represent cash paid to creditors. These individual amounts will be posted to the creditors' accounts in the accounts payable subsidiary ledger. At the end of the month, the total of the accounts payable column is posted to the general ledger.

4. The Sundry column is used to record debits for any account that cannot be entered in the other special columns. These would include purchases of equipment, inventory, payment of expenses, and cash withdrawals. Each item is posted separately to the general ledger. The total of the Sundry column is not posted.

EXAMPLE 2

Cash Disbursements Journal   CD-1

Date	Description	P.R.	Check No.	Cash Cr.	Acct. Pay. Dr.	Sundry Dr.
Mar. 2	Agin Corp.	✓	1	600	600	
8	Rent Expense	53	2	220		220
15	Salaries Expense	54	3	1,900		1,900
18	Baker Corp.	✓	4	700	700	
21	Purchases	51	5	1,600		1,600
24	Salaries Expense	54	6	1,900		1,900
				6,920	1,300	5,620
				(11)	(21)	(✓)

General Ledger

Cash	11
	CD-1 Mar. 28 6,920

Rent Expense	53
Mar. 8 CD-1 220	

Accounts Payable	21
Mar. 28 CD-1 1,300	Bal. 23,700

Salaries Expense	54
Mar. 15 CD-1 1,900	
24 CD-1 1,900	

Purchases	51
Mar. 21 CD-1 1,600	

Accounts Payable Subsidiary Ledger

Agin Corp.	
Mar. 2 CD-1 600	Bal. 3,000*

Baker Corp.	
Mar. 18 CD-1 700	Bal. 700*

Connely Company	
	Bal. 9,000*

R. Davis Company	
	Bal. 11,000*

*From Section 7.4, Example 4.

8.4 DISCOUNTS

To induce a buyer to make payment before the amount is due, the seller may allow the buyer to deduct a certain percentage of the bill. If payment is due within a stated number of days after the date of invoice, the number of days will usually be preceded by the letter "n," signifying net. For example, bills due in 30 days would be indicated by n/30.

A 2 percent discount offered if payment is made within 10 days would be indicated by 2/10. If the buyer has a choice of either paying the amount less 2 percent within the 10-day period or paying the entire bill within 30 days, the terms would be written as 2/10, n/30.

EXAMPLE 3

A sales invoice totaling $1,000 and dated January 2 has discount terms of 2/10, n/30. If the purchaser pays on or before January 12 (10 days after the date of purchase), he or she may deduct $20 ($1,000 × 2%) from the bill and pay only $980. If the purchaser chooses not to pay within the discount period, he or she is obligated to pay the entire amount of $1,000 by February 1.

From the point of view of the seller, the discount is a sales discount; the purchaser would consider it a purchase discount. If a business experiences a great number of sales and purchase discounts, then special columns would be added in the cash receipts and cash disbursements journals.

Sales Discount appears as a reduction of Sales in the income statement. Purchases Discount appears as a reduction of Purchases in the Cost of Goods Sold section of the income statement.

8.5 COMBINATION CASH JOURNAL

Some companies, primarily for convenience, prefer to record all cash transactions (receipts and disbursements) in one journal. This combination cash journal uses basically the same account columns as the cash receipts and cash disbursements journals, but with a different arrangement of accounts.

This journal makes it easier on a day-to-day basis to keep track of changes in the Cash account, since the debit and credit to Cash are adjacent to one another.

EXAMPLE 4

The combination cash journal below is constructed from the same entries involved in the cash receipts journal (Example 1) and the cash disbursements journal (Example 2).

Combination Cash Journal

Cash Dr.	Cash Cr.	Ck. No.	Date	Account	P.R.	Sundry Dr.	Sundry Cr.	Acct. Pay. Dr.	Acct. Rec. Cr.	Sales Income Cr.
250			Mar. 2	Purchase Returns	52		250			
	600	1	2	Agin Corp.	✔			600		
350			4	Cash Sales	✔					350
	220	2	8	Rent Expense	53	220				
50			9	A. Anderson	✔				50	
350			14	B. Butler	✔				350	
	1,900	3	15	Salaries Expense	54	1,900				
	700	4	18	Baker Corp.	✔			700		
	1,600	5	21	Purchases	51	1,600				
200			22	Cash Sales	✔					200
	1,900	6	24	Salaries Expense	54	1,900				
100			29	C. Chase	✔				100	
1,300	6,920					5,620	250	1,300	500	550
(11)	(11)					(✔)	(✔)	(21)	(14)	(41)

Summary

1. Receipts of a firm include _____ and _____ .

2. For cash control purposes, cash handling and _____ must be separated.

3. The _____ journal is used to record all transactions that reduce cost.

4. The cash column in the cash receipts journal is _____, whereas the same column in the cash payments journal is _____ whenever cash is received or disbursed.

5. In order to record a cash disbursement, a _____ must be written and assigned a number.

6. _____ to Accounts Payable represent cash paid to creditors.

7. Accounts Payable is to the cash disbursements journal as _____ is to the cash receipts journal.

8. Sales Discounts and Purchase Discounts appear in the _____ statement as reductions of Sales and of Purchases, respectively.

9. Terms of 2/10, n/30 on a $800 purchase of March 6 paid within the discount period would provide a discount of _____ and a net cost of _____ .

10. The _____ journal contains all records of cash transactions (receipts and disbursements).

Answers: 1. cash, checks; 2. recording; 3. cash disbursements; 4. debited, credited; 5. check; 6. Debits; 7. Accounts Receivable; 8. income; 9. $16, $784; 10. combined cash

Solved Problems

8.1 A sales invoice totaling $3,000 and dated January 14 has discount terms of 2/10, n/30. If paid by January 23, what would be the entry (in general journal form) to record this transaction?

SOLUTION

Cash	2,940	
Sales Discount	60	
Accounts Receivable		3,000

8.2 The cash receipts journal below utilizes a special column for sales discounts. Record the following cash transactions in the journal:

May   2   Received a check for $588 from A. Banks in settlement of his $600 April invoice.
      12   Received $686 in settlement of the April invoice of $700 from J. Johnson.
      26   Received a check for $495 in settlement of B. Simpson's April account of $500.

Cash Receipts Journal   CR-1

Date	Account Cr.	P.R.	Cash Dr.	Sales Disc. Dr.	Acct. Rec. Cr.	Sundry Cr.

SOLUTION

Cash Receipts Journal   CR-1

Date	Account Cr.	P.R.	Cash Dr.	Sales Disc. Dr.	Acct. Rec. Cr.	Sundry Cr.
May 2	A. Banks		588	12	600	
12	J. Johnson		686	14	700	
26	B. Simpson		495	5	500	
			1,769	31	1,800	

8.3 The cash disbursements journal below utilizes the special column Purchases Discount. Record the cash transactions into the cash disbursements journal.

June 2 Paid J. Thompson $490 in settlement of our April invoice for $500, Check 24.

    10 Sent a check to B. Rang, $297, in settlement of the May invoice of $300, Check 25.

    21 Paid A. Johnson $588 in settlement of the $600 invoice of last month, Check 26.

Cash Disbursements Journal   CD-1

Date	Check No.	Account Dr.	P.R.	Cash Cr.	Purchases Disc. Cr.	Acct. Pay. Dr.	Sundry Dr.

SOLUTION

Cash Disbursements Journal   CD-1

Date	Check No.	Account Dr.	P.R.	Cash Cr.	Purchases Disc. Cr.	Acct. Pay. Dr.	Sundry Dr.
June 2	24	J. Thompson		490	10	500	
10	25	B. Rang		297	3	300	
21	26	A. Johnson		588	12	600	
				1,375	25	1,400	

8.4 Record the following transactions in the cash receipts journal:

Mar. 2 Received $600 from J. Kappala in full settlement of her account.

    10 Received $615 from B. Elder in full settlement of his account.

Mar. 14   Cash sales for a 2-week period, $4,400.

     28   Sold $200 of office supplies (not a merchandise item) to Smith Company as a courtesy.

     30   Owner made additional investment, $1,500.

     30   Cash sales for the last 2 weeks, $2,600.

Cash Receipts Journal   CR-1

Date	Account Cr.	P.R.	Cash Dr.	Acct. Rec. Cr.	Sales Income Cr.	Sundry Cr.

SOLUTION

Cash Receipts Journal   CR-1

Date	Account Cr.	P.R.	Cash Dr.	Acct. Rec. Cr.	Sales Income Cr.	Sundry Cr.
Mar. 2	J. Kappala	✓	600	600		
10	B. Elder	✓	615	615		
14	Cash Sales	✓	4,400		4,400	
28	Office Supplies	15	200			200
30	Capital	31	1,500			1,500
30	Cash Sales	✓	2,600		2,600	
			9,915	1,215	7,000	1,700

8.5   Post the information from Problem 8.4 into the accounts receivable subsidiary ledger.

Accounts Receivable Ledger

J. Kappala

Bal.	600		

B. Elder

Bal.	615		

SOLUTION

Accounts Receivable Ledger

J. Kappala

Bal.	600	CR-1 Mar. 2	600

B. Elder

Bal.	615	CR-1 Mar. 10	615

8.6 Post the cash receipts journal totals from Problem 8.4 to the accounts in the general ledger.

General Ledger

Cash		11		Capital		31
					Bal.	6,500

Accounts Receivable		12		Sales Income		41
Bal.	3,000					

Office Supplies		15
Bal.	3,500	

SOLUTION

General Ledger

Cash		11		Capital		31
Mar. 31 CR-1 9,915					Bal.	6,500
					CR-1 Mar. 30	1,500

Accounts Receivable		12		Sales Income		41
Bal.	3,000	CR-1 Mar. 31 1,215			CR-1 Mar. 31	7,000

Office Supplies		15
Bal.	3,500	CR-1 Mar. 28 200

8.7 Record the following transactions in the cash disbursements journal:

Mar. 1 Paid rent for the month, $320 (Check #16).
       7 Paid J. Becker $615 for his February invoice (Check #17).
      10 Bought store supplies for cash, $110 (Check #18).
      15 Paid salaries for the 2-week period, $685 (Check #19).
      23 Paid B. Cone for February invoice, $600 (Check #20).
      30 Paid salaries for the second half of the month, $714 (Check #21).

Cash Disbursements Journal   CD-1

Date	Check No.	Account Dr.	P.R.	Cash Cr.	Acct. Pay. Dr.	Sundry Dr.

SOLUTION

Cash Disbursements Journal   CD-1

Date	Check No.	Account Dr.	P.R.	Cash Cr.	Acct. Pay. Dr.	Sundry Dr.
Mar. 1	16	Rent Expense		320		320
7	17	J. Becker	✓	615	615	
10	18	Store Supplies		110		110
15	19	Salaries Expense		685		685
23	20	B. Cone	✓	600	600	
30	21	Salaries Expense		714		714
				3,044	1,215	1,829

8.8 Post the information from Problem 8.7 into the accounts payable subsidiary ledger.

Accounts Payable Ledger

J. Becker			B. Cone	
	Bal.	615		Bal.	600

SOLUTION

Accounts Payable Ledger

J. Becker				B. Cone			
Mar. 7 CD-1	615	Bal.	615	Mar. 23 CD-1	600	Bal.	600

8.9 Post the cash disbursements journal from Problem 8.7 to the accounts in the general ledger.

General Ledger

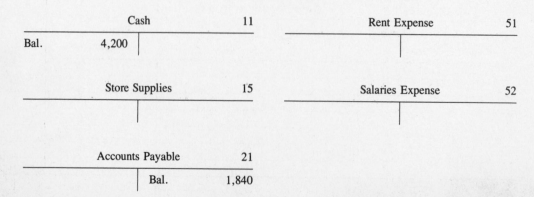

Cash	11		Rent Expense	51
Bal.	4,200			

Store Supplies	15		Salaries Expense	52

Accounts Payable	21
Bal.	1,840

SOLUTION

General Ledger

Cash	11
Bal. 4,200	CD-1 Mar. 31 3,044

Rent Expense	51
Mar. 1 CD-1 320	

Store Supplies	15
Mar. 10 CD-1 110	

Salaries Expense	52
Mar. 15 CD-1 685	
30 CD-1 714	

Accounts Payable	21
Mar. 31 CD-1 1,215	Bal. 1,840

8.10 All transactions affecting the cash account of Park Company for the month of January 198X are presented below:

Jan. 1 Received cash from Alden Company for the balance due on their account, $1,600, less 2 percent discount.

 5 Received payment from Walk Company on account, $1,550.

 8 Paid rent for the month, $650, Check #165.

 10 Purchased supplies for cash, $614, Check #166.

 14 Cash sales for the first half of the month, $5,280.

 15 Paid biweekly salaries, $1,600, Check #167.

 19 Received $406 in settlement of a $400 note receivable plus interest.

 19 Received payment from J. Cork of $500, less 1 percent discount.

 20 Paid B. Simmons $686 in settlement of our $700 invoice, Check #168.

 24 Paid $450 on account to L. Hann, Check #169.

 27 Paid H. Hiram $800, less 2 percent, on account, Check #170.

 30 Paid biweekly salaries, $1,680, Check #171.

Record the above transactions in both the cash receipts and the cash disbursements journals.

Cash Receipts Journal   CR-1

Date	Account Cr.	P.R.	Cash Dr.	Sales Disc. Dr.	Sales Income Cr.	Acct. Rec. Cr.	Sundry Cr.

Cash Disbursements Journal   CD-1

Date	Check No.	Account Dr.	P.R.	Cash Cr.	Pur. Disc. Cr.	Acct. Pay. Dr.	Sundry Dr.

SOLUTION

Cash Receipts Journal   CR-1

Date	Account Cr.	P.R.	Cash Dr.	Sales Disc. Dr.	Sales Income Cr.	Acct. Rec. Cr.	Sundry Cr.
Jan. 1	Alden Co.		1,568	32		1,600	
5	Walk Co.		1,550			1,550	
14	Cash Sales		5,280		5,280		
19	Notes Rec.						400
19	Interest Inc.		406				6
19	J. Cork		495	5		500	
			9,299	37	5,280	3,650	406

Cash Disbursements Journal   CD-1

Date	Check No.	Account Dr.	P.R.	Cash Cr.	Pur. Disc. Cr.	Acct. Pay. Dr.	Sundry Dr.
Jan. 8	165	Rent Expense		650			650
10	166	Supplies		614			614
15	167	Salaries Exp.		1,600			1,600
20	168	B. Simmons		686	14	700	
24	169	L. Hann		450		450	
27	170	H. Hiram		784	16	800	
30	171	Salaries Exp.		1,680			1,680
				6,464	30	1,950	4,544

Examination II

Part I: Multiple Choice

1. The type of transaction that would appear in the sales journal would be (*a*) sale of merchandise for cash; (*b*) sale of equipment for cash; (*c*) sale of equipment in exchange for a note; (*d*) sale of merchandise on account; (*e*) none of the above.

2. The receipt of cash arising from a sales transaction would be recorded in (*a*) the cash receipts journal; (*b*) the cash payments journal; (*c*) the sales journal; (*d*) the purchases journal; (*e*) none of the above.

3. The classification and normal balance of the sales discount account would be (*a*) expense, debit; (*b*) revenue, credit; (*c*) contra revenue, debit; (*d*) asset, debit; (*e*) none of the above.

4. If an item retailing for $1,000, subject to a trade discount of 25 percent, is paid for within the sales discount period, terms 2/10, n/30, the amount of the check received would be (*a*) $1,000; (*b*) $750; (*c*) $740; (*d*) $735; (*e*) none of the above.

5. Each time an entry is recorded in the purchases journal, the credit would be entered in the (*a*) purchase column; (*b*) accounts payable column; (*c*) supply column; (*d*) accounts receivable column; (*e*) none of the above.

6. Which of the following items would be recorded in the purchases journal? (*a*) supplies purchased on account; (*b*) equipment purchased on account; (*c*) merchandise purchased on account; (*d*) all of the above; (*e*) none of the above.

7. The controlling account in the general ledger that summarizes the debits and credits to the individual accounts in the customer's ledger is entitled (*a*) Accounts Receivable; (*b*) Accounts Payable; (*c*) Sales; (*d*) Purchases; (*e*) none of the above.

8. The item that reflects the payment of cash is known as a (an) (*a*) check; (*b*) invoice; (*c*) voucher; (*d*) draft; (*e*) none of the above.

9. Infrequent sales returns would appear in which journal? (*a*) sales; (*b*) sales returns; (*c*) general; (*d*) cash receipts; (*e*) cash payments.

10. The combined cash journal would be used for (*a*) all cash received during the month; (*b*) all payments made in cash during the month; (*c*) any item that has to do with either income or outgo of cash; (*d*) all of the above; (*e*) none of the above.

Part II: Problems

1. In the table below, indicate in which of the five journals each transaction is to be recorded.

	Cash Payments	Cash Receipts	Sales Income	Purchases	General
(*a*) Sale of merchandise for cash					
(*b*) Sale of merchandise on account					
(*c*) Cash refunded to a customer					
(*d*) Receipt of cash from a customer in settlement of an account					

	Cash Payments	Cash Receipts	Sales Income	Purchases	General
(e) Purchase of merchandise for cash					
(f) Purchase of merchandise on account					
(g) Payment of salaries					
(h) Note payable sent to a creditor in settlement of an account					
(i) Payment of interest on the mortgage					
(j) Received a note in settlement of a customer's account					

2. S. Perkowski began business on March 1. The transactions completed by the Company for the month of March are listed below. Record these transactions, using the various journals provided.

March 1 Deposited $18,000 in a bank account for the operation of Perkowski Company.
2 Paid rent for the month, $600, Check #1.
4 Purchased equipment on account from Anton Equipment, $10,000.
7 Purchased merchandise on account from Baily Company, $1,200.
7 Cash sales for the week, $1,650.
10 Issued Check #2 of $150 for store supplies.
11 Sold merchandise on account to Manny Company, $600.
12 Sold merchandise on account to Nant Company, $350.
14 Paid biweekly salaries of $740, Check #3.
14 Cash sales for the week, $1,800.
16 Purchased merchandise on account from Cotin Company, $1,000.
17 Issued Check #4 to Baily Company for Mar. 7 purchase, less 2 percent.
18 Bought $250 worth of store supplies from Salio Supply House on account.
19 Returned defective merchandise of $200 to Cotin Company and received credit.
19 Sold merchandise on account to Olin Company, $645.
21 Issued Check #5 of $500 to Andon Equipment in part payment of equipment purchase.
22 Received check from Nant Company in settlement of their Mar. 12 purchase, less 2 percent discount.
22 Purchased merchandise from Canny Corporation for cash, $750, Check #6.
23 Cash sales for the week, $1,845.
24 Purchased merchandise on account from Daily Corporation, $850.
25 Sold merchandise on account to Pallit Corporation, $740.
26 Purchased additional supplies on account, $325, from Salio Supply House.
27 Received check from Manny Company in settlement of their account, less 1 percent discount.
30 Cash sales for the week, $1,920.
30 Received $300 on account from Olin Company.
31 Paid biweekly salaries, $810, Check #7.

General Journal J-1

Date	Description	P.R.	Debit	Credit

Cash Receipts Journal   CR-1

Date	Account Cr.	P.R.	Cash Dr.	Sales Disc. Dr.	Acct. Rec. Cr.	Sales Income Cr.	Sundry Cr.

Cash Disbursements Journal   CD-1

Date	Check No.	Account Dr.	P.R.	Cash Cr.	Pur. Disc. Cr.	Acct. Pay. Dr.	Sundry Dr.

Purchases Journal   P-1

Date	Account Cr.	P.R.	Acct. Pay. Cr.	Pur. Dr.	Store Supp. Dr.	Office Supp. Dr.	Sundry		
							Acct. Dr.	P.R.	Amt.

Sales Journal   S-1

Date	Account Debited	P.R.	Accounts Receivable Dr. Sales Income Cr.

3. Based on the work above, post all transactions to the appropriate accounts in the general ledger, the accounts receivable ledger, and the accounts payable ledger.

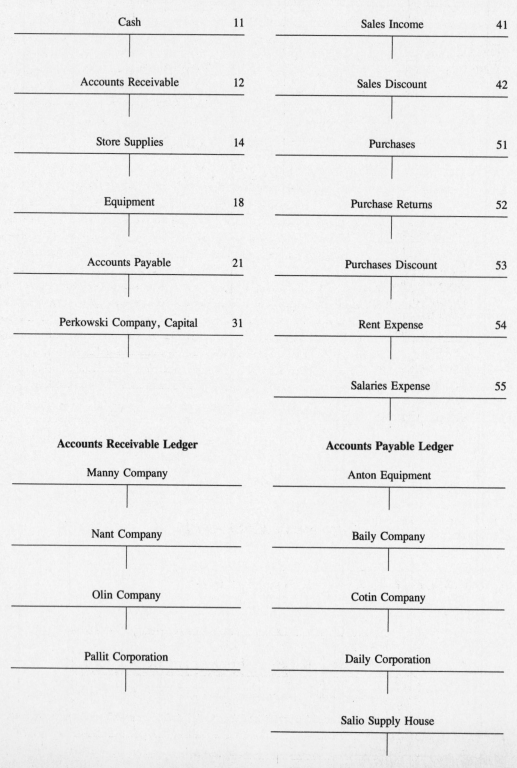

General Ledger

Cash	11		Sales Income	41

Accounts Receivable	12		Sales Discount	42

Store Supplies	14		Purchases	51

Equipment	18		Purchase Returns	52

Accounts Payable	21		Purchases Discount	53

Perkowski Company, Capital	31		Rent Expense	54

			Salaries Expense	55

Accounts Receivable Ledger

Manny Company

Nant Company

Olin Company

Pallit Corporation

Accounts Payable Ledger

Anton Equipment

Baily Company

Cotin Company

Daily Corporation

Salio Supply House

4. Based on the information above, prepare (*a*) a schedule of accounts receivable; (*b*) a schedule of accounts payable; (*c*) a trial balance.

(*a*)

Perkowski Company
Schedule of Accounts Receivable
March 31, 198X

Olin Company	
Pallit Corporation	

(*b*)

Perkowski Company
Schedule of Accounts Payable
March 31, 198X

Anton Equipment	
Cotin Company	
Daily Corporation	
Salio Supply House	

(*c*)

Perkowski Company
Trial Balance
March 31, 198X

Cash		
Accounts Receivable		
Store Supplies		
Equipment		
Accounts Payable		
Perkowski Company, Capital		
Sales Income		
Sales Discount		
Purchases		
Purchase Returns		
Purchases Discount		
Rent Expense		
Salaries Expense		

Answers to Examination II

Part I

1. (*d*); 2. (*a*); 3. (*c*); 4. (*d*); 5. (*b*); 6. (*d*); 7. (*a*); 8. (*a*); 9. (*c*); 10. (*d*)

Part II

1.

	Cash Payments	Cash Receipts	Sales Income	Purchases	General
(*a*)		✓			
(*b*)			✓		
(*c*)	✓				
(*d*)		✓			

	Cash Payments	Cash Receipts	Sales Income	Purchases	General
(e)	✔				
(f)				✔	
(g)	✔				
(h)					✔
(i)	✔				
(j)					✔

2.

General Journal   J-1

Date	Description	P.R.	Debit	Credit
Mar. 19	Accounts Payable, Cotin Co.	21/✔	200	
	Purchase Returns	52		200
	Defective goods			

Cash Receipts Journal   CR-1

Date	Account Cr.	P.R.	Cash Dr.	Sales Disc. Dr.	Acct. Rec. Cr.	Sales Income Cr.	Sundry Cr.
Mar. 1	Perkowski Company, Capital	31	18,000				18,000
7	Cash Sales	✔	1,650			1,650	
14	Cash Sales	✔	1,800			1,800	
22	Nant Company	✔	343	7	350		
23	Cash Sales	✔	1,845			1,845	
30	Manny Company	✔	594	6	600		
30	Cash Sales	✔	1,920			1,920	
30	Olin Company	✔	300		300		
			26,452	13	1,250	7,215	18,000
			(11)	(42)	(12)	(41)	(✔)

Cash Disbursements Journal   CD-1

Date	Check No.	Account Dr.	P.R.	Cash Cr.	Pur. Disc. Cr.	Acct. Pay. Dr.	Sundry Dr.
Mar. 2	1	Rent Expense	54	600			600
10	2	Store Supplies	14	150			150
14	3	Salaries Expense	55	740			740
17	4	Baily Company	✔	1,176	24	1,200	
21	5	Anton Equipment	✔	500		500	
22	6	Purchases	51	750			750
31	7	Salaries Expense	55	810			810
				4,726	24	1,700	3,050
				(11)	(52)	(21)	(✔)

Purchases Journal   P-1

Date	Account Cr.	P.R.	Acct. Pay. Cr.	Pur. Dr.	Store Supp. Dr.	Office Supp. Dr.	Sundry		
							Acct. Dr.	P.R.	Amt.
Mar. 4	Anton Equipment	✓	10,000				Equip.	18	10,000
7	Baily Company	✓	1,200	1,200					
16	Cotin Company	✓	1,100	1,100					
18	Salio Supply House	✓	250		250				
24	Daily Corporation	✓	850	850					
26	Salio Supply House	✓	325		325				
			13,725	3,150	575				10,000
			(21)	(51)	(14)				(✓)

Sales Journal   S-1

Date	Account Debited	P.R.	Accounts Receivable Dr. Sales Income Cr.
Mar. 11	Manny Company	✓	600
12	Nant Company	✓	350
19	Olin Company	✓	645
25	Pallit Corporation	✓	740
			2,335
			(12)(41)

3.   **General Ledger**

Cash 11		Sales Income 41

Cash   11
Mar. 31 CR-1 26,452 | CD-1 Mar. 31 4,726
          21,726

Sales Income   41
                      | S-1 Mar. 31 2,335
                      | CR-1   31 7,215
                      | 9,550

Accounts Receivable   12
Mar. 31 S-1 2,335 | CR-1 Mar. 31 1,250
          1,085

Sales Discount   42
Mar. 31 CR-1   13 |

Store Supplies   14
Mar. 10 CD-1 150 |
     31 P-1   575 |
          725 |

Purchases   51
Mar. 22 CD-1 750 |
     31 P-1 3,150 |
          3,900 |

Equipment   18
Mar. 4 P-1 10,000 |

Purchase Returns   52
                   | J-1 Mar. 19 200

Accounts Payable   21
Mar. 19 J-1   200 | P-1 Mar. 31 13,725
     31 CD-1 1,700 | 11,825

Purchases Discount   53
                   | CD-1 Mar. 31 24

General Ledger, cont.

Perkowski Company, Capital			31
	CR-1 Mar. 1	18,000	

Rent Expense		54
Mar. 2 CD-1	600	

Salaries Expense		55
Mar. 14 CD-1	740	
31 CD-1	810	
1,550		

Accounts Receivable Ledger

Manny Company

Mar. 11 S-1	600	CR-1 Mar. 30	600

Nant Company

Mar. 12 S-1	350	CR-1 Mar. 22	350

Olin Company

Mar. 19 S-1	645	CR-1 Mar. 30	300

Pallit Corporation

Mar. 25 S-1	740		

Accounts Payable Ledger

Anton Equipment

Mar. 21 CD-1	500	P-1 Mar. 4	10,000

Baily Company

Mar. 17 CD-1	1,200	P-1 Mar. 7	1,200

Cotin Company

Mar. 19 J-1	200	P-1 Mar. 16	1,100

Daily Corporation

		P-1 Mar. 24	850

Salio Supply House

		P-1 Mar. 18	250
		P-1 26	325

4. (a)

Perkowski Company	
Schedule of Accounts Receivable	
March 31, 198X	
Olin Company	$ 345
Pallit Corporation	740
	$1,085

(b)

Perkowski Company	
Schedule of Accounts Payable	
March 31, 198X	
Anton Equipment	$ 9,500
Cotin Company	900
Daily Corporation	850
Salio Supply House	575
	$11,825

(c)

Perkowski Company
Trial Balance
March 31, 198X

Cash	$21,726	
Accounts Receivable	1,085	
Store Supplies	725	
Equipment	10,000	
Accounts Payable		$11,825
Perkowski Company, Capital		18,000
Sales Income		9,550
Sales Discount	13	
Purchases	3,900	
Purchase Returns		200
Purchases Discount		24
Rent Expense	600	
Salaries Expense	1,550	
	$39,599	$39,599

PART III: Specific Bookkeeping and Accounting Topics

Chapter 9

Summarizing and Reporting via the Worksheet

9.1 INTRODUCTION

The recording of transactions and the adjusting and closing procedures have been discussed in previous chapters. It is reasonable to expect that among the hundreds of computations and clerical tasks involved, some errors will occur, such as posting a debit as a credit. Today many financial records are maintained on the computer or on mechanical bookkeeping systems. The use of machine time to correct errors can be very costly and may provoke questions from financial managers.

One of the best ways yet developed of avoiding errors in the permanent accounting records, and also of simplifying the work at the end of the period, is to make use of an informal record called the *worksheet*.

9.2 WORKSHEET PROCEDURES FOR A SERVICE BUSINESS

We are already familiar with the types of accounts found in a service business—that is, a business in which revenue comes from services rendered—so we shall first discuss the worksheet for such a business.

The worksheet is usually prepared in pencil on a large sheet of accounting stationery called *analysis paper*. On the worksheet, the ledger accounts are adjusted, balanced, and arranged in proper form for preparing the financial statements. All procedures can be reviewed quickly, and the adjusting and closing entries can be made in the formal records with less chance of error. Moreover, with the data for the income statement and balance sheet already proved out on the worksheet, these statements can be prepared more quickly.

For a typical service business, we may suppose the worksheet to have eight money columns; namely a debit and a credit column for four groups of figures:

1. Trial balance
2. Adjustments
3. Income statement
4. Balance sheet

The steps in completing the worksheet are then:

1. Enter the trial balance figures from the ledger.
2. Enter the adjustments.
3. Extend the adjusted trial balance figures to either the income statement or balance sheet columns.
4. Total the income statement columns and the balance sheet columns.
5. Enter the net income or net loss.

EXAMPLE 1

From the following trial balance and adjustment information, prepare an eight-column worksheet.

T. Dembofsky
Trial Balance
December 31, 198X

	Dr.	Cr.
Cash	$ 7,000	
Accounts Receivable	3,500	
Prepaid Rent	3,000	
Supplies	800	
Equipment	6,200	
Accounts Payable		$ 4,500
T. Dembofsky, Capital		12,000
Fees Income		10,000
Salaries Expense	4,600	
General Expense	1,400	
	$26,500	$26,500

Adjustment information:

(a)	Rent Expired for Year	$1,200
(b)	Supplies on Hand	$ 200
(c)	Salaries Accrued	$ 400

T. Dembofsky
Worksheet
December 31, 198X

Account Title	Trial Balance Dr.	Trial Balance Cr.	Adjustments Dr.	Adjustments Cr.	Income Statement Dr.	Income Statement Cr.	Balance Sheet Dr.	Balance Sheet Cr.
Cash	7,000						7,000	
Accounts Receivable	3,500						3,500	
Prepaid Rent	3,000			(a) 1,200			1,800	
Supplies	800			(b) 600			200	
Equipment	6,200						6,200	
Accounts Payable		4,500						4,500
T. Dembofsky, Capital		12,000						12,000
Fees Income		10,000				10,000		
Salaries Expense	4,600		(c) 400		5,000			
General Expense	1,400				1,400			
	26,500	26,500						
Rent Expense			(a) 1,200		1,200			
Supplies Expense			(b) 600		600			
Salaries Payable				(c) 400				400
			2,200	2,200	8,200	10,000	18,700	16,900
Net Income					1,800			1,800
					10,000	10,000	18,700	18,700

Use the following procedures:

1. **Enter the trial balance figures.** The balance of each general ledger account is entered in the appropriate trial balance column of the worksheet. The balances summarize all the transactions for December before any adjusting entries have been applied.

2. **Enter the adjustments.** After the trial balance figures have been entered and the totals are in agreement, the adjusting entries should be entered in the second pair of columns. The related debits and credits are keyed by letters so that they may be rechecked quickly for any errors. The letters should be in proper sequence, beginning with the accounts at the top of the page.

   (a) *Rent.* Rent may be paid in advance, at which time the debit would be to Prepaid Rent (an asset). As it expires, the Prepaid Rent account will be reduced as it must reflect only what has been prepaid. The entry to record the expired rent is

Rent Expense	1,200	
Prepaid Rent		1,200

   The account name, Rent Expense, should be written in at the bottom of the worksheet.

   (b) *Supplies.* This firm may have purchased $800 worth of supplies to last for a few years. Only the cost of the supplies used during each year is considered as an operating expense for that period; the unused portion is deferred to future periods. For this reason, the purchase of supplies is debited to an asset account and adjusted at the end of the year. Because supplies of $200 were still on hand at the close of the period, it is understood that $600 had been used and should be charged to the expense.

Supplies Expense	600	
Supplies		600

   The account Supplies Expense should be written in at the bottom of the worksheet.

   (c) *Salaries.* The salaries amount in the trial balance column would include only the payments that have been recorded and paid during the month. The portion that was *earned* in December but paid in the following year, because the weekly pay period ended in January, would not be included. Therefore an adjusting entry is needed to reflect the $400 earned but not yet paid.

Salaries Expense	400	
Salaries Payable		400

   The account title Salaries Payable should also be written in on the worksheet.

3. **Extend the trial balance figures and the adjustment figures to either the income statement or balance sheet columns.** The process of extending the balance horizontally should begin with the account at the top of the sheet. The revenue and expense accounts should be extended to the income statement columns; the assets, liabilities, and capital to the balance sheet columns. Each figure is extended to only one of the columns. After the adjusted trial balance column totals have been proved out, then the income statement columns and the balance sheet columns should also prove out.

4. **Total the income statement columns and the balance sheet columns.** The difference between the debit and credit totals in both sets of columns should be the same amount, which represents net income or net loss for the period.

5. **Enter the net income or net loss.** In Example 1, the credit column total in the income statement is $10,000, the debit column total is $8,200. The credit column, or income side, is the larger, representing a net income of $1,800 for the month. Since net income increases capital, the net income figure should go on the credit side of the balance sheet. The balance sheet credit column total of $16,900 plus net income of $1,800 totals $18,700, which equals the debit column total. Since both the income statement columns and balance sheet columns are in agreement, it is a simple matter to prepare the formal income statement and balance sheet.

   If there had been a loss, the debit or expense column in the income statement would have been the larger and the loss amount would have been entered in the credit column in order to balance the two columns. As a loss would decrease the capital, it would be entered in the balance sheet debit column.

9.3   WORKSHEET PROCEDURES FOR A MERCHANDISING BUSINESS

Merchandising (trading) businesses are those whose income derives largely from buying or selling goods rather than from rendering services. In addition to the accounts discussed in Section 9.2, the worksheet for a merchandising business will carry: Inventory, Cost of Goods Sold, Purchases, Transportation-In, and Purchase Returns.

Let us discuss these new accounts separately and then illustrate their handling on the worksheet.

Inventory and Cost of Goods Sold

Inventory represents the value of goods on hand either at the beginning or the end of the accounting period. The beginning balance would be the same amount as the ending balance of the previous period. Generally, not all purchases of merchandise are sold in the same period; so unsold merchandise must be counted and priced and the total recorded in the ledger as Ending Inventory. The amount of this inventory will be shown as an asset in the balance sheet. The amount of goods sold during the period will be shown as Cost of Goods Sold in the income summary.

EXAMPLE 2

Partial Income Summary

Sales Income			$98,200
Cost of Goods Sold			
Inventory, January 1		$38,100	
Purchases	$42,100		
Purchase Returns	300	41,800	
Goods Available for Sale		$79,900	
Less: Inventory Dec. 31		42,500	
Cost of Goods Sold			37,400
Gross Profit on Sales			$60,800

EXAMPLE 3

Trial balances of the Magda Sirras Company, as of December 31, are as follows:

Cash	$ 14,200	
Accounts Receivable	6,500	
Merchandise Inventory	38,100	
Supplies	4,200	
Prepaid Insurance	8,000	
Equipment	15,100	
Accumulated Depreciation		$ 3,400
Accounts Payable		11,200
M. Sirras, Capital		37,200
M. Sirras, Drawing	2,400	
Sales Income		98,200
Purchases	42,100	
Purchase Returns		300
Salaries Expense	11,200	
Rent Expense	4,500	
Misc. General Expense	4,000	
	$150,300	$150,300

The following additional information for year-end adjustments is (a) merchandise inventory on December 31, $42,500; (b) supplies inventory, December 31, $4,000; (c) insurance expired during this year, $2,000; (d) depreciation for the current year, $800; (e) salaries accrued on December 31, $400.

M. Sirras
Worksheet
December 31, 198X

Account Title	Trial Balance Dr.	Trial Balance Cr.	Adjustments Dr.	Adjustments Cr.	Income Statement Dr.	Income Statement Cr.	Balance Sheet Dr.	Balance Sheet Cr.
Cash	14,200						14,200	
Accounts Receivable	6,500						6,500	
Merchandise Inventory	38,100		(a) 42,500	(a) 38,100			42,500	
Supplies	4,200			(b) 200			4,000	
Prepaid Insurance	8,000			(c) 2,000			6,000	
Equipment	15,100						15,100	
Accumulated Deprec.		3,400		(d) 800				4,200
Accounts Payable		11,200						11,200
M. Sirras, Capital		37,200						37,200
M. Sirras, Drawing	2,400						2,400	
Sales Income		98,200				98,200		
Purchases	42,100				42,100			
Purchase Returns		300				300		
Salaries Expense	11,200		(e) 400		11,600			
Rent Expense	4,500				4,500			
Misc. Gen. Expense	4,000				4,000			
	150,300	150,300						
Exp. and Inc. Summary			(a) 38,100	(a) 42,500	38,100	42,500		
Supplies Expense			(b) 200		200			
Insurance Expense			(c) 2,000		2,000			
Depreciation Expense			(d) 800		800			
Salaries Payable				(e) 400				400
			84,000	84,000	103,300	141,000	90,700	53,000
Net Income					37,700			37,700
					141,000	141,000	90,700	90,700

The only significant difference from Example 1 arises from the presence of the account Merchandise Inventory. The inventory appearing in the trial balance is the inventory at the end of the previous month. The inventory at the end of December amounted to $42,500, and this is debited to Merchandise Inventory and credited to Expense and Income Summary in the adjustments columns:

Merchandise Inventory	42,500	
Expense and Income Summary		42,500

The Beginning Inventory of $38,100 must now be closed out to Expense and Income Summary as follows:

Expense and Income Summary	38,100	
Merchandise Inventory		38,100

The net effect of these entries is indicated below.

Note also that both amounts of the Expense and Income Summary are carried over to the income statement columns rather than only its net amount.

Summary

1. Because the worksheet is an informal statement, it is prepared in _____.

2. The balances that appear in the first two columns of the worksheet originate from the _____.

3. All changes in accounts appear in the _____ columns of the worksheet.

4. If the total of the debit column of the income statement in the worksheet is larger than the total of the credit column of the income statement, the balance is said to be a _____ for the period.

5. Ending inventory will appear in the _____ column of the worksheet.

6. The account affected by the two inventory entries is _____.

7. Beginning inventory plus net purchases will equal _____.

8. _____ businesses are those whose income comes from buying or selling goods.

9. The amount of goods sold during the period will be shown as _____ in the income summary.

10. The Transportation-In account is combined with the _____ account in the income statement.

Answers: 1. pencil; 2. ledger; 3. adjustment; 4. net loss; 5. balance sheet; 6. Expense and Income Summary; 7. goods available for sale; 8. Merchandising; 9. cost of goods sold; 10. Purchases

Solved Problems

9.1 Joe Hurt owns and operates Rent-a-Wreck Company, a used car rental business. Below is a trial balance before the month-end adjustments.

Trial Balance

	Dr.	Cr.
Cash	$ 1,940	
Accounts Receivable	1,575	
Supplies	1,740	
Prepaid Rent	2,900	
Equipment	16,500	
Accounts Payable		$ 1,000
Joe Hurt, Capital		21,650
Joe Hurt, Drawing	2,500	
Rental Income		7,125
Salaries Expense	1,800	
Utilities Expense	540	
Miscellaneous Expense	280	
	$29,775	$29,775

Listed below are the month-end adjustments:

(*a*) Inventory of supplies at end of month, $975

(*b*) Rent for the month, $900

(*c*) Depreciation expense for month, $500

(*d*) Salaries payable, $200

Prepare an adjusted trial balance and make the necessary adjusting entries.

Account Title	Trial Balance		Trial Balance Adjustments		Adjusted Trial Balance	
	Dr.	Cr.	Dr.	Cr.	Dr.	Cr.

Adjusting entries:

(a)

(b)

(c)

(d)

SOLUTION

Account Title	Trial Balance Dr.	Trial Balance Cr.	Trial Balance Adjustments Dr.	Trial Balance Adjustments Cr.	Adjusted Trial Balance Dr.	Adjusted Trial Balance Cr.
Cash	1,940				1,940	
Accounts Receivable	1,575				1,575	
Supplies	1,740			(a) 765	975	
Prepaid Rent	2,900			(b) 900	2,000	
Equipment	16,500				16,500	
Accounts Payable		1,000				1,000
J. Hurt, Capital		21,650				21,650
J. Hurt, Drawing	2,500				2,500	
Rental Income		7,125				7,125
Salaries Expense	1,800		(d) 200		2,000	
Utilities Expense	540				540	
Miscellaneous Expense	280				280	
	29,775	29,775				
Supplies Expense			(a) 765		765	
Rent Expense			(b) 900		900	
Depreciation Expense			(c) 500		500	
Accumulated Depreciation				(c) 500		500
Salaries Payable				(d) 200		200
Total Adjustments			2,365	2,365		
Total Adjusted Trial Balance					30,475	30,475

Adjusting entries:

(a)	Supplies Expense	765	
	Supplies		765
(b)	Rent Expense	900	
	Prepaid Rent		900
(c)	Depreciation Expense	500	
	Accumulated Depreciation		500
(d)	Salaries Expense	200	
	Salaries Payable		200

9.2 From the partial view of the worksheet below, determine the net income or loss.

Income Statement		Balance Sheet	
Dr.	Cr.	Dr.	Cr.
19,500	36,200	54,200	37,500

SOLUTION

$$\begin{array}{rl} 36,200 & \text{(total credits of income statement)} \\ -19,500 & \text{(total debits of income statement)} \\ \hline 16,700 & \text{(net income)} \end{array}$$

	Income Statement		Balance Sheet	
	Dr.	Cr.	Dr.	Cr.
	19,500	36,200	54,200	37,500
Net Income	16,700			16,700
	36,200	36,200	54,200	54,200

9.3 The following selected accounts are taken from the ledger of C. Gold. Place check marks in the appropriate columns to which the accounts will be extended in the worksheet.

Title	Income Statement		Balance Sheet	
	Dr.	Cr.	Dr.	Cr.
(1) Cash				
(2) Accounts Receivable				
(3) Accounts Payable				
(4) C. Gold, Drawing				
(5) C. Gold, Capital				
(6) Expense and Income Summary				
(7) Sales Income				
(8) Depreciation Expense				
(9) Salaries Payable				

SOLUTION

Title	Income Statement Dr.	Income Statement Cr.	Balance Sheet Dr.	Balance Sheet Cr.
(1) Cash			✔	
(2) Accounts Receivable			✔	
(3) Accounts Payable				✔
(4) C. Gold, Drawing			✔	
(5) C. Gold, Capital				✔
(6) Expense and Income Summary	✔	✔		
(7) Sales Income		✔		
(8) Depreciation Expense	✔			
(9) Salaries Payable				✔

9.4   From the following trial balances and adjustments information, prepare an eight-column worksheet.

W. Gurney Company
Trial Balance
December 31, 198X

Account Title	Trial Balance Dr.	Trial Balance Cr.	Adjustments Dr.	Adjustments Cr.	Income Statement Dr.	Income Statement Cr.	Balance Sheet Dr.	Balance Sheet Cr.
Cash	8,000							
Accounts Receivable	3,500							
Prepaid Rent	3,000							
Supplies	800							
Equipment	6,200							
Accounts Payable		5,500						
W. Gurney, Capital		12,000						
Fees Income		10,000						
Salaries Expense	4,600							
General Expense	1,400							
	27,500	27,500						

Adjustments:

(*a*)   Rent expired for year, $1,000

(*b*)   Supplies on hand, $300

(*c*)   Salaries accrued, $400

SOLUTION

W. Gurney Company
Worksheet
December 31, 198X

Account Title	Trial Balance Dr.	Trial Balance Cr.	Adjustments Dr.	Adjustments Cr.	Income Statement Dr.	Income Statement Cr.	Balance Sheet Dr.	Balance Sheet Cr.
Cash	8,000						8,000	
Accounts Receivable	3,500						3,500	
Prepaid Rent	3,000			(a) 1,000			2,000	
Supplies	800			(b) 500			300	
Equipment	6,200						6,200	
Accounts Payable		5,500						5,500
W. Gurney, Capital		12,000						12,000
Fees Income		10,000				10,000		
Salaries Expense	4,600		(c) 400		5,000			
General Expense	1,400				1,400			
	27,500	27,500						
Rent Expense			(a) 1,000		1,000			
Supplies Expense			(b) 500		500			
Salaries Payable				(c) 400				400
			1,900	1,900	7,900	10,000	20,000	17,900
Net Income					2,100			2,100
					10,000	10,000	20,000	20,000

9.5   From the information in Problem 9.4, prepare all adjusting and closing entries.

Adjusting Entries

(a)

(b)

(c)

Closing Entries

(a)

(b)

(c)

SOLUTION

Adjusting Entries

(a)	Rent Expense	1,000	
	Prepaid Rent		1,000
(b)	Supplies Expense	500	
	Supplies		500
(c)	Salaries Expense	400	
	Salaries Payable		400

Closing Entries

(a)	Fees Income	10,000	
	Expense and Income Summary		10,000
(b)	Expense and Income Summary	7,900	
	Salaries Expense		5,000
	General Expense		1,400
	Rent Expense		1,000
	Supplies Expense		500
(c)	Expense and Income Summary	2,100	
	W. Gurney, Capital		2,100

9.6 From the data of Problem 9.4, prepare the income statement and balance sheet.

W. Gurney Company		
Income Statement		
For the Period Ending December 31, 198X		
Fees Income		
Expenses:		
Salaries Expense		
Rent Expense		
Supplies Expense		
General Expense		
Total Expenses		
Net Income		

W. Gurney Company
Balance Sheet
December 31, 198X

ASSETS		LIABILITIES AND CAPITAL		
Current Assets:		Liabilities:		
Cash		Accounts Payable		
Accounts Receivable		Salaries Payable		
Prepaid Rent		Total Liabilities		
Supplies		Capital:		
Total Current Assets		Capital, Jan. 1, 198X		
Fixed Assets:		Add: Net Income		
Equipment		Capital, Dec. 31, 198X		
Total Assets		Total Liabilities and Capital		

SOLUTION

W. Gurney Company
Income Statement
For the Period Ending December 31, 198X

Fees Income		$10,000
Expenses:		
Salaries Expense	$5,000	
Rent Expense	1,000	
Supplies Expense	500	
General Expense	1,400	
Total Expenses		7,900
Net Income		$ 2,100

W. Gurney Company
Balance Sheet
December 31, 198X

ASSETS		LIABILITIES AND CAPITAL		
Current Assets:		Liabilities:		
Cash	$ 8,000	Accounts Payable		$ 5,500
Accounts Receivable	3,500	Salaries Payable		400
Prepaid Rent	2,000	Total Liabilities		$ 5,900
Supplies	300	Capital:		
Total Current Assets	$13,800	Capital, Jan. 1, 198X	$12,000	
Fixed Assets:		Add: Net Income	2,100	
Equipment	6,200	Capital, Dec. 31, 198X		14,100
Total Assets	$20,000	Total Liabilities and Capital		$20,000

9.7 Hy Sharp owns the Real Sharp Knife Shop. Hy completed a trial balance sheet and has asked you, his accountant, to complete his year-end financial statements. Upon examining his books, you discover the following adjusting entries that must be made to complete the worksheet for the year-end financial statements. Complete the worksheet.

(*a*) Insurance expired, $2,100

(*b*) Mortgage payment made on last day of year but not recorded, paid with check (cash), $2,400

(*c*) Supplies on hand at year-end, $5,900

(*d*) Salaries owed at year-end, $1,950

(*e*) Depreciation for the year, $7,100

(*f*) Rent expired on storage building, $3,200

Account Title	Trial Balance Dr.	Trial Balance Cr.	Adjustments Dr.	Adjustments Cr.	Income Statement Dr.	Income Statement Cr.	Balance Sheet Dr.	Balance Sheet Cr.
Cash	12,600							
Accounts Receivable	16,900							
Prepaid Rent	9,600							
Prepaid Insurance	7,400							
Supplies	14,100							
Equipment	42,900							
Accounts Payable		1,100						
Notes Payable		1,200						
Mortgage Notes Payable		24,500						
Hy Sharp, Capital		17,200						
Hy Sharp, Drawing	16,200							
Sales Income		104,150						
Salaries Expense	26,500							
Utilities Expense	1,950							
	148,150	148,150						

SOLUTION

Account Title	Trial Balance Dr.	Cr.	Adjustments Dr.	Cr.	Income Statement Dr.	Cr.	Balance Sheet Dr.	Cr.
Cash	12,600			(b) 2,400			10,200	
Accounts Receivable	16,900						16,900	
Prepaid Rent	9,600			(f) 3,200			6,400	
Prepaid Insurance	7,400			(a) 2,100			5,300	
Supplies	14,100			(c) 8,200			5,900	
Equipment	42,900						42,900	
Accounts Payable		1,100						1,100
Notes Payable		1,200						1,200
Mortgage Notes Payable		24,500	(b) 2,400					22,100
Hy Sharp, Capital		17,200						17,200
Hy Sharp, Drawing	16,200						16,200	
Sales Income		104,150				104,150		
Salaries Expense	26,500		(d) 1,950		28,450			
Utilities Expense	1,950				1,950			
	148,150	148,150						
Insurance Expense			(a) 2,100		2,100			
Supplies Expense			(c) 8,200		8,200			
Salaries Payable				(d) 1,950				1,950
Depreciation Expense			(e) 7,100		7,100			
Accum. Depreciation				(e) 7,100				7,100
Rent Expense			(f) 3,200		3,200			
			24,950	24,950	51,000	104,150	103,800	50,650
Net Income					53,150			53,150
					104,150	104,150	103,800	103,800

9.8 The Mills Company purchased merchandise costing $150,000. What is the cost of goods sold under each assumption below?

	Beginning Inventory	Ending Inventory
(a)	100,000	60,000
(b)	75,000	50,000
(c)	50,000	30,000
(d)	0	10,000

SOLUTION

	Beginning Inventory	+ Purchases	− Ending Inventory	= Cost of Goods Sold
(a)	100,000	150,000	60,000	190,000
(b)	75,000	150,000	50,000	175,000
(c)	50,000	150,000	30,000	170,000
(d)	0	150,000	10,000	140,000

9.9   For each situation below, determine the missing figures.

	Beginning Inventory	Purchases During Period	Ending Inventory	Cost of Goods Sold
(a)	$18,000	$40,000	———	$35,000
(b)	———	41,000	$15,000	42;000
(c)	21,000	37,000	20,000	———
(d)	27,000	———	25,000	38,000

SOLUTION

(a) $23,000, (b) $16,000, (c) $38,000, (d) $36,000

9.10   Compute the cost of goods sold from the following information: Beginning Inventory, $30,000; Purchases, $70,000; Purchase Returns, $3,000; Transportation-In, $1,000; Ending Inventory, $34,000. (Transportation-In is to be added to the cost.)

SOLUTION

Beginning Inventory		$30,000
Purchases	$70,000	
Purchase Returns	3,000	
Net Purchases	$67,000	
Transportation-In	1,000	68,000
Total Available		$98,000
Ending Inventory		34,000
Cost of Goods Sold		$64,000

9.11   Prepare an income statement based upon the data below.

(a) Merchandise inventory, Jan. 1, 198X, $30,000

(b) Merchandise inventory, Dec. 31, 198X, $24,000

(c) Purchases, $66,000

(d) Sales income, $103,000

(e) Purchase returns, $2,000

(f) Total selling expenses, $15,500

(g) Total general expenses, $12,400

(h) Sales returns, $3,000

Income Statement

SOLUTION

Income Statement

Sales Income		$103,000
Less: Sales Returns		3,000
Net Sales		$100,000
Cost of Goods Sold:		
Merchandise Inventory, Jan. 1	$30,000	
Purchases	$66,000	
Less: Purchase Returns	2,000	64,000
Goods Available for Sale		$94,000
Less: Merchandise Inventory, Dec. 31		24,000
Cost of Goods Sold		70,000
Gross Profit		$ 30,000
Expenses:		
Total Selling Expenses	$15,500	
Total General Expenses	12,400	
Total Expenses		27,900
Net Profit		$ 2,100

9.12 Journalize the following data:

(a) Merchandise inventory, January 1, $31,800; December 31, $38,500.

(b) Prepaid insurance before adjustment, $1,540. It was found that $460 had expired during the year.

(c) Office supplies physically counted on December 31 were worth $120. The original balance of Supplies on Hand was $750.

(d) Office salaries for a 5-day week ending on Friday average $2,500. The last payday was on Friday, December 27.

(a) _____

(b) _____

(c) _____

(d) _____

SOLUTION

		Dr.	Cr.
(a)	Expense and Income Summary	31,800	
	Merchandise Inventory		31,800
	Merchandise Inventory	38,500	
	Expense and Income Summary		38,500
(b)	Insurance Expense	460	
	Prepaid Insurance		460
(c)	Office Supplies Expense	630	
	Office Supplies		630
(d)	Office Salaries Expense	1,000	
	Salaries Payable (December 30 and 31)		1,000

9.13 A section of the worksheet is presented below. Enter the adjustment required for Inventory, if it is assumed that Ending Inventory was $39,000.

	Trial Balance		Adjustments	
Title	Dr.	Cr.	Dr.	Cr.
Merchandise Inventory	32,400			
Expense and Income Summary				

SOLUTION

Title	Trial Balance Dr.	Trial Balance Cr.	Adjustments Dr.	Adjustments Cr.
Merchandise Inventory	32,400		39,000	32,400
Expense and Income Summary			32,400	39,000

9.14 Using the information in Problem 9.13, extend the accounts in the worksheet. What classification does the Inventory of $39,000 represent?

Title	Income Statement Dr.	Income Statement Cr.	Balance Sheet Dr.	Balance Sheet Cr.
Merchandise Inventory				
Expense and Income Summary				

SOLUTION

Title	Income Statement Dr.	Income Statement Cr.	Balance Sheet Dr.	Balance Sheet Cr.
Merchandise Inventory			39,000	
Expense and Income Summary	32,400	39,000		

Merchandise inventory of $39,000 represents the value of the goods on hand and is classified as a current asset.

9.15 John Bright runs Bright Light, a light fixture store. John has completed his trial balance for the fiscal year just ended and has asked you, his accountant, to complete the worksheet and make any adjustments necessary. Below are the necessary adjustments that you have discovered.

(a) Merchandise inventory on December 31, $27,400

(b) Inventory of office supplies on December 31, $850

(c) Rent expired during the year, $3,000

(d) Depreciation expense (building), $3,250

(e) Depreciation expense (equipment), $2,500

(f) Salaries accrued, $1,150

(g) Insurance expired, $2,000

Complete the worksheet and show the necessary adjusting entries as of the end of the fiscal year December 31, 198X.

Account Title	Trial Balance		Adjustments		Income Statement		Balance Sheet	
	Dr.	Cr.	Dr.	Cr.	Dr.	Cr.	Dr.	Cr.
Cash	14,000							
Accounts Receivable	14,500							
Prepaid Rent	4,200							
Merchandise Inventory	21,700							
Office Supplies	1,950							
Prepaid Insurance	3,650							
Building	65,000							
Acc. Deprec.—Build.		32,500						
Equipment	28,500							
Acc. Deprec.—Equip.		9,000						
Accounts Payable		4,250						
John Bright, Capital		46,800						
John Bright, Drawing	16,900							
Income Summary								
Sales Income		137,400						
Salaries Expense	41,700							
Advertising Expense	8,400							
Utilities Expense	8,700							
Miscellaneous Expense	750							
	229,950	229,950						
Office Supplies Expense								
Rent Expense								
Insurance Expense								
Deprec. Exp.—Build.								
Deprec. Exp.—Equip.								
Salaries Payable								
Net Income								

Adjusting Entries

(a)	Dec. 31			
(b)	31			
(c)	31			
(d)	31			

Adjusting Entries, cont.

(e)	Dec. 31			
(f)	31			
(g)	31			

SOLUTION

Account Title	Trial Balance Dr.	Trial Balance Cr.	Adjustments Dr.	Adjustments Cr.	Income Statement Dr.	Income Statement Cr.	Balance Sheet Dr.	Balance Sheet Cr.
Cash	14,000						14,000	
Accounts Receivable	14,500						14,500	
Prepaid Rent	4,200			(d) 3,000			1,200	
Merchandise Inventory	21,700		(b) 27,400	(a) 21,700			27,400	
Office Supplies	1,950			(c) 1,100			850	
Prepaid Insurance	3,650			(e) 2,000			1,650	
Building	65,000						65,000	
Acc. Deprec.—Build.		32,500		(f) 3,250				35,750
Equipment	28,500						28,500	
Acc. Deprec.—Equip.		9,000		(g) 2,500				11,500
Accounts Payable		4,250						4,250
John Bright, Capital		46,800						46,800
John Bright, Drawing	16,900						16,900	
Income Summary			(a) 21,700	(b) 27,400	21,700	27,400		
Sales Income		137,400				137,400		
Salaries Expense	41,700		(h) 1,150		42,850			
Advertising Expense	8,400				8,400			
Utilities Expense	8,700				8,700			
Miscellaneous Expense	750				750			
	229,950	229,950						
Office Supplies Expense			(c) 1,100		1,100			
Rent Expense			(d) 3,000		3,000			
Insurance Expense			(e) 2,000		2,000			
Deprec. Exp.—Build.			(f) 3,250		3,250			
Deprec. Exp.—Equip.			(g) 2,500		2,500			
Salaries Payable				(h) 1,150				1,150
			62,100	62,100	94,250	164,800	170,000	99,450
Net Income					70,550			70,550
					164,800	164,800	170,000	170,000

Adjusting Entries

(a)	Dec. 31	Expense and Income Summary	21,700	
		Merchandise Inventory		21,700
(b)	31	Merchandise Inventory	27,400	
		Expense and Income Summary		27,400
(c)	31	Office Supplies Expense	1,100	
		Office Supplies		1,100
(d)	31	Rent Expense	3,000	
		Prepaid Rent		3,000
(e)	31	Depreciation Expense	3,250	
		Depreciation Expense	2,500	
		Accumulated Depreciation—Building		3,250
		Accumulated Depreciation—Equipment		2,500
(f)	31	Salaries Expense	1,150	
		Salaries Payable		1,150
(g)	31	Insurance Expense	2,000	
		Prepaid Insurance		2,000

9.16 From the information in the following T accounts, prepare the necessary closing entries at December 31.

Cash		Accounts Receivable		Supplies Expense	
8,175		1,750		1,250	

Wages Expense		T. Tom, Capital		T. Tom, Drawing	
19,200			37,500	11,950	

Rent Expense		Fuel Expense		Insurance Expense	
3,175		1,325		4,750	

Equipment		Miscellaneous Expense		Sales Income	
75,090		235			89,400

Closing Entries

(a)			
(b)			
(c)			
(d)			

SOLUTION

Closing Entries

(a)	Sales Income	89,400	
	Expense and Income Summary		89,400
(b)	Expense and Income Summary	29,935	
	Wages Expense		19,200
	Insurance Expense		4,750
	Rent Expense		3,175
	Fuel Expense		1,325
	Supplies Expense		1,250
	Miscellaneous Expense		235
(c)	Expense and Income Summary	59,465	
	T. Tom, Capital		59,465
(d)	T. Tom, Capital	11,950	
	T. Tom, Drawing		11,950

9.17 From the trial balance of the Manell Sales Company, as of December 31, which follows, prepare an eight-column worksheet, using the following additional information for year-end adjustments: (a) merchandise inventory on December 31, $42,000; (b) supplies inventory, December 31, $4,000; (c) insurance expired during this year, $2,000; (d) depreciation for the current year, $800; (e) salaries accrued on December 31, $400.

Mannell Sales Company
Trial Balance

Cash	$ 15,000	
Accounts Receivable	6,500	
Merchandise Inventory	38,100	
Supplies	4,200	
Prepaid Insurance	8,000	
Equipment	15,100	
Accumulated Depreciation		$ 4,400
Accounts Payable		11,200
Manell, Capital		37,000
Manell, Drawing	2,400	
Sales Income		98,200
Purchases	42,100	
Purchase Returns		300
Salaries Expense	11,200	
Rent Expense	4,500	
Misc. General Expense	4,000	
	$151,100	$151,100

Manell Sales Company
Worksheet

Account Title	Trial Balance		Adjustments		Income Statement		Balance Sheet	
	Dr.	Cr.	Dr.	Cr.	Dr.	Cr.	Dr.	Cr.

SOLUTION

Manell Sales Company
Worksheet

Account Title	Trial Balance Dr.	Trial Balance Cr.	Adjustments Dr.	Adjustments Cr.	Income Statement Dr.	Income Statement Cr.	Balance Sheet Dr.	Balance Sheet Cr.
Cash	15,000						15,000	
Accounts Receivable	6,500						6,500	
Merchandise Inventory	38,100		(a) 42,000	(a) 38,100			42,000	
Supplies	4,200			(b) 200			4,000	
Prepaid Insurance	8,000			(c) 2,000			6,000	
Equipment	15,100						15,100	
Accumulated Deprec.		4,400		(d) 800				5,200
Accounts Payable		11,200						11,200
Manell, Capital		37,000						37,000
Manell, Drawing	2,400						2,400	
Sales Income		98,200				98,200		
Purchases	42,100				42,100			
Purchase Returns		300				300		
Salaries Expense	11,200		(e) 400		11,600			
Rent Expense	4,500				4,500			
Misc. Gen. Expense	4,000				4,000			
	151,100	151,100						
Exp. and Inc. Sum.			(a) 38,100	(a) 42,000	38,100	42,000		
Supplies Expense			(b) 200		200			
Insurance Expense			(c) 2,000		2,000			
Depreciation Expense			(d) 800		800			
Salaries Payable				(e) 400				400
			83,500	83,500	103,300	140,500	91,000	53,800
Net Income					37,200			37,200
					140,500	140,500	91,000	91,000

9.18   From the information in Problem 9.17, prepare all necessary adjusting and closing entries.

Adjusting Entries

(a)

(b)

(c)

(d)

(e)

Closing Entries

(a)			
(b)			
(c)			
(d)			

SOLUTION

Adjusting Entries

(a)	Merchandise Inventory	42,000	
	Expense and Income Summary		42,000
	Expense and Income Summary	38,100	
	Merchandise Inventory		38,100
(b)	Supplies Expense	200	
	Supplies		200
(c)	Insurance Expense	2,000	
	Prepaid Insurance		2,000
(d)	Depreciation Expense	800	
	Accumulated Depreciation		800
(e)	Salaries Expense	400	
	Salaries Payable		400

Closing Entries

(a)	Sales Income	98,200	
	Purchase Returns	300	
	Expense and Income Summary		98,500
(b)	Expense and Income Summary	65,200	
	Purchases		42,100
	Salaries Expense		11,600
	Rent Expense		4,500
	Misc. General Expense		4,000
	Supplies Expense		200
	Insurance Expense		2,000
	Depreciation Expense		800

Closing Entries, cont.

(c)	Expense and Income Summary	37,200	
	Manell, Capital		37,200
(d)	Manell, Capital	2,400	
	Manell, Drawing		2,400

9.19 From the information in Problem 9.18, prepare all financial statements.

Manell Sales Company

Income Statement

For the Period Ending December 31, 198X

Manell Sales Company

Capital Statement

For the Period Ending December 31, 198X

Manell Sales Company
Balance Sheet
December 31, 198X

SOLUTION

Manell Sales Company
Income Statement
For the Period Ending December 31, 198X

Sales Income		$98,200
Cost of Goods Sold:		
Merchandise Inventory, Jan. 1	$38,100	
Purchases	$42,100	
Less: Purchase Returns	300	41,800
Goods Available for Sale		$79,900
Less: Merchandise Inventory, Dec. 31		42,000
Cost of Goods Sold		37,900
		$60,300
Operating Expenses:		
Salaries Expense	$11,600	
Rent Expense	4,500	
Insurance Expense	2,000	
Supplies Expense	200	
Depreciation Expense	800	
Misc. General Expense	4,000	
Total Expenses		23,100
Net Income		$37,200

Manell Sales Company		
Capital Statement		
For the Period Ending December 31, 198X		

Capital, Jan. 1, 198X		$37,000
Net Income	$37,200	
Less: Drawing	2,400	34,800
Increase in Capital		$71,800
Capital, Dec. 31, 198X		

Manell Sales Company		
Balance Sheet		
December 31, 198X		

ASSETS		
Current Assets:		
Cash	$15,000	
Accounts Receivable	6,500	
Merchandise Inventory	42,000	
Supplies	4,000	
Prepaid Insurance	6,000	
Total Current Assets		$73,500
Fixed Assets:		
Equipment	$15,100	
Less: Accumulated Depreciation	5,200	9,900
Total Assets		$83,400
LIABILITIES AND CAPITAL		
Current Liabilities:		
Accounts Payable	$11,200	
Salaries Payable	400	
Total Current Liabilities		$11,600
Capital, Dec. 31, 198X		71,800
Total Liabilities and Capital		$83,400

9.20   Jessie James, owner of the Money Shop, a small loan business whose fiscal year ends on September 30, has asked you, his accounting clerk, to prepare a trial balance and make all the necessary adjustments to complete a worksheet. Below is a list of the year-end adjusting entries you found necessary. Complete the worksheet and show the adjusting entries.

(a)   A $2,000 note received from a customer on September 30 was not posted to the ledger. There was also $200 of interest received on the note (use the interest income account for the $200).

(b)   The notes payable of $2,000 was paid on September 30 but was not entered in the ledger. There was $125 of interest paid on the note.

(c) $400 of supplies were used during the year.

(d) $2,000 of the prepaid rent has expired as of September 30.

(e) $1,200 of the prepaid advertising has expired as of September 30.

(f)   Depreciation expense on office equipment was $300.

(g)   Accrued salaries at September 30 was $700.

Account Title	Trial Balance		Adjustments		Income Statement		Balance Sheet	
	Dr.	Cr.	Dr.	Cr.	Dr.	Cr.	Dr.	Cr.
Cash	10,500							
Accounts Receivable	11,750							
Notes Receivable	14,100							
Supplies	725							
Prepaid Rent	3,025							
Prepaid Advertising	1,325							
Office Equipment	1,800							
Accounts Payable		475						
Notes Payable		2,000						
Jessie James, Capital		19,450						
Jessie James, Drawing	9,200							
Interest Income		46,650						
Utilities Expense	1,325							
Miscellaneous Exp.	325							
Salaries Expense	14,500							
	68,575	68,575						

Adjusting Entries

(a)	Sept. 30			
(b)	30			
(c)	30			
(d)	30			
(e)	30			

Adjusting Entries, cont.

(f)	Sept. 30			
(g)	30			

SOLUTION

Account Title	Trial Balance Dr.	Trial Balance Cr.	Adjustments Dr.	Adjustments Cr.	Income Statement Dr.	Income Statement Cr.	Balance Sheet Dr.	Balance Sheet Cr.
Cash	10,500		(a) 2,200	(b) 2,125			10,575	
Accounts Receivable	11,750						11,750	
Notes Receivable	14,100			(a) 2,000			12,100	
Supplies	725			(c) 400			325	
Prepaid Rent	3,025			(d) 2,000			1,025	
Prepaid Advertising	1,325			(e) 1,200			125	
Office Equipment	1,800						1,800	
Accounts Payable		475						475
Notes Payable		2,000	(b) 2,000					
Jessie James, Capital		19,450						19,450
Jessie James, Drawing	9,200						9,200	
Interest Inc.		46,650		(a) 200		46,850		
Utilities Expense	1,325				1,325			
Miscellaneous Expense	325				325			
Salaries Expense	14,500		(g) 700		15,200			
	68,575	68,575						
Interest Expense			(b) 125		125			
Supplies Expense			(c) 400		400			
Rent Expense			(d) 2,000		2,000			
Advertising Expense			(e) 1,200		1,200			
Depreciation Expense			(f) 300		300			
Accum. Deprec.				(f) 300				300
Salaries Payable				(g) 700				700
			8,925	8,925	20,875	46,850	46,900	20,925
Net Income					25,975			25,975
					46,850	46,850	46,900	46,900

Adjusting Entries

(a)	Sept. 30	Cash	2,200	
		Interest Income		200
		Notes Receivable		2,000
(b)	30	Notes Payable	2,000	
		Interest Expense	125	
		Cash		2,125

Adjusting Entries, cont.

(c)	30	Supplies Expense	400	
		Supplies		400
(d)	30	Rent Expense	2,000	
		Prepaid Rent		2,000
(e)	30	Advertising Expense	1,200	
		Prepaid Advertising		1,200
(f)	30	Depreciation Expense	300	
		Accumulated Depreciation		300
(g)	30	Salaries Expense	700	
		Salaries Payable		700

Chapter 10

Payroll

10.1 GROSS PAY

The pay rate at which employees are paid is generally arrived at through negotiations between the employer and the employees. The employer, however, must conform with all applicable federal and state laws (minimum wage, and so on). One law requires that workers, excluding salaried workers or workers in industries such as hotels and restaurants, be compensated at one and one-half times their regular pay for hours worked over forty (40).

Gross pay for wage earners is generally computed by using an individual time card.

Time Card

Name _____		Pay Rate/Hour _____	
Week Ended _____			
	Time In	Time Out	Hours
Monday	_____	_____	_____
Tuesday	_____	_____	_____
Wednesday	_____	_____	_____
Thursday	_____	_____	_____
Friday	_____	_____	_____
Approved _____		Total Hours for Week	_____

EXAMPLE 1

The computation of Carol Johnson's gross pay appears below.

Time Card

Name ____Carol Johnson____		Pay Rate/Hour ____$7.50____	
Week Ended ____7/18/8X____			
	Time In	Time Out	Hours
Monday	8:00 A.M.	4:00 P.M.	8
Tuesday	8:00 A.M.	6:00 P.M.	10
Wednesday	8:00 A.M.	7:00 P.M.	11
Thursday	8:00 A.M.	4:00 P.M.	8
Friday	8:00 A.M.	5:00 P.M.	9
Approved _____		Total Hours for Week	46

Regular pay: 40 hours × $7.50   = $300.00
Overtime pay: 6 hours × $1\frac{1}{2}$ × $7.50 =   67.50
Gross pay: = $367.50

10.2 DEDUCTIONS FROM GROSS PAY

Federal Withholding Taxes

Federal income taxes are withheld from gross pay on a pay-as-you-go-system. The amount to withhold from each employee is determined after consideration of the following four factors:

1. The amount of gross pay
2. The taxpayer's filing status (married or single)
3. The number of exemptions claimed by the taxpayer
4. The payroll period

The employee's filing status and number of exemptions claimed is determined by referring to Form W-4 filled out by each employee when he or she began to work.

Form **W-4** (Rev. January 1986)	Department of the Treasury—Internal Revenue Service **Employee's Withholding Allowance Certificate**	OMB No. 1545-0010 Expires: 11-30-87

1 Type or print your full name | **2** Your social security number

Home address (number and street or rural route)

City or town, state, and ZIP code

3 Marital Status
- ☐ Single   ☐ Married
- ☐ Married, but withhold at higher Single rate
- **Note:** If married, but legally separated, or spouse is a nonresident alien, check the Single box.

4 Total number of allowances you are claiming (from line F of the worksheet on page 2) . . . .

5 Additional amount, if any, you want deducted from each pay . . . . **$**

6 I claim exemption from withholding because (see instructions and check boxes below that apply):

  a ☐ Last year I did not owe any Federal income tax and had a right to a full refund of **ALL** income tax withheld, **AND**

  b ☐ This year I do not expect to owe any Federal income tax and expect to have a right to a full refund of **ALL** income tax withheld. If both a and b apply, enter the year effective and "EXEMPT" here . . . ▶ | Year 19

  c If you entered "EXEMPT" on line 6b, are you a full-time student? . . . . ☐Yes ☐No

Under penalties of perjury, I certify that I am entitled to the number of withholding allowances claimed on this certificate, or if claiming exemption from withholding, that I am entitled to claim the exempt status.

Employee's signature ▶   **Date** ▶   , 19

7 Employer's name and address (**Employer: Complete 7, 8, and 9 only if sending to IRS**) | **8** Office code | **9** Employer identification number

Fig. 10-1

How many exemptions can an employee claim? An employee is entitled to one personal exemption and one for his or her spouse and each dependent.

EXAMPLE 2

Bill MacDonald's gross pay for the week is $355. He is married and claims four exemptions. The federal tax to be withheld is $47.30. (Tables that follow are used for example only and are not official.)

MARRIED Persons—WEEKLY Payroll Period

And the wages are—		And the number of withholding allowances claimed is—										
		0	1	2	3	④	5	6	7	8	9	10 or more
At least	But less than	The amount of income tax to be withheld shall be—										
$320	$330	$54.20	$50.60	$47.00	$43.40	$39.80	$37.10	$34.70	$32.20	$29.80	$27.30	$24.90
330	340	56.70	53.10	49.50	45.90	42.30	38.80	36.40	33.90	31.50	29.00	26.60
340	350	59.20	55.60	52.00	48.40	44.80	41.20	38.10	35.60	33.20	30.70	28.30
350	360	62.00	58.10	54.50	50.90	⑪⑦.30	43.70	40.10	37.30	34.90	32.40	30.00
360	370	64.80	60.80	57.00	53.40	49.80	46.20	42.60	39.00	36.60	34.10	31.70
370	380	67.60	63.60	59.50	55.90	52.30	48.70	45.10	41.50	38.30	35.80	33.40
380	390	70.40	66.40	62.30	58.40	54.80	51.20	47.60	44.00	40.40	37.50	35.10
390	400	73.20	69.20	65.10	61.10	57.30	53.70	50.10	46.50	42.90	39.30	36.80
400	410	76.00	72.00	67.90	63.90	59.80	56.20	52.60	49.00	45.40	41.80	38.50
410	420	78.80	74.80	70.70	66.70	62.60	58.70	55.10	51.50	47.90	44.30	40.70

EXAMPLE 3

Barbara Ledina earns $175 for the week. She is single and claims zero exemptions. The amount of the tax to be withheld is $30.10.

SINGLE Persons—WEEKLY Payroll Period

And the wages are—		And the number of withholding allowances claimed is—										
		⓪	1	2	3	4	5	6	7	8	9	10 or more
At least	But less than	The amount of income tax to be withheld shall be—										
$120	$125	$18.00	$14.90	$12.00	$9.20	$6.40	$4.10	$1.80	$0	$0	$0	$0
125	130	19.20	15.90	13.00	10.20	7.30	4.90	2.60	.20	0	0	0
130	135	20.30	17.00	14.00	11.20	8.30	5.70	3.40	1.00	0	0	0
135	140	21.50	18.20	15.00	12.20	9.30	6.50	4.20	1.80	0	0	0
140	145	22.60	19.30	16.00	13.20	10.30	7.40	5.00	2.60	.30	0	0
145	150	23.80	20.50	17.10	14.20	11.30	8.40	5.80	3.40	1.10	0	0
150	160	25.50	22.20	18.90	15.70	12.80	9.90	7.00	4.60	2.30	0	0
160	170	27.80	24.50	21.20	17.80	14.80	11.90	9.00	6.20	3.90	1.60	0
170	180	30.10	26.80	23.50	20.10	16.80	13.90	11.00	8.10	5.50	3.20	.90
180	190	32.40	29.10	25.80	22.40	19.10	15.90	13.00	10.10	7.20	4.80	2.50

Social Security Taxes (Federal Insurance Contributions Act)

Currently (1987) the amount to be withheld from an employee's pay is 7.15 percent of the first $43,800 of earnings.

EXAMPLE 4

Flo Cagen has earned $43,700 to date. She then received $600 gross pay for the week. What is the amount of the FICA tax to be withheld?

$$(\$100) \times (7.15\%) = \$7.15$$

$100 brings the employee's earnings up to $43,800, the maximum.

EXAMPLE 5

Lou Harmin has earned $21,000 to date. His gross pay for the week is $500. How much Social Security (FICA) is to be withheld from his pay?

$$(\$500) \times (7.15\%) = \$35.75$$

EXAMPLE 6

Doris Hartmann has earned $44,200 to date. Her gross pay for the week is $700. How much Social Security is to be withheld from her pay?

None. She is already over the maximum of $43,800.

State and Local Taxes Withheld

Most states and some cities impose a tax on the gross earnings of each residential employee. These taxes are also withheld from the employee's pay and turned over periodically by the employer to the appropriate agency.

Other Deductions

All the deductions discussed so far have been mandatory. Often, through agreement with the employer, amounts will be withheld for retirement plans, union dues, savings bonds, insurance, and other deductions.

EXAMPLE 7

Harold Eccleston earned $575 for the week. Deductions from his pay were: Federal Withholding, $82.00; FICA, $41.11; State Tax, $23; Union Dues, $16. What is his net pay?

$$\begin{aligned} \text{Net pay} &= \$575 - (\$82 + \$41.11 + \$23 + \$16) \\ &= \$575 - \$162.11 \\ &= \$412.89 \end{aligned}$$

10.3 THE PAYROLL SYSTEM

The payroll system generally consists of input data (time cards), a payroll register (to compute the payroll each payroll period), individual earnings cards (a separate record for each employee), paychecks, and a system for recording both the payroll and the related employer taxes with appropriate liabilities.

Individual Time Card

Although the overall payroll is recorded in a payroll register, it is also necessary to know both the earnings and the deductions for *each* employee separately. These individual records facilitate the preparation of required governmental reports and assist the employer in maintaining control over payroll expenditures. They also act as convenient references to basic employee information such as earnings to date, exemptions, filing status, and employee classification. Information from the payroll register is posted *immediately* after recording the payroll to the individual earnings cards.

Individual Earnings Card

Name	_____	Filing Status	_____
Address	_____	Exemptions Claimed	_____
	_____	Position	_____
S.S. No.	_____	Pay Rate ____ Per ____	

First Quarter

| Payroll Period | Gross | | | Deductions | | | | | Net | |
	Reg.	Ot.	Total	FICA	Fed. With.	State With.	Oth. Ded.	Total Ded.	Net Pay	Ck. No.
First quarter										

Payroll Register

A payroll register is a specially designed form used at the close of each payroll period (weekly, biweekly, and so on) to summarize and compute the payroll for the period. Although the design of this form may vary slightly depending on desired information and the degree of automation, most contain the same basic information.

Refer to the payroll register (Table 10.1) and note that it is broken into five sections:

(1) Computation of gross earnings (regular, overtime, total).

(2) Taxable earnings (information only), used as a reference to computer FICA tax withheld or paid by the employer and unemployment tax payable by the employer.

(3) Deductions from gross pay—a place is provided for each tax withheld and for miscellaneous deductions (coded).

(4) Net pay. This is the employee's take-home pay. This may be checked by adding the total of deductions to the net pay. The result should be the gross pay.

(5) Gross salaries charged to specific accounts.

EXAMPLE 8

Using the data in Table 10.2, record the payroll as of June 15 for Atlas Company in Table 10.3.

10.4 RECORDING THE PAYROLL

The payroll is generally recorded initially in the general journal. Since the payroll register is the input for the entry, it is generally totaled for the payroll period and proved before any entry is made.

Table 10.1 Payroll Register

Date	Name	(1) Gross Pay Reg.	Ot.	Total	(2) Taxable FICA	Unemp.	(3) Deductions Fed. With.	State With.	Code	Oth. Ded.	Total Ded.	(4) Net Net Pay	Ck. No.	(5) Distribution Office Salaries	Factory Salaries

Table 10.2 Payroll Data

Name	(Prior to Payroll) Earnings to Date	Gross Pay Reg.	Ot.	Total	Classification	Fed. With.	State With.	FICA	Other Deductions
P. Smith	$5,800	$360	$45	$405	Office	$38.00	$17.00	$28.96	Union A, $11.00
S. Jones	8,200	320	—	320	Office	45.00	15.30	22.88	
R. Campbell	6,900	280	84	364	Factory	31.00	13.30	26.03	Union A, $9.00

Table 10.3 Payroll Register

Date	Name	Gross Pay Reg.	Ot.	Total	Taxable FICA	Unemp.	Deductions Fed. With.	State With.	Code	Oth. Ded.	FICA	Total Ded.	Net Net Pay	Ck. No.	Distribution Office Salaries	Factory Salaries
6/15	P. Smith	$360	$45	$ 405	$ 405	$405	$ 38.00	$17.00	A	$11.00	$28.96	$ 94.96	$310.04	44	$405	
6/15	S. Jones	320	—	320	320	-0-*	45.00	15.30		-0-	22.88	83.18	236.82	45	320	
6/15	R. Campbell	280	84	364	364	100*	31.00	13.30	A	9.00	26.03	79.33	284.67	46		$364
	Total	$960	$129	$1,089	$1,089	$505	$114.00	$45.60		$20.00	$77.87	$257.47	$831.53		$725	$364

*Only first $7,000 is subject to unemployment tax.

185

EXAMPLE 9

From the data summarized in Example 8, record the payroll in general journal form.

General Journal

Date	Description	P.R.	Debit	Credit
June 15	Office Salaries Expense		725.00	
	Factory Salaries Expense		364.00	
	FICA Withholding Tax Payable			77.87
	Federal Withholding Tax Payable			114.00
	State Withholding Tax Payable			45.60
	Union Dues Payable			20.00
	Salaries Payable			831.53
	To record the payroll for the week ended June 15			

Payroll Taxes Imposed on the Employer

1. *Social Security (Federal Insurance Contributions Act).* Not only is Social Security (FICA) withheld from the employee's pay, but a matching amount is paid in by the employer. The employer's contribution is generally computed by multiplying the total *taxable* payroll for the current period by 7.15 percent. The two 7.15 percent contributions (7.15 percent from the employee; 7.15 percent from the employer) are reported quarterly by the employer on federal Form 941.

2. *Unemployment taxes.* Employers are required to pay unemployment taxes to both the federal and state governments. Under current legislation, the tax is imposed only on the first $7,000 of each employee's earnings. Although the typical state unemployment tax rate is 3.5 percent, rates vary from 0 to 5 percent depending on the state, the nature of the business, and the employer's experience with unemployment. For the current year (1987), the official federal unemployment tax rate is 6.2 percent. However, as long as the employer is up to date on the state tax, the employer is allowed an automatic credit of 5.4 percent no matter what rate the employer actually pays. The effective federal unemployment tax rate is therefore 0.8 percent.

Recording the Employer's Taxes

When the payroll is recorded, the employer must also record his or her liability for taxes imposed on him or her, as well as those imposed on the employees.

EXAMPLE 10

From the data summarized in the payroll register in Table 10.3, record the employer's taxes for the payroll period. (Assume a 4 percent state unemployment tax rate and a 0.8 percent federal rate.)

General Journal

Date	Description	P.R.	Debit	Credit
June 15	Payroll Tax Expense		102.11	
	FICA Withholding Tax Payable*			77.87
	State Unemployment Insurance Payable†			20.20
	Federal Unemployment Insurance Payable†			4.04
	To record the employers taxes for the week ended June 15			

---

*Must match employee's contribution.

†Note that by reference to the payroll register (taxable unemployment), only $505.00 is subject to the tax.

Summary

1. Compensation is paid at the rate of time and one-half when an employee works more than _____ hours.

2. The amount of federal income tax withheld from a person is based on the individual's _____ and _____ .

3. Form _____ will yield information pertaining to the number of exemptions an employee is filing.

4. The rate of FICA tax is _____ percent.

5. FICA is reported _____ by the employer on Form _____ .

6. The payroll _____ is the input for the payroll entry.

7. Generally, all payroll entries are recorded in the _____ journal.

8. The two types of payroll taxes imposed on the employer are _____ and _____ .

9. The payroll tax expense entry is recorded in the _____ journal.

10. The one tax that is paid by the employee and matched by the employer is _____ .

Answers: 1. 40; 2. filing status, number of exemptions; 3. W-4; 4. 7.15%; 5. quarterly, 941; 6. register; 7. general; 8. FICA, unemployment; 9. general; 10. FICA

Solved Problems

10.1 Below is a time card for Laura Anthony. Complete the hours section of her time card and compute her gross pay.

Time Card

Name	Laura Anthony	Pay Rate/Hour	$8.00	
Week Ended	9/20/8X			
	Time In	Time Out	Hours	
Monday	8:00 A.M.	4:00 P.M.	_____	
Tuesday	8:00 A.M.	4:00 P.M.	_____	
Wednesday	8:00 A.M.	6:00 P.M.	_____	
Thursday	8:00 A.M.	7:30 P.M.	_____	
Friday	8:00 A.M.	6:30 P.M.	_____	
Approved _____		Total Hours for Week	_____	

SOLUTION

Time Card

Name	Laura Anthony	Pay Rate/Hour	$8.00
Week Ended	9/20/8X		

	Time In	Time Out	Hours
Monday	8:00 A.M.	4:00 P.M.	8
Tuesday	8:00 A.M.	4:00 P.M.	8
Wednesday	8:00 A.M.	6:00 P.M.	10
Thursday	8:00 A.M.	7:30 P.M.	$11\frac{1}{2}$
Friday	8:00 A.M.	6:30 P.M.	$10\frac{1}{2}$

Approved _____	Total Hours for Week	48

Regular pay: 40 hours × $8.00   = $320.00
Overtime pay: 8 hours × $12.00* =   96.00
Total gross pay   = $416.00

*Time and one-half rate.
8 hours overtime × 1.5 = $12.00 per hour for overtime
$12.00 × 8 hours overtime = $96.00 for overtime

10.2 How many exemptions are permitted to be claimed on Form W-4 in the following cases:

(a) Taxpayer and spouse (nonworking)

(b) Taxpayer, spouse, and two children

(c) Taxpayer and mother she fully supports

SOLUTION

(a) 2; (b) 4; (c) 3

10.3 Based on the withholding tables appearing on page 182, how much will be withheld in each of the following situations:

(a) Employee, single, claiming one exemption, earns $156 for the week.

(b) Employee, married, has gross pay of $406 weekly. Claims five exemptions.

SOLUTION

(a) $22.20; (b) $56.20

10.4 How much FICA tax will be withheld from the following employees?

	Employee	Amount Earned Prior to Current Payroll	Amount Earned This Week	Amount Withheld for FICA
(a)	I. Blanton	$26,000	$600	?
(b)	P. Burday	43,600	700	?
(c)	M. Fleming	45,000	750	?

SOLUTION

(a) $42.90 ($600 × 7.15%)

(b) $14.30 ($200 balance × 7.15%)

(c) $0 (Maximum of $43,800 has been reached.)

10.5   Complete the table below based on the employer's payroll obligation. Assume a state rate of 4 percent and a federal rate of 0.8 percent.

Employee	Amount Earned This Week	Accumulated Earnings	FICA	Federal Unemployment	State Unemployment
(a) B. Orzech	$550	$5,300	$39.33	?	?
(b) M. Felson	475	6,725	33.96	?	?
(c) H. Hendricks	610	7,900	43.62	?	?

SOLUTION

	Federal Unemployment	State Unemployment
(a)	$4.40	$22.00
(b)	2.20*	11.00†
(c)	None	None

---

*Federal rate is 0.8 percent on first $7,000; balance subject to tax is $275.00.

†State rate is 4 percent on first $7,000; balance subject to tax is $275.00.

10.6   Judy Bagon worked 44 hours during the first week in February of the current year. The pay rate is $9.00 per hour. Withheld from her wages were FICA 7.15 percent; federal income tax $47.00; hospitalization $7.20. Prepare the necessary payroll entry.

SOLUTION

Salaries Expense	414.00*	
FICA Taxes Payable		29.60
Federal Income Tax Payable		47.00
Hospitalization Payable		7.20
Salaries Payable		330.20

*40 hours × $9 = $360.00   (regular)
 4 hours × $13.50 =   54.00   (overtime)
                     $414.00

10.7 Based on the information in Problem 10.6, what is the entry to record the employer's payroll tax if it is assumed the state tax rate is 4 percent and the federal unemployment rate is 0.8 percent? (Prior to payroll) earnings to date = $5,100.00.

SOLUTION

Payroll Tax Expense	49.47	
FICA Taxes Payable		29.60
Federal Unemployment Insurance Payable		3.31
State Unemployment Insurance Payable		16.56

10.8 The total payroll for the Berchid Realty Company for the week ending May 30 was $26,000. Of the total amount, $19,000 was subject to FICA tax, $3,800 held for federal income tax, $1,500 held for pension saving plan, and the balance paid in cash. Present the journal entry necessary to record the payroll for this week, assuming that the FICA tax rate is 7.15 percent.

Salaries Expense		
FICA Taxes Payable		
Federal Income Taxes Payable		
Pension Savings Payable		
Cash		

SOLUTION

Salaries Expense	26,000.00	
FICA Taxes Payable		1,358.50
Federal Income Taxes Payable		3,800.00
Pension Savings Payable		1,500.00
Cash		19,341.50

10.9 Based on Problem 10.8, present the employer's payroll tax entry, assuming a state tax rate of 4 percent and federal unemployment 0.8 percent and that of the total payroll, $12,000 was subject to federal and state unemployment.

Payroll Tax Expense		
FICA Taxes Payable		
Federal Unemployment Insurance Payable		
State Unemployment Insurance Payable		

SOLUTION

Payroll Tax Expense	1,934.50	
FICA Taxes Payable		1,358.50*
Federal Unemployment Insurance Payable		96.00
State Unemployment Insurance Payable		480.00

*Matched.

10.10 For the week ending June 30, the Benezran Company had a total gross payroll of $54,000. Of that amount, earnings subject to FICA were $41,500 and the amount subject to unemployment compensation tax was $11,200. Present the journal entry to record the employer's payroll tax for the week, assuming the following rates: FICA 7.15 percent, state unemployment 4 percent, federal unemployment 0.8 percent.

SOLUTION

Payroll Tax Expense	3,504.85	
FICA Taxes Payable		2,967.25
State Unemployment Insurance Payable		448.00
Federal Unemployment Insurance Payable		89.60

10.11 Below is the payroll data for three of the employees of the S. Board Company:

Employee	Amount Earned to Date	Gross Pay for Week
L. Benjamin	$7,400	$500.00
R. Hochian	6,800	400.00
C. Murphy	5,400	300.00

The company is located in a state that imposes an unemployment insurance tax of 3 percent on the first $7,000. Federal unemployment tax is 0.8 percent; FICA tax is 7.15 percent. Present the entry necessary to record the employer's payroll tax expense.

SOLUTION

	FICA	State	Federal
Benjamin	$35.75 (500 × 7.15%)	None	None
Hochian	28.60 (400 × 7.15%)	$ 6.00 (200 × 3%)	$1.60 (200 × 0.8%)
Murphy	21.45 (300 × 7.15%)	9.00 (300 × 3%)	2.40 (300 × 0.8%)
	$85.80	$15.00	$4.00

Payroll Tax Expense	104.80	
FICA Taxes Payable		85.80
State Unemployment Insurance Payable		15.00
Federal Unemployment Insurance Payable		4.00

10.12 Based on the information below, complete the March 28 payroll register for the J. Rakosi Medical Center.

Name	Earnings to Date	Gross Pay Reg.	Ot.	Total	Federal Withholding	Other Deductions
J. Erin	$7,400	$280	$63	$343	$35	Union, $12
M. Ribble	6,900	400	75	475	77	Union, $10
W. Mondstein	7,100	380	—	380	42	—
M. Yamura	3,700	410	—	410	44	—

Payroll Register

Date	Name	Gross Pay Reg.	Ot.	Total	Taxable FICA	Unemp.	Deductions FICA	Fed. With.	Oth. Ded.	Net Net Pay

SOLUTION

Payroll Register

Date	Name	Gross Pay Reg.	Ot.	Total	Taxable FICA	Unemp.	Deductions FICA	Fed. With.	Oth. Ded.	Net Net Pay
3/28	J. Erin	280	63	343	343	—	24.52	35.00	U-12.00	271.48
	M. Ribble	400	75	475	475	100	33.96	77.00	U-10.00	354.04
	W. Mondstein	380	—	380	380	—	27.17	42.00	—	310.83
	M. Yamura	410	—	410	410	410	29.32	44.00	—	336.68
	Totals	1,470	138	1,608	1,608	510	114.97	198.00	22.00	1,273.03

10.13 Based on the information in Problem 10.12, present the payroll journal entry needed.

SOLUTION

Salaries Expense	1,608.00	
FICA Taxes Payable		114.97
Federal Income Taxes Payable		198.00
Union Dues Payable		22.00
Salaries Payable		1,273.03

10.14 Based on the information presented in the payroll register of Problem 10.12, present the necessary payroll tax expense entry for the employer. Assume a state tax rate of 4 percent and a federal rate of 0.8 percent.

SOLUTION

Payroll Tax Expense	139.45	
FICA Taxes Payable		114.97
Federal Unemployment Insurance Payable		4.08*
State Unemployment Insurance Payable		20.40*

*The total amount of the payroll subject to the $7,000 maximum earned limitation for unemployment insurance is $510 (M. Ribble, $100.00; M. Yamura, $410.00).

10.15 Below is the payroll information for the Link Company for the week ending June 9, 198X (FICA tax rate 7.15%).

Office salaries were $68,400, of which $54,200 was subject to FICA tax, $6,740 was withheld for federal withholding tax, and $2,960 was withheld for state taxes. Prepare the necessary journal entry.

SOLUTION

Office Salaries Expense	68,400.00	
FICA Taxes Payable		3,875.30
Federal Taxes Payable		6,740.00
State Taxes Payable		2,960.00
Salaries Payable		54,824.70

10.16 From the preceding information, what would be the journal entry to record the employer's payroll tax expense for the week if $44,700 was subject to unemployment tax? Use a 3.5% state tax and 0.8% federal rate.

SOLUTION

Payroll Tax Expense	5,797.40	
FICA Taxes Payable		3,875.30*
State Unemployment Taxes Payable		1,564.50
Federal Unemployment Taxes Payable		357.60

*Employer has to match FICA tax.

Chapter 11

Negotiable Instruments

11.1 INTRODUCTION

A large proportion of all business transactions are credit transactions. One way of extending credit is by the acceptance of a promissory note, a contract in which one person (the maker) promises to pay another person (the payee) a specific sum of money at a specific time, with or without interest. A promissory note is used for the following reasons:

1. The holder of a note can usually obtain money by taking the note to the bank and selling it (discounting the note).

2. The note is a written acknowledgment of a debt and is better evidence than an open account. It takes precedence over accounts in the event that the debtor becomes bankrupt.

3. The note facilitates the sale of merchandise on long-term or installment plans.

For a note to be negotiable, it must meet the requirements of the Uniform Negotiable Instrument Law. This legislation states that the instrument:

1. Must be in writing and signed by the maker

2. Must contain an order to pay a definite sum of money

3. Must be payable to order on demand or at a fixed future time

EXAMPLE 1

The promissory note below contains the following information:

(1) Face or principal—the amount of the note

(2) Date of the note—date note was written

(3) Term period—time allowed for payment

(4) Payee—individual to whom payment must be made

(5) Face or principal—[see (1)]

(6) Interest—percentage of annual interest

(7) Maturity date—date the note is to be paid

(8) Maker—person liable for payment of the note

$$\$ 2{,}000^{(1)} \qquad \text{New York, NY} \quad \text{April 4,}^{(2)} 198X$$

90 days[3] _____ after date I promise to pay to

the order of ___Barbara Ledina[4]_____

Two thousand and 00/100[5] —————————————— Dollars

at 14 percent per annum at Second National Bank[6] _____

Value received

Due July 3, 198X[7] ___J. Lerner[8]_____

11.2 METHODS OF COMPUTING INTEREST

For the sake of simplicity, interest is commonly computed on the basis of a 360-day year divided into 12 months of 30 days each. Two widely used methods are (1) the cancellation method and (2) the 6 percent, 60-days method.

EXAMPLE 2   The Cancellation Method

The basic formula is

$$\text{Interest} = \text{principal} \times \text{rate} \times \text{time}$$

Consider a note for $400 at 6 percent for 90 days. The principal is the face amount of the note ($400). The rate of interest is written as a fraction: $6\%/100\% = 6/100$. The time, if less than a year, is expressed as a fraction by dividing the number of days the note runs by the number of days in a year: 90/360. Thus,

$$\text{Interest} = \$400 \times \frac{6}{100} \times \frac{90}{360} = \$6$$

EXAMPLE 3   The 6 Percent, 60-Days Method

This is a variation of the cancellation method, based on the fact that 60 days, or $\frac{1}{6}$ year, at 6 percent is equivalent to 1 percent, so that the interest is obtained simply by shifting the decimal point of the principal two places to the left. The method also applies to other time periods or other interest rates. For instance:

$400 Note	**30 Days**	**6%**
(a) Determine the interest for 60 days.		$4.00
(b) Divide the result by 2 (30 days is one-half of 60 days).	*Ans.*	$2.00

$400 Note	**45 Days**	**6%**
(a) Determine the interest for 30 days.		$2.00
(b) Determine the interest for 15 days.		$1.00
(c) Add the interest for 30 days and 15 days.	*Ans.*	$3.00

$400 Note	**60 Days**	**5%**
(a) Determine the interest at 6 percent.		$4.00
(b) Determine the interest at 1 percent by taking one-sixth of the above amount.		$ .67
(c) Multiply the interest at 1 percent by the rate desired, 0.67×5.	*Ans.*	$3.35

Determining Maturity Date

The maturity days are the number of days after the note has been issued and may be determined by:

1. Subtracting the date of the note from the number of days in the month in which it was written.

2. Adding the succeeding full months (in terms of days), stopping with the last full month before the number of days in the note are exceeded.

3. Subtracting the total days of the result of steps 1 and 2 above from the time of the note. The resulting number is the due date in the upcoming month.

EXAMPLE 4

The maturity date of a 90-day note dated April 4 would be computed as follows:

Time of note:		90
April	30	
Date of note:	4	26
May		31
June		30
Total:		87
Maturity date:	July	3

If the due date of a note is expressed in months, the maturity date can be determined by counting that number of expressed months from the date of writing:

EXAMPLE 5

A 5-month note dated March 17 would be due for payment on August 17. A 1-month note dated March 31 would mature on April 30.

11.3 ACCOUNTING FOR NOTES PAYABLE AND NOTES RECEIVABLE

A promissory note is a note payable from the standpoint of the maker; it is a note receivable from the standpoint of the payee.

Notes Payable

A note payable is a written promise to pay a creditor an amount of money in the future. Notes are used by a business to (1) purchase items, (2) settle an open account, or (3) borrow money from a bank.

1. *Purchase items*

EXAMPLE 6

Office Equipment costing $2,000 was purchased by giving a note.

Office Equipment	2,000	
Notes Payable		2,000

2. *Settle an open account*

EXAMPLE 7

There are times when a corporation must issue a note payable for settlement of an account payable. Assume that the Harmin Agency bought merchandise from Laska Corporation for $500, terms 2/10, n/30. The entry would be recorded in the purchases journal and would appear in the general ledger as:

Purchases		Accounts Payable	
500			500

However, 30 days later, the agency is unable to pay and gives to the Laska Company a 12 percent, 60-day note for $500 to replace its open account. When the Harmin Agency issues the note payable, an entry is made in the general journal that will decrease the accounts payable and increase the notes payable.

Accounts Payable	500	
Notes Payable		500

Accounts Payable		Notes Payable	
500	500		500

Note that the Harmin Agency still owes the debt to the Laska Company. However, it now becomes a different form of an obligation, as it is a written, signed promise in the form of a note payable.

When the maker pays the note in 60 days at 12 percent, the amount of his payment will be the total of the principal and interest and will be recorded in the cash disbursements journal.

3. ***Borrow money from a bank.*** On occasions, businesses find that it may be necessary to borrow money by giving a note payable to the bank. Frequently, banks require the interest that will be owed to them to be paid in advance. This is accomplished by deducting the amount of the interest from the principal immediately when the loan is made and is known as *discounting a note payable*. The proceeds will be that amount of money that the maker of the note receives after the discount has been taken from the principal.

EXAMPLE 8

Assume that the Rhulen Agency seeks to borrow $3,000 for 60 days at 14 percent from the Commercial National Bank. The bank will deduct the interest ($70.00) from the $3,000 principal and will give the difference of $2,930 (proceeds) to the Rhulen Agency.

The entry recorded in the cash receipts journal of the Rhulen Agency would be

Cash	2,930	
Interest Expense	70	
Notes Payable		3,000

Sixty days after the issuance of the instrument, the note becomes due, and the Rhulen Agency sends a check for the face of the note ($3,000). Because the interest was deducted immediately when the loan was made, no further interest will be paid at that time. The entry to record the payment of the note will be made in the cash payments journal:

Notes Payable	3,000	
Cash		3,000

Note: When a business issues many notes payable, a special subsidiary book, known as the notes payable register, may be used. This register will give the complete data for all notes issued and paid by the business. It must be noted, however, that this is merely a source of information and not a journal, as no postings are made from it to the ledger.

Notes Receivable

A note received from a customer is an asset because it becomes a claim against the buyer for the amount due.

EXAMPLE 9

Assume that Ira Sochet owes S. Wyde $400 and gives him a 15 percent, 90-day note in settlement. On Mr. Wyde's books, the entry is:

Notes Receivable	400	
Accounts Receivable		400

Only the principal ($400) is recorded when the note is received, since it represents the amount of the unpaid account. The interest is not due until the date of collection, 90 days later. At that time, the interest earned (income) will be part of the entry recognizing the receipt of the proceeds from the note:

Cash	415	
Notes Receivable		400
Interest Income		15

11.4 DISCOUNTING

The negotiability of a notes receivable enables the holder to receive cash from the bank before the due date. This is known as *discounting*.

Once the interest to be paid has been determined, the procedure for discounting a note is quite simple. We define the maturity value of a note by

1.   Maturity value = face of note + interest income

where the face is the principal and the interest income is computed as in Section 11.2. The holder of a note may discount it at the bank prior to its due date. He or she will receive the maturity value, less the discount, or interest charge imposed by the bank for holding the note for the unexpired portion of its term. In other words,

2.   Discount = maturity value × discount rate × unexpired time

and

3.   Net proceeds = maturity value − discount

EXAMPLE 10

Mr. Wyde holds a $400, ninety-day, 15 percent note written on April 10. (See Example 9.) As the holder of the note, he decides to discount it on May 10. The bank's rate of discount will be assumed to be 15 percent. The interest on the note, as found in Example 9, amounts to $15. Hence,

1.   Maturity value = $400 + $15 = $415

Since, at the time of discounting, Mr. Wyde has held the note for only 30 days, the bank will have to wait 90 − 30 = 60 days until it can receive the maturity value. The discount charge is then

2. $$\text{Discount} = \$415 \times \frac{15}{100} \times \frac{60}{360} = \$10.38$$

and Mr. Wyde receives

3.   Net proceeds = $415 − $10.38 = $404.62

In this example, the bank's discount rate happened to be equal to the interest rate of the note; this need not always be the case.

11.5 DISHONORED NOTES RECEIVABLE

If the issuer of a note does not make payment on the due date, the note is said to be dishonored. It is no longer negotiable, and the amount is charged back to Accounts Receivable. The reasons for transferring the dishonored notes receivable to the accounts receivable account are: (1) the Notes Receivable account is then limited to current notes that have not yet matured; and (2) the Accounts Receivable account will then show the dishonoring of the note, giving a better picture of the transaction.

EXAMPLE 11

A $600, sixty-day, 14 percent note written by C. Babcock was dishonored on the date of maturity. The entry runs:

Accounts Receivable, C. Babcock	614	
Notes Receivable		600
Interest Income		14

Observe that the interest income is recorded and is charged to the customer's account.

When a payee discounts a note receivable, he or she creates a contingent (potential) liability. This occurs because there is a possibility that the maker may dishonor the note. Bear in mind that the payee has already received payment from the bank in advance of the maturity date. The payee is, therefore, contingently liable to the bank to make good on the amount (maturity value) in the event of default by the maker. Any protest fee arising from the default of the note is charged to the maker of the note and is added to the amount to be charged against his or her account.

EXAMPLE 12

An $800, ninety-day, 14 percent note, dated May 1, is discounted on May 31 at 14 percent. Upon presentation on the due date, the note is dishonored. The entry will be:

Accounts Receivable	828*	
Cash		828

*$800   (face)
   28   (interest)
$828   (maturity value)

Had the bank issued a protest fee of $3, the amount charged to the customer would be $831.

11.6 DRAFTS

In addition to promissory notes, drafts are sometimes used when a settlement of a business obligation occurs.

A draft is an order by the seller (drawer) to the buyer (drawee) stating that the buyer must pay a certain amount of money to a third party (payee).

EXAMPLE 13

If the seller is not acquainted with the buyer, he or she may draw a draft on the buyer and attach to it a bill of lading for the purchase. (A bill of lading is prepared by the transportation company.) The draft and bill of lading are sent to the bank, at which time the bank presents the documents to the buyer. When the buyer pays the amount of the draft to the bank, he or she receives the bill of lading and obtains the purchase from the transportation company. The bank forwards the amount collected to the seller, deducting from it a service charge.

Summary

1. If Robert Glatt issues a $800 note to Richard Tobey, Glatt is called the _____ and Tobey the _____.

2. What effect does the acceptance of a note receivable, in settlement of an account, have on the total assets of a firm?

3. The holder of a note can usually obtain money by taking it to a bank and _____ it.

4. A note is written evidence of a _____.

5. When a payee discounts a note receivable, he or she creates a _____ liability.

6. The face of a note plus the interest due is known as _____.

7. Banks will normally take their discount on the _____ of the note.

8. A written promise to pay a creditor an amount of money in the future is known as a
    _____ .

9. The _____ will be that amount of money that the maker of the note receives after the discount
    has been taken from the principal.

10. If many notes are issued by a firm, a _____ may be needed.

Answers: 1. maker, payee; 2. no effect—both are current assets; 3. discounting; 4. debit (obligation); 5. contingent;
6. maturity value; 7. maturity value; 8. note payable; 9. proceeds; 10. notes payable register

Solved Problems

11.1   Below is an example of a note receivable.

> July 1, 198X
>
> I, Ruth Brent, promise to pay Concord, Inc., $900, 90 days from
> date, at 14 percent interest.
>
> Ruth Brent

(*a*) Who is the maker of the note? (*b*) Who is the payee of the note? (*c*) What is the maturity date of
the note? (*d*) What is the maturity value of the note?

SOLUTION

(*a*) Ruth Brent; (*b*) Concord, Inc.; (*c*) Sept. 29; (*d*) $931.50

11.2   A note written on August 1 and due on November 15 was discounted on October 15. (*a*) How many
days was the note written for? (*b*) How many days did the bank charge for in discounting the note?

SOLUTION

(*a*)	Aug. 2–31	30 days		(*b*)	Oct. 16–31	16 days
	Sept. 1–30	30 days			Nov. 1–15	15 days
	Oct. 1–31	31 days				31 days *Ans.*
	Nov. 1–15	15 days				
		106 days *Ans.*				

11.3   Determine the interest on the following notes: (*a*) $750 principal, 14 percent interest, 96 days; (*b*)
$800 principal, 12 percent interest, 90 days.

SOLUTION

(*a*)	$750	14%	60 days	$17.50	(*b*)	$800	12%	60 days	$16
		14%	30 days	8.75			12%	30 days	8
		14%	6 days	1.75				90 days	$24 *Ans.*
			96 days	$28.00 *Ans.*					

11.4 A $4,000, ninety-day, 14 percent note receivable in settlement of an account, dated June 1, is discounted at 14 percent on July 1. Compute the proceeds of the note.

SOLUTION

$4,000.00	Principal
140.00	Interest income (90 days, 14%)
$4,140.00	Maturity value
96.60	Discount (60 days, 14% of maturity value)
$4,043.40	Proceeds

11.5 What are the entries needed to record the information in Problem 11.4 (*a*) on June 1? (*b*) on July 1?

(*a*)

(*b*)

SOLUTION

(*a*)	Notes Receivable	4,000.00	
	Accounts Receivable		4,000.00
(*b*)	Cash	4,043.40	
	Interest Income		43.40
	Notes Receivable		4,000.00

11.6 A $6,000, fourteen percent, 120-day note receivable, dated September 1, is discounted at 14 percent on October 1. What is the entry needed on October 1?

SOLUTION

$6,000.00	Principal
280.00	Interest income (120 days at 14%)
$6,280.00	Maturity value
219.80	Discount (90 days, 14% of maturity value)
$6060.20	Proceeds

Cash	6,060.20	
Notes Receivable		6,000.00
Interest Income		60.20

11.7   Based on the information in Problem 11.6, what entry would be needed if the note were discounted immediately?

SOLUTION

$6,000.00	Principal
280.00	Interest income (120 days at 14%)
$6,280.00	Maturity value
293.07	Discount (120 days, 14% of maturity value)
$5,986.93	Proceeds

Cash	5,986.93	
Interest Expense	13.07	
Notes Receivable		6,000.00

Note: The proceeds are less than the principal because the note was discounted immediately at the same rate.

11.8   Record the following transactions in the books of John Agin Company:

(*a*)   May 1   Received a $6,000, ninety-day, 15 percent note in settlement of the Stolloff account.

(*b*)   May 31   Discounted the note at 15 percent at the bank.

(*c*)   July 30   Stolloff paid the note in full.

(*a*)		—	
(*b*)			
(*c*)			

SOLUTION

(*a*)	Notes Receivable	6,000.00	
	Accounts Receivable, Stolloff Company		6,000.00
(*b*)	Cash	6,069.37*	
	Interest Income		69.37
	Notes Receivable		6,000.00

*$6,000.00	Principal
225.00	Interest income
$6,225.00	Maturity value
155.63	Discount
$6,069.37	Proceeds

(*c*)   No entry

11.9 If, in Problem 11.8, Stolloff dishonored his obligation on July 30 and a $5 protest fee was imposed by the bank, what entry would be required to record this information?

SOLUTION

Accounts Receivable, Stolloff Company	6,230	
Cash		6,230

*6,225 (maturity value) + $5 (protest fee) = $6,230.

11.10 Record the following transactions in the books of Carl Bresky:

(a) Sept. 5 Received an $8,000, ninety-day, 12 percent note in settlement of the M. Ribble account and immediately discounted it at 12 percent at the bank.

(b) Dec. 4 M. Ribble dishonored the note, and a protest fee of $2 was imposed.

(c) Dec. 31 M. Ribble paid her obligation, including the protest fee.

(a)

(b)

(c)

SOLUTION

(a)	Notes Receivable	8,000.00	
	Accounts Receivable—M. Ribble		8,000.00
	Cash	7,992.80*	
	Interest Expense	7.20	
	Notes Receivable		8,000.00

$8,000.00	Principal
240.00	Interest income
$8,240.00	Maturity value
247.20	Discount
$7,992.80	Proceeds

(b)	Accounts Receivable—M. Ribble	8,242*	
	Cash		8,242
	*(Maturity value + protest fee)		
(c)	Cash	8,242	
	Accounts Receivable—M. Ribble		8,242

11.11 The Erin Corporation borrowed $5,000 for 90 days at 16 percent from the Sullivan National Bank. What entries are needed to (*a*) record the loan and (*b*) record the repayment?

(*a*)

(*b*)

SOLUTION

(*a*)

Cash	4,800	
Interest Expense	200*	
Notes Payable		5,000

* Interest for 90 days at 16 percent deducted in advance.

(*b*)

Notes Payable	5,000	
Cash		5,000

11.12 Based on the information in Problem 11.11, what entry would be necessary if, after 90 days, M. Erin was unable to repay the loan and was granted another 90-day renewal?

SOLUTION

Interest Expense	200*	
Cash		200

* Only the interest has to be paid, since the note was renewed.

11.13 Record the following transactions in the books of B. K. Logging:

(*a*) June 1   Received a $10,000, ninety-day, 14% note in settlement of the McGraw account (dated June 1).

(*b*) July 1   Discounted the note at 16% at local bank.

(*c*) Aug. 30   Received notice that McGraw dishonored the note; paid the bank on the note plus $10 protest fee.

(*d*)   30   Contacted McGraw and received full payment on the same day.

Journal Entries

June 1			
July 1			

Journal Entries, cont.

Aug. 30			
30			

SOLUTION

Journal Entries

June 1	Notes Receivable	10,000	
	Accounts Receivable		10,000
July 1	Cash	10,074	
	Interest Income		74
	Notes Receivable		10,000
Aug. 30	Accounts Receivable	10,360	
	Cash		10,360
30	Cash	10,360	
	Accounts Receivable		10,360

July 1: $\$10,000 \times 14\% = \$1,400 \times \dfrac{90 \text{ days}}{360 \text{ days}} = \$350 \text{ interest}$

$10,000   Principal
   350   Interest
$10,350   Maturity value
   276   Discount
$10,074   Proceeds

August 30: $10,350 + $10 (protest fee)

11.14 Hill Top Diner borrowed $8,000 for 120 days at 15.75 percent from the local bank. The note was dated January 1. Show the entries recording the loan and the payback of the note.

Journal Entries

Jan. 1			
May 1			

SOLUTION

Journal Entries

Jan. 1	Cash	7,580	
	Interest Expense	420	
	Notes Payable		8,000
May 1	Notes Payable	8,000	
	Cash		8,000

11.15 Received a $20,000, ninety-day, 14.50 percent note from Sun Town Company on account (note was dated November 1). Sun Town paid the note on the due date. Show the entries for this transaction.

Journal Entries

Nov. 1			
Jan. 30			

SOLUTION

Journal Entries

Nov. 1	Notes Receivable	20,000	
	Accounts Receivable		20,000
Jan. 30	Cash	20,725	
	Interest Income		725
	Notes Receivable		20,000

11.16 From the preceding problem, what would the adjusting entry be on December 31 if that was the last day of the accounting period?

Journal Entry

Dec. 31			

SOLUTION

Journal Entry

Dec. 31	Interest Receivable	483.33	
	Interest Income		483.33*

*$20,000 × 14.5% × $\frac{1}{6}$ (November and December)

Chapter 12

Cash and Its Control

12.1 INTRODUCTION

In most firms, transactions involving the receipt and disbursement of cash far outnumber any other kinds of transactions. Cash is, moreover, the most liquid asset and most subject to theft and fraud. It is therefore essential to have a system of accounting procedures and records that will maintain adequate control over cash.

Cash is a medium of exchange and includes such items as currency, coin, demand deposits, savings deposits, petty cash funds, bank drafts, cashier's checks, personal checks, and money orders.

12.2 CONTROLLING CASH RECEIPTS

In a very small business, the owner-manager can maintain control through personal contact and supervision. This kind of direct intervention must, in a larger firm, be replaced by a system of internal control, exercised through accounting reports and records.

The specific controls applied to cash receipts may be summarized as:

1. All receipts should be banked promptly.
2. Receipts from cash sales should be supported by sales tickets, cash register tapes, and so on.
3. Accountability should be established each time cash is transferred.
4. Persons receiving cash should not make disbursements of cash, record cash transactions, or reconcile bank accounts.

12.3 CONTROLLING CASH DISBURSEMENTS

Payments must be made only by properly authorized persons, equivalent value must be received, and documents must adequately support the payment. Following are specific internal controls relating to cash disbursements:

1. All disbursements, except petty cash payments, should be made by prenumbered check.
2. Vouchers and supporting documents should be submitted for review when checks are signed.
3. Persons who sign checks should not have access to cash receipts, should not have custody of funds or record cash entries, and should not reconcile bank accounts.

12.4 CONTROLLING CASH BALANCES

The basic principle of separation of duties is evident in the specific controls for cash balances:

1. Bank reconciliations should be prepared by persons who do not receive cash or sign checks.
2. Bank statements and paid checks should be received unopened by the person reconciling the account.
3. All cash funds on hand should be closely watched and surprise counts made at intervals.

If the rules of Section 12.2 are followed, then it is clear that the monthly bank statement can be made a powerful control over cash balances—hence, the importance of reconciling bank balances.

12.5   BANK STATEMENTS

Checks

A business opens a checking account to gain the privilege of placing its deposits in a safe place and the ability also to write checks. When an account is opened, each person who is authorized to write checks on that account must sign a signature card. The bank keeps the signature card on file and compares it when checks are submitted. The check becomes a written notice by the depositor directing the bank to deduct a specific sum of money from the checking account and to pay that amount to the person or company written on the check. A check involves three parties:

1. Drawer—the firm that writes the check
2. Drawee—the bank on which the check is drawn
3. Payee—the person or company to whom the check is to be paid

Checks offer several advantages. The checkbook stubs provide a record of the cash paid out, while the cancelled checks provide proof that money has been paid to the person legally entitled to it. Also, the use of checks is the most convenient form of paying bills, because checks can be sent safely through the mail. If a check is lost or stolen, the depositors can request the bank not to pay (a stop order).

Endorsements

When a check is given to the bank for deposit, the depositor signs the check on the back to show that he or she accepts responsibility for the amount of that check. The depositor's signature is known as an *endorsement*. This endorsement transfers the ownership of the check and guarantees to the individual that the depositor will guarantee its payment. Different kinds of endorsements serve different needs:

1. *Blank endorsement.* A blank endorsement consists only of the name of the endorser. Its disadvantage lies in the fact that a lost or stolen check with a blank endorsement may be cashed by the finder or thief. Therefore, this type of endorsement should not be used unless the depositor is at the bank ready to make a deposit (Fig. 12-1).
2. *Endorsement in full.* Endorsement in full states that the check can be cashed or transferred only on the order of the person named in the endorsement (Fig. 12-2).
3. *Restrictive endorsement.* A restrictive endorsement limits the receiver of the check as to the use he or she can make of the funds collected. Usually this type of endorsement is done when checks are prepared for deposit (Fig. 12-3).

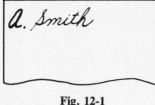   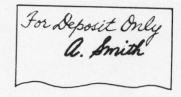

Fig. 12-1   Fig. 12-2   Fig. 12-3

Reconciliation

Banks customarily mail monthly statements to those firms that have checking accounts with them. These statements show the cash balance from the beginning of the month, all the deposits and payments recorded during the month, daily balances, and the ending balance. Cancelled checks, records of deposit, and other documents that support the data shown on the bank statement are forwarded to the depositor along with the statement. Examples of such documents might be a deduction (debit memorandum) for a bank service charge or an addition (credit memorandum) for the proceeds of a note collected by the bank for the depositor.

Usually the balance of the bank statement and the balance of the depositor's account will not agree. To prove the accuracy of both records, the reconciling differences have to be found and any necessary entries made. The reconciling items will fall into two broad groups: (1) those on the depositor's books but not recorded by the bank, and (2) those on the bank statement but not on the books.

Items on Books but Not on Bank Statement

Outstanding checks. Outstanding checks are those issued by the depositor but not yet presented to the bank for payment. The total of these checks is to be deducted from the bank balance.

Deposits in transit. Deposits in transit comprise cash receipts recorded by the company but too late to be deposited. The total of such deposits is to be added to the bank balance.

Bookkeeping errors. Bookkeeping errors arise in recording amounts of checks; for example, a transposition of figures. The item should be added to the bank balance if it was previously overstated on the books. If the item was previously understated on the books, the amount should be deducted.

Items on Bank Statement but Not on Books

Service charges. The bank generally deducts amounts for bank services. The exact amount is usually not known by the depositor until the statement is received. The amount should be deducted from the book balance.

NSF (nonsufficient funds) checks. NSF checks have been deposited but cannot be collected because of insufficient funds in the account of the drawer of the check. The bank then issues a debit memorandum charging the depositor's account. The amount should be deducted from the book balance.

Collections. The bank collects notes and other items for a small fee. The bank then adds the proceeds to the account and issues a credit memorandum to the depositor. Often there are unrecorded amounts at the end of the month. The amounts should be added to the book balance.

Bank errors. Bank errors should not be entered on the books. They should be brought to the attention of the bank and corrected by the bank. Journal entries should be made for any adjustments to the book accounts. The statement used in accounting for the differences between the bank balance and the depositor's balance is known as a *bank reconciliation*.

EXAMPLE 1

The following information was available when the L. Etkind Company began to reconcile its bank balance on June 30, 198X: balance per depositor's books, $1,640; balance per bank statement, $2,420; deposit in transit, $150; checks outstanding—no. 650 for $300 and no. 645 for $240; collection of $400 note plus interest of $8, $408; collection fee for note, $10; bank service charge, $8.

L. Etkind Company
Bank Reconciliation
June 30, 198X

Balance per bank		$2,420	Balance per books		$1,640
Add: Deposit in transit		150	Add: Proceeds of note		408
		$2,570			$2,048
Less:			Less:		
Outstanding checks			Collection fee	$10	
No. 650	$300		Service charge	8	
No. 645	240	540			18
Adjusted balance		$2,030	Adjusted balance		$2,030

Only reconciling items in the depositor's section (right side, above) are to be recorded on the books. The reconciling items in the bank section (left side, above) have already been recorded on the books and merely have not yet reached the bank. They will normally be included in the next bank statement.

To complete the reconcilement, the following two journal entries will be needed:

Entry 1   Cash   408
                                         Notes Receivable   400
                                         Interest Income   8

Entry 2   Service Charge Expense   18
                                         Cash   18

12.6   PETTY CASH

To eliminate the necessity of writing checks in very small amounts, it is customary to maintain a petty cash fund from which small disbursements are made. Examples are postage, delivery expense, telegrams, and so on.

Each disbursement from the petty cash fund should be accounted for by a receipt (a bill presented and signed by the payee at the time of payment). If no bill is presented, the one responsible for the fund should prepare a receipt similar to the one illustrated below and have the payee sign it. This is known as a *petty cash voucher*.

The face of the voucher should contain the following data:

(1) Receipt number

(2) Date of disbursement

(3) Name of payee

(4) Amount of the expenditure

(5) Purpose for which the expenditure was made

(6) Account affected by the expenditure

(7) Signature of payee

Petty Cash Voucher

```
(1)  No. _____     (2)  Date _____

(3)  Paid to _____     (4)  Amount $_____

(5)  Reason _____

(6)  Account to be charged _____

(7)  Received by _____
```

Under the *imprest* system, a fund is established for a fixed petty cash amount, and this fund is periodically reimbursed by a single check for amounts expended. The steps in setting up and maintaining the petty cash fund are as follows:

1. An estimate is made of the total of the small amounts likely to be disbursed over a short period, usually a month. A check is drawn for the estimated total and put into the fund. The only time an entry is made in the petty cash account is for the initial establishment of the fund, unless at some later time it is determined that this fund must be increased or decreased.

EXAMPLE 2

Petty Cash   100
     Cash   100

2. The individual in charge of petty cash usually keeps the money in a locked box along with petty cash vouchers. The petty cash voucher, when signed by the recipient, acts as a receipt and provides information concerning the transaction. As each payment is made, the voucher is entered in the petty cash record under the heading, "Payments."

3. The amount paid is then distributed to the account affected.

4. The columns are to be totaled in order to determine the amount chargeable to each account.

EXAMPLE 3

Petty Cash Record

Date	Explanation	Voucher	Receipts	Payments	Postage	Del.	Sundry
Jan. 1	Established		$100.00				
2	Postage on Sales	1		$ 10.00	$10.00		
4	Telegram	2		6.00	6.00		
8	Taxi Fare	3		10.00		$10.00	
10	Coffee for Overtime	4		4.00			$ 4.00
15	Stamps	5		18.00	18.00		
26	Cleaning Windows	6		12.00			12.00
			$100.00	$ 60.00	$34.00	$10.00	$16.00
	Balance			40.00			
			$100.00	$100.00			
Feb. 1	Balance		$ 40.00				
	Replenished Fund		60.00				

5. A check is then drawn in an amount equalling the total amount disbursed.

6. When the check is cashed, the money is replaced in the fund to restore it to the original amount.

7. Each amount listed in the distribution section of the petty cash fund is entered as a debit to the individual expense. The total amount of the check is credited to Cash.

The petty cash fund established in Example 2 would yield the following entry for the first month:

Postage Expense	34.00	
Delivery Expense	10.00	
Sundry Expense	16.00	
Cash		60.00

8. Proof of petty cash is obtained by counting the currency and adding the amount of all the vouchers in the cash box. The total should agree with the amount in the ledger for the petty cash fund. If it does not, the entry in the cash disbursements journal that records the reimbursement of the petty cash fund will have to include an account known as *Cash Short and Over*. A cash shortage is debited, a cash overage is credited to this account. Cash Short and Over is closed out at the end of the year into the expense and income account and is treated as a general expense (if a debit balance) or miscellaneous income (if a credit balance).

Summary

1. The most liquid asset and also the one most subject to theft and fraud is _____.

2. All disbursements, except petty cash payments, should be made by _____.

3. A written notice by a depositor instructing his bank to deduct a specific sum from his account and to pay it to the person assigned is known as a _____ .

4. A check involves three parties: the _____ , who writes the check; the _____ , the bank on which it is drawn; and the _____ , the person to whom it is to be paid.

5. The signature on the back of a check showing that the individual accepts responsibility for that amount is known as an _____ .

6. The _____ endorsement poses the greatest threat in the event of a lost or stolen check.

7. A bank service charge is evidenced by a _____ .

8. A check that has been deposited but cannot be collected because of insufficient funds is labeled _____ and is deducted from the _____ balance.

9. Under the _____ , a fund is established for a fixed petty cash amount that is reimbursed by a single check for amounts expended.

10. If a proof of petty cash is impossible, the account _____ will have to be used.

Answers: 1. cash; 2. prenumbered check; 3. check; 4. drawer, drawee, payee; 5. endorsement; 6. blank; 7. debit memorandum; 8. NSF, book; 9. imprest system; 10. Cash Short and Over

Solved Problems

12.1   Below is an example of a check.

(a) Who is the drawer?

(b) Who is the drawee?

(c) Who is the payee?

SOLUTION

(a) B. Smith

(b) Whiteside County Bank

(c) Jason Sloane

12.2 (*a*) Assume that J. Lerner, banking at 1st City Bank, wishes a full endorsement for A. Levy. Present below the needed endorsement.

(*b*) A blank endorsement is needed instead.

(*c*) A restrictive endorsement for a deposit is needed instead.

Full Endorsement	Blank Endorsement	Restrictive Endorsement

SOLUTION

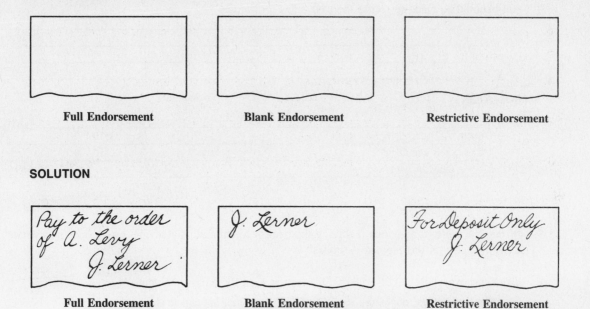

Full Endorsement	Blank Endorsement	Restrictive Endorsement

12.3 Indicate for items 1–8 below, in order to produce equal adjusted balances for A & J Company, whether they should be

(*a*) Added to the bank statement balance

(*b*) Deducted from the bank statement balance

(*c*) Added to the depositor's balance

(*d*) Deducted from the depositor's balance

(*e*) Exempted from the bank reconciliation statement

1. Statement includes a credit memorandum, representing the collection of the proceeds of a note left at the bank.

2. A credit memorandum representing the proceeds of a loan, made to A & J Company by the bank.

3. Deposits in transit.

4. Seven outstanding checks were not recorded on the statement.

5. A customer's check that A & J Company had deposited was returned with "nonsufficient funds" stamped across the face.

6. The bank erroneously charged someone else's check against A & J's account.

7. A & J Company was credited on the bank statement with the receipt from another depositor.

8. A $96 check was erroneously recorded in A & J's check stubs as $69.

SOLUTION

1. (*c*); 2. (*c*); 3. (*a*); 4. (*b*); 5. (*d*); 6. (*a*); 7. (*b*); 8. (*d*)

12.4 At the close of the day, the total cash sales as determined by the sales registers were $1,580. However, the total cash receipts amounted to only $1,570. The error cannot be located at the present time. What entry should be made to record the cash sales for the day?

SOLUTION

Cash	1,570	
Cash Short and Over	10	
Sales Income		1,580

12.5 Of the following transactions involving the bank reconciliation statement, which ones necessitate an adjusting entry on the depositor's books?

(*a*) Outstanding checks of $3,000 did not appear on the bank statement.

(*b*) The last 2 days' deposited receipts, $2,850, did not appear on the bank statement.

(*c*) The depositor's check for $120 for supplies was written in her records as $210.

(*d*) Bank service charge, $4.

(*e*) A note left at the bank for collection, $822, was paid and credited to the depositor's account.

SOLUTION

(*c*)	Cash	90	
	Supplies		90
(*d*)	Service Charge Expense	4	
	Cash		4
(*e*)	Cash	822	
	Notes Receivable		822

12.6   Using the following data, reconcile the bank account of the Kemper Motor Company.

1.   Bank balance, $7,780.

2.   Depositor's balance, $6,500.

3.   Note collected by bank, $1,000, plus interest of $30; a collection charge of $10 was made by the bank.

4.   Outstanding checks, $410.

5.   Deposit in transit, $150.

SOLUTION

Balance per bank statement	$7,780	Balance per Kemper's books	$6,500
Add: Deposit in transit	150	Add: Note collected by bank	
	$7,930	Note	$1,000	
Less:		Interest	30	1,030
Outstanding checks	410		$7,530
		Less: Collection charge	10
Adjusted balance	$7,520	Adjusted balance	$7,520

12.7   Prepare the adjusting entries needed for Problem 12.6

SOLUTION

Cash	1,030	
Notes Receivable		1,000
Interest Income		30
Service Charge Expense	10	
Cash		10

12.8   Correct the following incorrect bank reconciliation proof.

Kaney Company
Bank Reconciliation
December 31, 198X

Balance per depositor's books		$7,250
Add:		
Note collected by bank including interest	515	
Deposit in transit	1,200	
Bank error charging Kane's check to Kaney account	860	
Total		$9,825
Deduct:		
Check from customer of J. Brown deposited and		
returned by bank as NSF	$ 150	
Service charge	5	
Check for $250 written in Kaney's ledger for		
supplies and checkbook stubs as $150	100	
Outstanding checks	1,100	1,355
		$8,470
Less: Unexplained difference		1,920
Balance per bank statement		$6,550

SOLUTION

Kaney Company
Bank Reconciliation
December 31, 198X

Balance per bank statement	$6,550	Balance per depositor's books			$7,250
Add:		Add:			
Deposit in transit	1,200	Note collected by bank			515
Error	860				$7,765
	$8,610				
		Less:			
Less:		NSF	$150		
Outstanding checks	1,100	Bank service charge	5		
Adjusted balance	$7,510	Error	100		255
		Adjusted balance			$7,510

12.9 Prepare the adjusting entries needed for Problem 12.8.

SOLUTION

Cash	515	
Notes Receivable		515
Service Charge Expense	5	
Accounts Receivable—J. Brown	150	
Supplies	100	
Cash		255

12.10 Halls Gift Shop prepares monthly bank reconciliations. From the following data, prepare the July bank reconciliation.

1. Balance per bank statement, $21,700
2. Balance per checkbook, $15,178
3. Note collected by bank, $525 plus $41 interest
4. Outstanding checks:

No. 947	$1,117
No. 953	2,728
No. 957	573
No. 963	1,789
No. 971	770

5. Bank service charge, $19
6. Deposit in transit, $1002

Halls Gift Shop
Bank Reconciliation
July 31, 198X

SOLUTION

Halls Gift Shop
Bank Reconciliation
July 31, 198X

Balance per bank statement	$21,700
Add: Deposit in transit	1,002
	$22,702
Less: Outstanding checks	6,977
Correct bank balance	$15,725

Halls Gift Shop
Bank Reconciliation, cont.
July 31, 198X

Balance per checkbook	$15,178
Note plus interest collected by bank	566
	$15,744
Less: Bank service charge	19
Correct book balance	$15,725

12.11 From the following data, prepare a bank reconciliation for the Big Red Company for the month of May:

1. Balance per bank statement, $7,915
2. Balance per checkbook, $5,140
3. Deposit in transit, $475
4. Outstanding checks, $2,170
5. Note collected by bank, $1,000 plus $110 interest
6. Bank service charge, $21
7. A check written in the amount of $98 for supplies was entered in the checkbook as $89.

Big Red Company
Bank Reconciliation
May 31, 198X

BANK	BOOK

SOLUTION

Big Red Company
Bank Reconciliation
May 31, 198X

BANK		BOOK	
Balance per bank statement	$7,915	Balance per checkbook	$5,140
Plus: Deposit in transit	475	Plus: Note and interest	1,110
	8,390		$6,250
Less: Outstanding checks	2,170	Less: Checkbook error	9
			$6,241
		Less: Bank service charge	$ 21
Correct bank balance	$6,220		$6,220

12.12 Transactions for the Fred Saltzman Co. for the month of January, pertaining to the establishment of a petty cash fund, were as follows:

Jan. 1   Established an imprest petty cash fund of $50.
     31   Box contained $6 cash and paid vouchers for transportation, $14; freight, $16; charity, $4; office supplies, $6; miscellaneous expense, $4.

What are the journal entries necessary to record the petty cash information?

SOLUTION

Petty Cash	50	
Cash		50
Transportation Expense	14	
Freight Expense	16	
Charity Expense	4	
Office Supplies Expense	6	
Miscellaneous Expense	4	
Cash		44

12.13 If, in Problem 12.12, the cash on hand was $9, record the January 31 reimbursement.

SOLUTION

Transportation Expense	14	
Freight Expense	16	
Charity Expense	4	
Office Supplies Expense	6	
Miscellaneous Expense	4	
Cash		41
Cash Short and Over		3

12.14 If, in Problem 12.12, the cash on hand was only $2, record the January 31 reimbursement. What will happen to the Short and Over account?

SOLUTION

Transportation Expense	14	
Freight Expense	16	
Charity Expense	4	
Office Supplies Expense	6	
Miscellaneous Expense	4	
Cash Short and Over	4	
Cash		48

Examination III

1. For each individual situation below, determine the missing figures.

	Beginning Inventory	Purchases During Period	Return Purchases	Ending Inventory	Cost of Goods Sold
(a)	$22,000	$16,000	$1,000	$ 7,000	?
(b)	41,000	23,000	3,000	?	$37,000
(c)	?	22,000	1,000	26,000	40,000

2. (a) Construct the cost of goods sold section of the income statement based on the following information: Sales Income, $84,000; Inventory (Beginning), $28,000; Inventory (Ending), $22,000; Purchases, $51,000; Purchases Returns, $2,000.

   (b) What is the gross profit of the firm?

3. Journalize the following adjusting data as of December 31:

   (a) Merchandise inventory, January 1, $46,000; December 31, $48,000.

   (b) Office supplies physically counted on December 31 were $1,250. The original balance of supplies on hand were $2,100.

   (c) Prepaid insurance before adjustment, $3,850. It was found that $2,700 had expired during the year.

   (d) Salaries for a 5-day week ending on Friday were $3,500. The last payday was on the previous Friday, December 28.

4. Sandra Sarazzin worked 49 hours during the second week in March of the current year. Her pay rate is $6.40 per hour. Withheld from her wages were FICA, 7.15 percent; federal income tax, $51; hospitalization, $8; union dues, $6. Determine the necessary payroll entry.

5. The total payroll for the Randolf Company for the week ending April 30 was $17,000. Of the total amount, $12,000 was subject to FICA tax: $2,800 held for federal income tax; $900 for hospitalization; and the balance paid in cash.

   (a) Present the journal entry necessary to record the payroll for this week, assuming that the FICA tax is 7.15 percent.

   (b) Present the employer's payroll tax entry, assuming a state tax of 4 percent, a federal rate of 0.8 percent, and that of the total payroll, $5,000, was subject to federal and state unemployment.

6. Journalize the following separate entries:

   (a) W. Schoop discounted his own $4,000 note from City Bank for 120 days at 12 percent.

   (b) W. Schoop discounted at 12 percent E. Orlian, 90-day, 12 percent, $3,000 note immediately upon receipt.

7. Apr. 5 A. Offengender bought $2,100 worth of goods from T. Vadka Company on account.
   May 1 Vadka received a 90-day, 12 percent note in settlement of A. Offengender's account.
      31 Vadka discounted the note at 12 percent.
   July 30 The bank informed Vadka that the discounted note has been dishonored and will charge Vadka the maturity value plus a protest fee of $5.00.
   Aug. 1 Received the full amount owed from Offengender.

   Prepare all necessary entries on the books of Vadka to reflect the above transactions.

8. Prepare a bank reconciliation statement based on the information below:

   (*a*) Bank balance, $3,400.

   (*b*) Checkbook balance, $3,120.

   (*c*) Outstanding checks, $1,140.

   (*d*) Deposits in transit, $1,800.

   (*e*) A $1,000 note was collected by the bank; interest added to it was $15. Bank service charge for collection, $5.

   (*f*) A $16 check we had deposited was returned for nonsufficient funds.

   (*g*) Check 12 for $82 was inadvertently recorded in our check stubs as $28.

Answers to Examination III

1. (*a*) $30,000

   (*b*) $24,000

   (*c*) $45,000

2. (*a*)

Cost of Goods Sold:		
Inventory (Beginning)		$28,000
Purchases	$51,000	
Purchase Returns	2,000	49,000
Goods Available for Sale		$77,000
Inventory (Ending)		22,000
Cost of Goods Sold		$55,000

   (*b*)

Sales	$84,000
Cost of Goods Sold	− 55,000
Gross Profit	$29,000

3. (*a*)

Expense and Income Summary	46,000	
Merchandise Inventory		46,000

Merchandise Inventory	48,000	
Expense and Income Summary		48,000

   (*b*)

Office Supplies Expense	850	
Office Supplies		850

   (*c*)

Insurance Expense	2,700	
Prepaid Insurance		2,700

   (*d*)

Salaries Expense	700	
Salaries Payable		700

(Monday, December 31, 3500 ÷ 5)

4.   Salaries Expense   342.40*
                        FICA Taxes Payable   24.48
                        Federal Income Tax Payable   51.00
                        Hospitalization Payable   8.00
                        Union Dues Payable   6.00
                        Salaries Payable   252.92

                    * 40 hours × $6.40 = $256.00 (regular)
                        9 hours × $9.60 =   86.40 (overtime)
                                          $342.40 total compensation

5. (a)   Salaries Expense   17,000
                        FICA Taxes Payable   858
                        Federal Income Taxes Payable   2,800
                        Hospitalization Payable   900
                        Cash   12,442

       (b)   Payroll Tax Expense   1,098
                        FICA Taxes Payable   858
                        Federal Unemployment Insurance Payable   40
                        State Unemployment Insurance Payable   200

6. (a)   Cash   3,840
                        Interest Expense   160
                            Notes Payable   4,000

       (b)   Cash   2,997.30*
                        Interest Expense   2.70
                            Notes Receivable   3,000.00

                    * $3,000.00 Principal
                          90.00 Interest income
                      $3,090.00 Maturity value
                          92.70 Discount
                      $2,997.30 Proceeds

7.   Apr. 15 Accounts Receivable   2,100.00
                         Sales Income   2,100.00

             May 1   Notes Receivable   2,100.00
                         Accounts Receivable   2,100.00

                 31   Cash   2,119.74*
                         Notes Receivable   2,100.00
                         Interest Income   19.74

             * $2,100.00 Principal
                  63.00 Interest income (90 days, 12%)
               $2,163.00 Maturity value
                  43.26 Discount (60 days balance, 12%)
               $2,119.74 Proceeds

July 30	Accounts Receivable	2,168.00†	
	Cash		2,168.00
Aug. 1	Cash	2,168.00	
	Accounts Receivable		2,168.00

† Maturity value	$2,163.00
Protest fee	5.00
	$2,168.00

8.

Bank Reconciliation Statement

Bank Balance	$3,400	Check balance		$3,120
Add: Deposit in transit	1,800	Add:		
	$5,200	Notes receivable	$1,000	
		Interest income	15	1,015
				$4,135
Less: Outstanding checks	1,140	Less:		
		Service charge	$ 5	
		NSF	16	
		Error	54	75
Bank balance corrected	$4,060	Checkbook balance corrected		$4,060

Chapter 13

Partnerships: Formation and Division of Profits and Losses

13.1 CHARACTERISTICS OF THE PARTNERSHIP

According to the Uniform Partnership Act, a partnership is "an association of two or more persons to carry on as co-owners of a business for profit." Generally speaking, partnership accounting is like that for the sole proprietorship, except in regard to owners' equity. The partnership uses a capital account and a drawing account for each partner.

The partnership has the following characteristics:

Articles of copartnership. Good business practice calls for a written agreement among the partners that contains provisions on the formation of the partnership, capital contributions of each partner, profit and loss distribution, admission and withdrawal of partners, withdrawal of funds, and dissolution of the business.

Unlimited liability. All partners have unlimited liability and are individually responsible to creditors for debts incurred by the partnership. The debts of the business can be satisfied not only by the assets of the partnership but also by the personal assets of the partners.

Co-ownership of property. All property invested in the business by the partners, as well as that purchased with the partnership's funds, becomes the property of all partners jointly. Therefore, each partner has an interest in the partnership in proportion to his or her capital balance, rather than a claim against specific assets.

Participation in profits and losses. Profits and losses are distributed among the partners according to the partnership agreement. If no agreement exists, profit and losses must be shared equally.

Limited life. A partnership may be dissolved by bankruptcy, death of a partner, mutual agreement, or court order.

13.2 FORMATION OF THE PARTNERSHIP

When a partnership is formed, each partner's capital account is credited for his or her initial investment, and the appropriate asset account is debited. If noncash assets are invested, these should be recorded at an agreed amount.

If liabilities are to be assumed by the partnership, they are credited to the respective liability accounts.

EXAMPLE 1

Walter Gurney has agreed to go into partnership with Ted Drew.

Drew's Accounts	Drew's Ledger Balances	Agreed Valuation
Cash	$18,000	$18,000
Supplies	3,000	2,000

Drew's Accounts	Drew's Ledger Balances	Agreed Valuation
Accounts Receivable	$ 6,000	$ 6,000
Equipment	18,000	
Accumulated Depreciation—Equipment	4,000	12,000
Notes Payable	8,000	8,000

The entry to record the initial investment of Drew in the firm of Drew and Gurney would be:

Cash	18,000	
Supplies	2,000	
Accounts Receivable	6,000	
Equipment	12,000	
Notes Payable		8,000
Drew, Capital		30,000

13.3 DIVISION OF NET INCOME AND LOSS

Partnership profits and losses may be divided in any manner the partners may agree upon. In general, a partner may be expected to share in proportion to the amount of capital and/or services he or she contributes. In the absence of a clear agreement, the law provides that all partners share equally, regardless of the differences in time devoted or capital contributed.

Below are outlined the principal methods for profit and loss distribution. For simplicity, the examples are limited to two partners.

Fixed or Capital Basis

Profits and losses are generally divided equally, in a fixed ratio, or in a ratio based on the amounts of capital contributed by the partners.

EXAMPLE 2

Drew and Gurney have capital balances of $30,000 and $20,000, respectively. The net income for the first year of operations was $15,000. If the partners have decided to share on an equal basis, the journal entry for the allocation of the net income will be:

Expense and Income Summary	15,000	
Drew, Capital		7,500
Gurney, Capital		7,500

If, however, capital investment is to be the determining factor, the entry will run as follows:

Expense and Income Summary	15,000	
Drew, Capital		9,000*
Gurney, Capital		6,000†

$$* \quad \frac{30,000}{30,000 + 20,000}(15,000)$$

$$† \quad \frac{20,000}{30,000 + 20,000}(15,000)$$

Interest Basis

Under this method, each partner is paid interest on his or her capital investment, and the remaining net income is divided in a fixed ratio or on some other basis. Thus, a partner's share depends partially on his or her capital investment.

EXAMPLE 3

Instead of the equal split in Example 2, each partner is to receive 6 percent interest on his or her capital balance, the remaining net income to be shared equally. The entry would be:

Expense and Income Summary	15,000	
Drew, Capital		7,800
Gurney, Capital		7,200

which is computed as follows:

	Drew	Gurney	Total
Interest on investment	$1,800	$1,200	$ 3,000
Balance	6,000	6,000	12,000
Totals	$7,800	$7,200	$15,000

Salary Basis

The partners may agree to give recognition to contributions in the form of services, while the remaining net income may be divided equally or in a fixed ratio.

EXAMPLE 4

Assume that the partnership of Drew and Gurney (Example 2) agree that a yearly salary allowance of $4,000 be given to Drew and $3,000 to Gurney, the balance to be divided equally. The entry would be:

Expense and Income Summary	15,000	
Drew, Capital		8,000
Gurney, Capital		7,000

which is computed as follows:

	Drew	Gurney	Total
Salaries	$4,000	$3,000	$ 7,000
Balance	4,000	4,000	8,000
Totals	$8,000	$7,000	$15,000

Salary-Plus-Interest Basis

Here, services rendered to the business and capital contribution jointly determine the income division. Each partner gets a salary, and, at the same time, interest on capital. If any balance remains, it is divided in an agreed ratio.

EXAMPLE 5

Drew and Gurney (Example 2) decide to allow a credit of 6 percent interest on capital balances, respective salaries of $4,000 and $3,000, and equal division of any remainder. The entry would be:

Expense and Income Summary	15,000	
Drew, Capital		8,300
Gurney, Capital		6,700

which is computed as follows:

	Drew	Gurney	Total
Interest	$1,800	$1,200	$ 3,000
Salaries	4,000	3,000	7,000
	$5,800	$4,200	$10,000
Balance	2,500	2,500	5,000
Totals	$8,300	$6,700	$15,000

In Example 5, as well as in Examples 3 and 4, the income of the business exceeded the total of the allowances to the partners. However, this may not always be the case. If the net income is less than the total of the allowances, the balance remaining is negative and is divided among the partners as though it were a loss.

EXAMPLE 6

Drew and Gurney (Example 2) decide to allow a credit of 6 percent interest on capital balances, respective salaries of $8,000 and $6,000, and equal division of the remainder. The entry would be:

Expense and Income Summary	15,000	
Drew, Capital		8,800
Gurney, Capital		6,200

which is computed as follows:

	Drew	Gurney	Total
Interest	$1,800	$1,200	$ 3,000
Salaries	8,000	6,000	14,000
	$9,800	$7,200	$17,000
Balance	− 1,000	− 1,000	− 2,000
Totals	$8,800	$6,200	$15,000

Summary

1. Partnership and sole proprietorship accounting are alike except in _____ .

2. Noncash assets are recorded at _____ amounts when the partnership is formed.

3. If profits and losses are not to be shared equally, the basis of distribution must be stated in the _____ .

4. Salaries and the interest on partners' capital balances are not included on the income statement but are shown on the _____ .

Answers: 1. owners' equity; 2. agreed; 3. partnership agreement; 4. capital statement

Solved Problems

13.1 Henderson and Erin have decided to form a partnership. Henderson invests the following assets at their agreed valuations, and he also transfers his liabilities to the new firm.

Henderson's Accounts	Henderson's Ledger Balances	Agreed Valuations
Cash	$17,500	$17,500
Accounts Receivable	7,200	7,000
Merchandise Inventory	12,200	10,000
Equipment	6,000	4,200
Accumulated Depreciation	1,000	
Accounts Payable	3,500	3,500
Notes Payable	3,600	3,600

Erin agrees to invest $26,000 in cash. Record (*a*) Henderson's investment, (*b*) Erin's investment.

(*a*)

(*b*)

SOLUTION

(*a*)	Cash	17,500	
	Accounts Receivable	7,000	
	Merchandise Inventory	10,000	
	Equipment	4,200	
	Accounts Payable		3,500
	Notes Payable		3,600
	Henderson, Capital		31,600
(*b*)	Cash	26,000	
	Erin, Capital		26,000

13.2 Adams, Bentley, and Carson have capital balances of $30,000, $25,000, and $20,000, respectively. Adams devotes three-fourths time; Bentley, half time; and Carson, one-fourth time. Determine their participation in net income of $37,500 if income is divided (*a*) in the ratio of capital investments, (*b*) in the ratio of time worked.

(a)   Adams

       Bentley

       Carson

       Net Income $37,500

(b)   Adams

       Bentley

       Carson

       Net Income $37,500

SOLUTION

(a) Total capital is $75,000. Hence:

Adams	($30,000/$75,000) $\times$ $37,500 =	$15,000
Bentley	($25,000/$75,000) $\times$ $37,500 =	12,500
Carson	($20,000/$75,000) $\times$ $37,500 =	10,000
Net income		$37,500

(b) The ratio is 3:2:1. Hence:

Adams	3/6 $\times$ $37,500 =	$18,750
Bentley	2/6 $\times$ $37,500 =	12,500
Carson	1/6 $\times$ $37,500 =	6,250
Net income		$37,500

13.3 The capital accounts of W. Dunn and S. Evans have balances of $35,000 and $25,000, respectively. The articles of copartnership refer to the distribution of net income as follows:

1. Dunn and Evans are to receive salaries of $9,000 and $6,000, respectively.

2. Each is to receive 6 percent on his capital account.

3. The balance is to be divided equally.

If net income for the firm is $32,000, (a) determine the division of net income and (b) present the entry to close the expense and income summary account.

(a)

	Dunn	Evans	Total
Salaries			
Interest			
Balance			
Share of net income			

(b)

SOLUTION

(a)

	Dunn	Evans	Total
Salaries	$ 9,000	$ 6,000	$15,000
Interest	2,100	1,500	3,600
	$11,100	$ 7,500	$18,600
Balance	6,700	6,700	13,400
Share of net income	$17,800	$14,200	$32,000

(b)

Expense and Income Summary	32,000	
Dunn, Capital		17,800
Evans, Capital		14,200

13.4   Redo Problem 13.3 for a net income of $12,000.

(a)

	Dunn	Evans	Total
Salaries			
Interest			
Balance			
Share of net income			

(b)

SOLUTION

(a)

	Dunn	Evans	Total
Salaries	$ 9,000	$6,000	$15,000
Interest	2,100	1,500	3,600
	$11,100	$7,500	$18,600
Balance	− 3,300	− 3,300	− 6,600
Share of net income	$ 7,800	$4,200	$12,000

(b)

Expense and Income Summary	12,000	
Dunn, Capital		7,800
Evans, Capital		4,200

13.5   During its first year of operations, the partnership Diamond, Ellis, and Frank earned $41,400. Journalize the entries needed to close the expense and income summary account and to allocate the net income to the partners under the following different assumptions:

(a)   The partners did not agree upon any method for sharing earnings.

(b)   The partners agreed to share earnings in the ratio of time invested. Diamond worked full time; Ellis, full time; Frank, half time.

(c)   The partners agreed to share earnings in the ratio of their capital investments (Diamond, $25,000; Ellis, $20,000; Frank, $15,000).

(a)

(b)

(c)

SOLUTION

(a)

Expense and Income Summary	41,400	
Diamond, Capital		13,800
Ellis, Capital		13,800
Frank, Capital		13,800

If no formal agreement exists, all profits and losses are assumed to be divided equally.

(b) The division ratio is $1:1:\frac{1}{2} = 2:2:1$.

Expense and Income Summary	41,400	
Diamond, Capital (2/5 × $41,400)		16,560
Ellis, Capital (2/5 × $41,400)		16,560
Frank, Capital (1/5 × $41,400)		8,280

(c) The division ratio is $25,000:20,000:15,000 = 5:4:3$.

Expense and Income Summary	41,400	
Diamond, Capital (5/12 × $41,400)		17,250
Ellis, Capital (4/12 × $41,400)		13,800
Frank, Capital (3/12 × $41,400)		10,350

13.6 The abbreviated income statement of James and Kelly for December 31, 198X, appears below:

Sales (net)	$240,000
Less: Cost of Goods Sold	105,000
Gross Profit	$135,000
Less: Expenses	65,000
Net Income	$ 70,000

The profit and loss agreement specifies that:

1. Interest of 5 percent is to be allowed on capital balances (James, $25,000; Kelly, $15,000).
2. Salary allowances to James and Kelly to be $6,000 and $4,000, respectively.

3. A bonus is to be given to James equal to 20 percent of net income without regard to interest or salary.

4. Remaining profits and losses are to be divided in the ratio of capital balances.

(a) Present the distribution of net income.

(b) Present the journal entry required to close the books.

(a)		James	Kelly	Total
Interest				
Salary				
Bonus				
Balance				
Net income				

(b)			

SOLUTION

(a)		James	Kelly	Total
Interest		$ 1,250	$ 750	$ 2,000
Salary		6,000	4,000	10,000
Bonus		14,000		14,000
		$21,250	$ 4,750	$26,000
Balance		27,500*	16,500*	44,000
Net income		$48,750	$21,250	$70,000

* $25,000	James	25/40 × $44,000 = $27,500
15,000	Kelly	15/40 × $44,000 = $16,500
$40,000	Total	

(b)	Expense and Income Summary	70,000	
	James, Capital		48,750
	Kelly, Capital		21,250

13.7 Kapela, Lesser, and Morton, with capital balances of $20,000, $30,000, and $25,000, respectively, split their profits and losses based on their capital balances. If the net profit for the year was $150,000, determine the distribution to each partner.

Kapela	
Lesser	
Morton	
Total cash	$150,000

SOLUTION

Kapela	$ 40,000	(20/75 × $150,000)
Lesser	60,000	(30/75 × $150,000)
Morton	50,000	(25/75 × $150,000)
Total cash	$150,000	

13.8 The capital accounts in the partnership of Frank Buck and John Doe are $57,500 and $87,500, respectively. The partnership agreement calls for a 15 percent interest on their capital accounts and the remaining sum to be shared equally. Net income for the year was $30,000. Show the division of the net income in good report form.

	Buck	Doe	Combined
Interest on capital balance			
Buck			
Doe			
Subtotal			
Balance			
Totals			

SOLUTION

	Buck	Doe	Combined
Interest on capital balance			
Buck, $57,500 × 15%	$ 8,625		$ 8,625
Doe, $87,500 × 15%		$13,125	13,125
Subtotal			$21,750
Balance ($30,000 − $21,750) divided equally	4,125	4,125	8,250
Totals	$12,750	$17,250	$30,000

13.9 From the information in Problem 13.8, show the journal entry to close the Income Summary account.

	Dr.	Cr.

SOLUTION

	Dr.	Cr.
Expense and Income Summary	30,000	
Buck, Capital		12,750
Doe, Capital		17,250

13.10 If Frank Buck and John Doe had the same partnership agreement and capital balances as above but incurred a net loss of $2,000, show the distribution in good report form.

	Buck	Doe	Combined
Buck			
Doe			
Subtotal			
Deficiency			
Totals			

SOLUTION

	Buck	**Doe**	**Combined**
Buck	$ 8,625		$ 8,625
Doe		$13,125	13,125
Subtotal			$21,750
Deficiency ($2,000 + 21,750) divided equally	(11,875)	(11,875)	23,750
Totals	($3,250)	$ 1,250	($2,000)

13.11 From the information above, show the journal entry to close the Income Summary account.

	Dr.	Cr.

SOLUTION

	Dr.	Cr.
Buck, Capital	3,250	
Income Summary		2,000
Doe, Capital		1,250

13.12 The partnership of Klein, Cross, and Budd had net income of $60,000 for the current year. The partnership agreement called for interest of 10 percent on average capital accounts, salaries of $5,000, $5,000, and $10,000, respectively, and the remaining sum divided in a 2:2:1 ratio. Average capital accounts were as follows:

Klein, Capital, $20,000

Cross, Capital, $20,000

Budd, Capital, $10,000

Show the division of the net income in good report form.

	Klein	**Cross**	**Budd**	**Combined**
Subtotal				
Salaries				
2:2:1 ratio balance				
Totals				

SOLUTION

	Klein	Cross	Budd	Combined
Klein ($20,000 × 10%)	$ 2,000			$ 2,000
Cross ($20,000 × 10%)		$ 2,000		2,000
Budd ($10,000 × 10%)			$ 1,000	1,000
Subtotal				$ 5,000
Salaries	5,000	5,000	10,000	20,000
	$ 7,000	$ 7,000	$11,000	$25,000
2:2:1 ratio balance	14,000	14,000	7,000	35,000
Totals	$21,000	$21,000	$18,000	$60,000

13.13 From the above information, show the journal entry to close the Expense and Income Summary account.

	Dr.	Cr.

SOLUTION

	Dr.	Cr.
Expense and Income Summary	60,000	
Klein, Capital		21,000
Cross, Capital		21,000
Budd, Capital		18,000

13.14 From the preceding problem, if there was a net income of $20,000 and the agreement was the same that income and losses were shared in a ratio of 2:2:1, show the division of the net income in good report form.

	Klein	Cross	Budd	Combined
Klein				
Cross				
Budd				
Subtotal				
Salaries				
Deficiency ratio 2:2:1				

SOLUTION

	Klein	Cross	Budd	Combined
Klein ($20,000 × 10%)	$2,000			$ 2,000
Cross ($20,000 × 10%)		$2,000		2,000
Budd ($10,000 × 10%)			$ 1,000	1,000
Subtotal				$ 5,000
Salaries	5,000	5,000	10,000	20,000
	$7,000	$7,000	$11,000	$25,000
Deficiency ratio 2 : 2 : 1	(2,000)	(2,000)	(1,000)	(5,000)
	$5,000	$5,000	$10,000	$20,000

13.15 Show the closing entry from the above information.

	Dr.	Cr.

SOLUTION

	Dr.	Cr.
Expense and Income Summary	20,000	
Klein, Capital		5,000
Cross, Capital		5,000
Budd, Capital		10,000

Chapter 14

Partnerships: Admission and Dissolution

14.1 ADMISSION OF A NEW PARTNER

The Uniform Partnership Act states that a partner may dispose of part or all of his or her interest in the firm without the consent of the remaining partners.

The individual who purchases the interest receives the selling partner's rights to share in income and expense. However, this purchaser is not a full partner, since he or she will have no vote or right to participate in partnership activities unless he or she is admitted to the firm.

Admission by Purchase of Interest

When the incoming partner purchases an interest from another partner, he or she pays the purchase price directly to the old partner. The only change required in the partnership's books is an entry transferring capital from the old partner's account to the account established for the new partner. Assets and liabilities of the business are not affected.

EXAMPLE 1

Drew and Gurney have capital balances of $30,000 and $20,000, respectively. T. Lambert is admitted to the partnership by purchasing half of Drew's interest for $18,000. The only entry required is the changing of the capital balances of the affected partners.

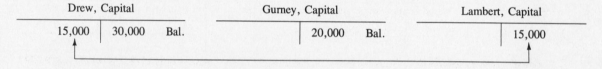

Lambert's admission results in the transfer of half of Drew's capital to Lambert, regardless of the amount paid by Lambert for his share of the partnership.

Admission by Contribution of Assets

The new partner may contribute assets to the partnership, thus increasing both the assets and the capital of the firm.

EXAMPLE 2

Assume that Lambert is to be admitted to the partnership of Drew and Gurney, whose total capital is $50,000 ($30,000 and $20,000, respectively) Lambert is to contribute $25,000 for a one-third interest in the new partnership. The entry to record his admission is

Cash	25,000	
Lambert, Capital		25,000

In Examples 1 and 2 it was assumed that the assets of Drew and Gurney were stated in terms of the current market prices when Lambert was admitted. Because of this, no adjustments were necessary in any of the assets prior to his admission. In some cases, when a new partner is admitted, assets may first have to be revalued or goodwill recognized in order to bring the capital accounts into line with current values.

1. *Revaluation of assets.* The book values of certain assets of the partnership must be adjusted before they agree with current prices. The net amount of the revaluation is then transferred to the capital

238

accounts of the old partners according to their income division agreement. If it appears that a number of assets need revaluation, whether to higher or lower figures, the adjustments may be made in a temporary account, Asset Revaluation, which will subsequently be closed to the partners' capital accounts.

EXAMPLE 3

Drew and Gurney share profits and losses equally. It was discovered that the supplies account is understated: The supplies carried on the books at $6,000 have a current replacement cost of $10,000. The following entry would be recorded prior to the admission of Lambert into the partnership:

Supplies	4,000	
Drew, Capital		2,000
Gurney, Capital		2,000

EXAMPLE 4

Before admitting Lambert to partnership, Drew and Gurney decide that: (*a*) $600 is to be written off the Accounts Receivable balance; (*b*) supplies carried at $6,000 are to be revalued at $8,000.

The entry to record the above revaluation is

Supplies	2,000	
Accounts Receivable		600
Asset Revaluation		1,400

After all adjustments have been made, Asset Revaluation is closed as follows:

Asset Revaluation	1,400	
Drew, Capital		700
Gurney, Capital		700

2. *Recognition of goodwill.* If a firm has the ability to earn more than the normal rate on its investment (because of a favorable location, established reputation, management skills, or better products or services), goodwill may be indicated, and an incoming partner may be charged for it. If so, the goodwill account is debited, while the old partners' accounts are credited in the ratios set up by the articles of partnership. On the other hand, if goodwill is created by the incoming partner, the goodwill account is debited, and the new partner's capital account credited.

EXAMPLE 5   Goodwill to the Old Partners

The capital balances of Drew and Gurney are $30,000 and $20,000, respectively. The partnership agrees to admit Lambert to their firm, who is to contribute cash of $20,000 and is to receive a one-fourth interest in the firm.

Though the total capital of the firm before the admission is $50,000, the parties agree that the firm was worth $60,000. This excess of $10,000 indicates the existence of goodwill; it will be allocated to the old partners in their profit-and-loss ratio, which is 1 : 1 in this case. The entries to record goodwill and the admission of the new partner are:

Goodwill	10,000	
Drew, Capital		5,000
Gurney, Capital		5,000
Cash	20,000	
Lambert, Capital		20,000*

$$* \tfrac{1}{4} (\$30{,}000 \;+\; \$20{,}000 \;+\; \$20{,}000 \;+\; \$10{,}000)$$

Drew   Gurney   Lambert   goodwill

EXAMPLE 6   Goodwill to the New Partner

Drew and Gurney, with capital balances of $30,000 and $20,000, respectively, agree to admit Lambert into the firm for a $15,000 investment, giving him a one-third share in profits and losses and granting him goodwill recognition of $10,000. The entry to record the above information would be:

Cash	15,000	
Goodwill	10,000	
Lambert, Capital		25,000*

$$* \tfrac{1}{3} \, (\underbrace{\$30,000}_{\text{Drew}} \; + \; \underbrace{\$20,000}_{\text{Gurney}} \; + \; \underbrace{\$25,000}_{\text{Lambert}})$$

14.2   LIQUIDATION OF A PARTNERSHIP

If the partners of a firm decide to discontinue the operation of the business, several accounting steps are necessary:

1. The accounts are adjusted and closed.

2. All assets are converted to cash.

3. All creditors are paid in full.

4. Any remaining cash is distributed among the partners according to the balances in their capital accounts (and not according to their profit and loss ratios).

EXAMPLE 7   Liquidation at a Gain

After Drew, Gurney, and Lambert have ceased business operations and adjusted and closed the accounts, the general ledger has the following post-closing trial balance:

Cash	$20,000	
Noncash Assets	65,000	
Liabilities		$10,000
Drew, Capital		15,000
Gurney, Capital		25,000
Lambert, Capital		35,000
	$85,000	$85,000

Assume for simplicity that all liabilities are paid at one time and that the noncash assets are sold in one transaction. Then, if the sale price is $80,000 and the partners share equally in profits and losses, we have the following liquidation schedule:

	Assets	=	Liabilities	+	Capital		
	Cash + Other		Accounts Pay.		Drew +	Gurney +	Lambert
Balances of capital accounts	$ 20,000 $65,000		$10,000		$15,000	$25,000	$35,000
Sale of assets	+ 80,000 − 65,000				+ 5,000	+ 5,000	+ 5,000
Balance after sale	$100,000		$10,000		$20,000	$30,000	$40,000
Payment of liabilities	− 10,000		10,000				
Balance after payment	$ 90,000				$20,000	$30,000	$40,000
Distribution to partners	− 90,000				− 20,000	− 30,000	− 40,000

The entries to record the liquidation are then:

Sale of Assets

Cash	80,000	
Other Assets		65,000
Drew, Capital		5,000
Gurney, Capital		5,000
Lambert, Capital		5,000

Payment of Liabilities

Liabilities	10,000	
Cash		10,000

Final Distribution to Partners

Drew, Capital	20,000	
Gurney, Capital	30,000	
Lambert, Capital	40,000	
Cash		90,000

EXAMPLE 8   Liquidation at a Loss

The data are as in Example 7 except that the noncash assets are now sold for $5,000.

	Assets	=	Liabilities	+	Capital		
	Cash +	Other	Accounts Pay.		Drew +	Gurney +	Lambert
Balances of capital accounts	$20,000	$65,000	$10,000		$15,000	$25,000	$35,000
Sale of assets	+ 5,000	− 65,000			− 20,000	− 20,000	− 20,000
Balance after sale	$25,000		$10,000		$(5,000)	$ 5,000	$15,000
Payment of liabilities	− 10,000		− 10,000				
Balance after payment	$15,000				$(5,000)	$ 5,000	$15,000
Distribution to partners	− 15,000					− 2,500	− 12,500
					$(5,000)	$ 2,500	$ 2,500

Notice that in the foregoing liquidation schedule the $60,000 loss on sale of the noncash assets was divided equally among the three partners. However, Drew's capital balance was not sufficient to absorb his share of the loss. This resulted in a debit balance ($5,000) in his capital account and becomes a claim of the partnership against him for that amount. The $5,000 deficit must be borne by the two remaining partners, and thus, in the distribution to partners, Gurney and Lambert each take an additional loss of $2,500.

The entries to record the liquidation are as follows:

Sale of Assets

Cash	5,000	
Drew, Capital	20,000	
Gurney, Capital	20,000	
Lambert, Capital	20,000	
Other Assets		65,000

Payment of Liabilities

Liabilities	10,000	
Cash		10,000

Distribution to Partners

Gurney, Capital	2,500	
Lambert, Capital	12,500	
Cash		15,000

Since there is a capital deficiency outstanding, one of three different possibilities will arise in the future: (1) Drew pays the deficiency in full; (2) Drew makes a partial payment; (3) Drew makes no payment. The entries corresponding to these possibilities are:

(1) Payment in Full

Cash	5,000	
Drew, Capital		5,000

Gurney, Capital	2,500	
Lambert, Capital	2,500	
Cash		5,000

(2) Partial Payment of $4,000

Cash	4,000	
Drew, Capital		4,000
Settlement of Drew's deficiency		

Gurney, Capital	500	
Lambert, Capital	500	
Drew, Capital		1,000
To close out the balance of Drew's account		

Gurney, Capital	2,000	
Lambert, Capital	2,000	
Cash		4,000
To distribute cash according to capital balances		

(3) No Payment

Gurney, Capital	2,500	
Lambert, Capital	2,500	
Drew, Capital		5,000

Summary

1. The book value of the partnership of Acme and Beam is $60,000, with each partner's account showing $30,000. If Caldwell were to purchase Beam's interest for $40,000, the amount credited to Caldwell's equity account would be _____.

2. In order to reflect higher current prices, certain assets of the partnership will be debited, with the corresponding credit to _____ .

3. A firm's superior earning power is recognized as _____ .

4. When a partnership decides to go out of business, the process of selling the assets, paying the creditors, and distributing the remaining cash to the partners is known as _____ .

5. The final distribution of cash to the partners is based on their _____ .

Answers: 1. $30,000;   2. Asset Revaluation;   3. goodwill;   4. liquidation;   5. capital balances

Solved Problems

14.1   The capital accounts of J. Phillips and H. Martin have balances of $25,000 each. E. Kurlander joins the partnership. What entry is necessary (*a*) if Kurlander purchases half of Phillip's investment for $15,000? (*b*) if Kurlander invests $15,000 in the firm?

(*a*)

(*b*)

SOLUTION

(*a*)	J. Phillips, Capital	12,500	
	E. Kurlander, Capital		12,500
(*b*)	Cash	15,000	
	E. Kurlander, Capital		15,000

14.2   L. Gelber and B. Orzech have capital balances of $20,000 and $30,000, respectively; H. Walker and W. Dunn are to be admitted to the partnership—Walker by purchasing half of Orzech's interest for $18,000 and Dunn by investing $10,000, for which he is to receive full equity value ($10,000).

(*a*)   What entry is needed to record the above information?
(*b*)   On a capital basis, what is Dunn's share of profits and losses?

(*a*)

(*b*)

SOLUTION

(a)

Cash	10,000	
B. Orzech, Capital	15,000	
H. Walker, Capital		15,000
W. Dunn, Capital		10,000

(b)

L. Gelber, Capital	$20,000
H. Walker, Capital	15,000
B. Orzech, Capital	15,000
W. Dunn, Capital	10,000
Total Capital	$60,000

$$\frac{\text{Dunn's investment}}{\text{Capital}} = \frac{\$10,000}{\$60,000} = \frac{1}{6} \quad \text{or} \quad 16\frac{2}{3}\%$$

14.3 The financial position of the partnership of Eccleston and Kapela, who share income in the ratio $3:2$, is shown below:

Eccleston-Kapela Company
Balance Sheet
April 30, 198X

ASSETS		LIABILITIES AND CAPITAL	
Current Assets	$ 65,000	Liabilities	$ 50,000
Equipment (net)	125,000	Eccleston, Capital	85,000
		Kapela, Capital	55,000
Total Assets	$190,000	Total Liabilities and Capital	$190,000

Both partners agree to admit a new partner, Rubin, into the firm. Prepare the necessary entries corresponding to each of the following options:

(a) Rubin purchases half of Kapela's interest for $30,000.

(b) Rubin invests $70,000 in the partnership and receives a one-third interest in capital and income.

(c) The original partners feel that goodwill should be recorded at a value of $20,000. Rubin's investment is to gain him a one-third interest in capital and income.

(a)

(b)

(c)

SOLUTION

(a)	Kapela, Capital	27,500	
	Rubin, Capital		27,500
(b)	Cash	70,000	
	Rubin, Capital		70,000
(c)	Goodwill	20,000	
	Eccleston, Capital		12,000
	Kapela, Capital		8,000
	Cash	80,000	
	Rubin, Capital		80,000*

* Eccleston and Kapela = $160,000; Capital = $\frac{2}{3}$; Rubin must put in $\frac{1}{3}$ or $80,000.

14.4 Before admitting Goldsmith to the partnership, Klapper and Babcock, who share profits and losses equally, decide that (a) Merchandise Inventory, recorded at $26,000, is to be revalued at $29,000; (b) $500 of Accounts Receivable is to be written off. Present journal entries to record the revaluations.

(a)			
(b)			

SOLUTION

(a)	Merchandise Inventory	3,000	
	Accounts Receivable		500
	Asset Revaluation		2,500
(b)	Asset Revaluation	2,500	
	Klapper, Capital		1,250
	Babcock, Capital		1,250

14.5 After the assets of the partnership have been adjusted to reflect current prices, the capital balances of B. Trane and J. Hochian are each $25,000. However, both partners agree that the partnership is worth $60,000. They decide to admit R. Berechad as an equal partner into their firm for a $30,000 investment. (a) Record the recognition of goodwill. (b) Record Berechad's investment. (c) What is the total capital of the firm?

(a)			

(b) _____

(c) _____

SOLUTION

(a)	Goodwill		10,000	
	B. Trane, Capital			5,000
	J. Hochian, Capital			5,000
(b)	Cash		30,000	
	R. Berechad, Capital			30,000

(c)	B. Trane, Capital	$30,000
	J. Hochian, Capital	30,000
	R. Berechad, Capital	30,000
	Total Capital	$90,000

14.6 If, in Problem 14.5, R. Berechad invested $20,000 for an equal share of equity, what would the entry be to record her admittance into the firm?

SOLUTION

Cash	20,000	
Goodwill	10,000	
R. Berechad, Capital		30,000

Since the total capital prior to Berechad's admittance was $60,000, an equal share would require an investment of $30,000, as in Problem 14.5. Therefore, the owners must have agreed to recognize the new partner's ability and awarded her capital credit (goodwill) of $30,000 − $20,000 = $10,000.

14.7 The following T accounts show the balances of the partnership of Bigelow and Holand as of June 30, 198X, prior to dissolution:

Cash		Merchandise Inventory	
35,000		12,600	

Equipment		Accumulated Depreciation	
15,000			12,000

Prepaid Insurance			Accounts Payable	
1,400				16,000

Bigelow, Capital			Holand, Capital	
	18,000			18,000

The partners share profits and losses equally. The terminating transactions are:

(a) Sold the merchandise for its market value, $16,500

(b) Realized $1,100 from the surrender of the insurance policies

(c) Sold the equipment for $2,000

(d) Distributed the gain to the partners' capital accounts

(e) Paid all liabilities

(f) Distributed the remaining cash

Present journal entries to record the above information.

(a)

(b)

(c)

(d)

(e)

(f)

SOLUTION

(a)	Cash	16,500	
	Merchandise Inventory		12,600
	Gain or Loss on Realization		3,900

(b)	Cash	1,100	
	Gain or Loss on Realization	300	
	Prepaid Insurance		1,400
(c)	Cash	2,000	
	Accumulated Depreciation	12,000	
	Gain or Loss on Realization	1,000	
	Equipment		15,000
(d)	Gain or Loss on Realization	2,600	
	Bigelow, Capital		1,300
	Holand, Capital		1,300
(e)	Accounts Payable	16,000	
	Cash		16,000
(f)	Bigelow, Capital	19,300	
	Holand, Capital	19,300	
	Cash		38,600

Summary of Transactions

Transaction	Cash	Other Assets	Liabilities	Bigelow, Capital	Holand, Capital
Balance	$35,000	$17,000	$16,000	$18,000	$18,000
(a)–(d)	+ 19,600	− 17,000		+ 1,300	+ 1,300
	$54,600		$16,000	$19,300	$19,300
(e)	− 16,000		− 16,000		
(f)	$38,600			$19,300	$19,300
	− 38,600			− 19,300	− 19,300

14.8 Sochet, Carlin, and Stadler, who divide profits and losses equally, have the following ledger balances as of December 31:

Cash	$36,000	Sochet, Capital	$15,000
Other Assets	18,000	Carlin, Capital	10,000
Liabilities	16,000	Stadler, Capital	13,000

The partners decide to liquidate and sell their noncash assets at a loss of $6,000. After meeting their obligations, they divide the remaining cash. Present all necessary entries.

(a)	Loss on realization:		

(b) Division of loss:

(c) Payment of liabilities:

(d) Division of remaining cash:

SOLUTION

(a)	Loss of realization:		
	Cash	12,000	
	Loss on Realization	6,000	
	Other Assets		18,000
(b)	Division of loss:		
	Sochet, Capital	2,000	
	Carlin, Capital	2,000	
	Stadler, Capital	2,000	
	Loss on Realization		6,000
(c)	Payment of liabilities:		
	Liabilities	16,000	
	Cash		16,000
(d)	Division of remaining cash:		
	Sochet, Capital	13,000	
	Carlin, Capital	8,000	
	Stadler, Capital	11,000	
	Cash		32,000

Summary of Transactions

Transaction	Cash	Other Assets	Liabilities	Sochet, Capital	Carlin, Capital	Stadler, Capital
Balance	$36,000	$18,000	$16,000	$15,000	$10,000	$13,000
(a), (b)	+ 12,000	− 18,000		− 2,000	− 2,000	− 2,000
	$48,000		$16,000	$13,000	$ 8,000	$11,000
(c)	− 16,000		− 16,000			
	$32,000			$13,000	$ 8,000	$11,000
(d)	− 32,000			− 13,000	− 8,000	− 11,000

14.9 Eccleston, Kapela, and Harmin, who share income and losses in the ratio 2:1:1, decide to liquidate their business on April 30. As of that date their post-closing trial balance reads:

Cash	$ 38,000	
Other Assets:	82,000	
Liabilities		$ 48,000
Eccleston, Capital		30,000
Kapela, Capital		22,000
Harmin, Capital		20,000
	$120,000	$120,000

Present the entries to record the following liquidating transactions:

(a) Sold the noncash assets for $12,000

(b) Distributed the loss to the partners

(c) Paid the liabilities

(d) Allocated the available cash to the partners

(e) The partner with the debit balance pays the amount he owes

(f) Any additional money is distributed

(a) _____

(b) _____

(c) _____

(d) _____

(e) _____

(f) _____

SOLUTION

(a)	Cash	12,000	
	Loss on Realization	70,000	
	Other Assets		82,000

(b)	Eccleston, Capital		35,000	
	Kapela, Capital		17,500	
	Harmin, Capital		17,500	
	Loss on Realization			70,000
(c)	Liabilities		48,000	
	Cash			48,000
(d)	Kapela, Capital		2,000	
	Cash			2,000
(e)	Eccleston, Capital		5,000	
	Cash			5,000
(f)	Cash		5,000	
	Kapela, Capital			2,500
	Harmin, Capital			2,500

Summary of Transactions

Transaction	Cash	Other Assets	Liabilities	Eccleston, Capital	Kapela, Capital	Harmin, Capital
Balance	$38,000	$82,000	$48,000	$30,000	$22,000	$20,000
(a), (b)	+ 12,000	− 82,000		− 35,000	− 17,500	− 17,500
	$50,000		$48,000	($ 5,000)	$ 4,500	$ 2,500
(c)	− 48,000		− 48,000			
	$ 2,000			($ 5,000)	$ 4,500	$ 2,500
(d)	− 2,000				− 2,000	
				($ 5,000)	$ 2,500	$ 2,500
(e)	+ 5,000			+ 5,000		
	$ 5,000				$ 2,500	$ 2,500
(f)	− 5,000				− 2,500	− 2,500

14.10 The trial balance of Blake and Carson, who share profits and losses equally, is as follows:

Cash	$ 40,000	
Other Assets:	60,000	
Accounts Payable		$ 30,000
Blake, Capital		45,000
Carson, Capital		25,000
	$100,000	$100,000

Both partners had decided to admit Davidoff into the partnership, as the business had grown steadily. Prior to Davidoff's admittance, the partners had agreed to record goodwill of $20,000. After this adjustment had been made, Davidoff invested sufficient cash so that he would have a one-third interest in the firm. However, the partners could not work together, and they decided to liquidate. The business, exclusive of the cash balance but including their liabilities, was sold for $32,000. Assuming that at the time of the sale, the balances of the accounts were as they appear above, prepare journal entries to record (*a*) the recognition of goodwill, (*b*) the acceptance of Davidoff into the partnership, (*c*) the sale of the business, (*d*) the distribution of the loss on realization, (*e*) the final division of cash.

(*a*)

(*b*)

(*c*)

(*d*)

(*e*)

SOLUTION

(*a*)	Goodwill	20,000	
	Blake, Capital		10,000
	Carson, Capital		10,000
(*b*)	Cash	45,000	
	Davidoff, Capital		45,000*
	*To produce three equal parts, Davidoff must invest one-half		
	of the existing capital ($70,000 + $20,000 goodwill).		
(*c*)	Cash	32,000	
	Accounts Payable	30,000	
	Loss on Realization	18,000	
	Other Assets		60,000
	Goodwill		20,000

(d)	Blake, Capital	6,000	
	Carson, Capital	6,000	
	Davidoff, Capital	6,000	
	Loss on Realization		18,000
(e)	Blake, Capital	49,000	
	Carson, Capital	29,000	
	Davidoff, Capital	39,000	
	Cash		117,000

Summary of Transactions

Transaction	Cash	Other Assets	Goodwill	Accounts Payable	Blake, Capital	Carson, Capital	Davidoff, Capital
Balance	$ 40,000	$60,000		$30,000	$45,000	$25,000	
(a)			$20,000		+ 10,000	+ 10,000	
	$ 40,000	$60,000	$20,000	$30,000	$55,000	$35,000	
(b)	+ 45,000						$45,000
	$ 85,000	$60,000	$20,000	$30,000	$55,000	$35,000	$45,000
(c), (d)	+ 32,000	− 60,000	− 20,000	− 30,000	− 6,000	− 6,000	− 6,000
	$117,000				$49,000	$29,000	$39,000
(e)	117,000				− 49,000	− 29,000	− 39,000

Chapter 15

The Corporation

15.1 CHARACTERISTICS OF THE CORPORATION

In essence, the corporation is an artificial being, created by law and having a continuous existence regardless of its changing membership. The members are the stockholders; they own the corporation but are distinct from it. As a separate legal entity, the corporation has all the rights and responsibilities of a person, such as entering into contracts, suing and being sued in its own name, and buying, selling, or owning property.

15.2 CORPORATE TERMINOLOGY

The *stockholders*, as owners of the business, have the right (1) to vote (one vote for every share of stock held), (2) to share in profits, (3) to transfer ownership, (4) to share in the distribution of assets in case of liquidation.

The *board of directors* is elected by the stockholders within the framework of the articles of incorporation. The board's duties include the appointing of corporate officers, determining company policies, and the distribution of profits.

A *share* of stock represents a unit of the stockholders' interest in the business. The par value of a share is an arbitrary amount established in the corporation's charter and printed on the face of each stock certificate. It bears no relation to the *market value*, that is, the current purchase or selling price. There are several categories of stock shares:

Authorized shares are shares of stock that a corporation is permitted to issue (sell) under its articles of incorporation.

Unissued shares are authorized shares that have not yet been offered for sale.

Subscribed shares are shares that a buyer has contracted to purchase at a specific price on a certain date. The shares will not be issued until full payment has been received.

Treasury stock represents shares that have been issued and later reacquired by the corporation.

Outstanding stock represents shares authorized, issued, and in the hands of stockholders. (Treasury stock is not outstanding, as it belongs to the corporation and not to the stockholders.)

15.3 ADVANTAGES OF THE CORPORATE FORM

The corporate form of business in the United States, when compared to the sole proprietorship or partnership, has several important advantages:

1. *Limited liability of stockholders.* Each stockholder is accountable only for the amount he or she invests in the corporation. If the company should fail, the creditors cannot ordinarily look beyond the assets of the corporation for settlement of their claims.

2. *Ready transfer of ownership.* Ownership of a corporation is evidenced by stock certificates; this permits stockholders to buy or sell their interests in a corporation without interfering with the management of the business. Through the medium of organized exchanges, millions of shares of stock change hands each day.

3. *Continued existence.* The death or incapacity of a partner may dissolve a partnership, but the corporation's existence is independent of the stockholders.

4. *Legal entity.* The corporation can sue and be sued, make contracts, buy and sell in its own name.

This is in contrast to the sole proprietorship, which must, by law, use individual names in all legal matters.

5. *Ease of raising capital.*   Advantages (1) and (2) above make the corporation an attractive investment for stockholders. Compare this to the partnership, where capital raising is restricted by the number of partners, the amounts of their individual assets, and the prospect of unlimited liability.

15.4 DISADVANTAGES OF THE CORPORATE FORM

Although the corporate form of business has the advantages listed above, it also has some disadvantages, such as the following:

1. *Taxation.*   The corporation must pay federal income taxes in the same manner as an individual and this results in double taxation of corporate income. Double taxation develops first from the taxing of the net profits and second from that portion of the profits distributed to the stockholders as individual income.

2. *Cost of organization.*   The corporation must secure state approval and legal assistance in forming this type of ownership. Requirements vary from state to state, but all states require (*a*) a minimum number of stockholders, (*b*) a minimum amount of capital, and (*c*) a payment of incorporation fees and taxes. The legal fees involved may run to thousands of dollars in large firms and must be added to the costs of state fees and taxes.

3. *Legal restrictions.*   The charter of the corporation of a state is the basis of the corporation's transactions and permits it to engage in only those activities that are stated or implied in the document. If the corporation wishes to operate in another state, it must either incorporate in that state also or pay a tax to the state. It is, therefore, apparent that the corporation is the most restricted form of business ownership.

15.5 EQUITY ACCOUNTING FOR THE CORPORATION

Accounting for the corporation is distinguished from accounting for the sole proprietorship or the partnership by the treatment of owners' (stockholders') equity, which, in the corporation, is separated into paid-in capital and retained earnings. The reason for this separation is that most states prohibit corporations from paying dividends from other than retained earnings. Paid-in capital is further divided, and so we have three major capital accounts:

Capital Stock.   This account shows the par value of the stock issued by the corporation.

Additional Paid-in Capital.   Amounts paid in beyond the par value of stock.

Retained Earnings.   The accumulated earnings arising from profitable operation of the business.

EXAMPLE 1   Operation at a Profit

Assume that on January 1, two separate businesses are formed, a sole proprietorship operated by Ira Sochet and a corporation having four stockholders. Assume further that the single owner invested $20,000 while the four stockholders each bought 500 shares of common stock at $10 per share. The entries to record the investments are:

Sole Proprietorship			*Corporation*		
Cash	20,000		Cash	20,000	
Ira Sochet, Capital		20,000	Common Stock		20,000

After a year's operations, the net income of each enterprise was $5,000. In the sole proprietorship, the Expense and Income Summary balance is transferred to the capital account; in the corporation, the balance is transferred to Retained Earnings. Thus:

Sole Proprietorship			*Corporation*	
Expense and Income Summary	5,000		Expense and Income Summary	5,000
Ira Sochet, Capital		5,000	Retained Earnings	5,000

The balance sheets of the two firms are identical except for the owners' equity sections, which appear as follows:

Sole Proprietorship		*Corporation*	
Ira Sochet, Capital, Jan. 1	$20,000	Common Stock, $10 par (2,000 shares authorized and issued)	$20,000
Add: Net Income	5,000	Retained Earnings	5,000
Ira Sochet, Capital, Dec. 31	$25,000	Stockholders' Equity	$25,000

EXAMPLE 2   Operation at a Loss

During the second year of operations, both firms in Example 1 lost $7,000, an amount that exceeds the first year's profits. Observe the difference in the two balance sheets:

Sole Proprietorship		*Corporation*	
Ira Sochet, Capital, Jan. 1	$25,000	Common Stock, $10 par (2,000 shares authorized and issued)	$20,000
Deduct: Net Loss	(7,000)	Deduct: Deficit	(2,000)*
Ira Sochet, Capital, Dec. 31	$18,000	Stockholders' Equity	$18,000

	* Retained Earnings	
	7,000	5,000

The $7,000 was treated as a net loss in the sole proprietorship; in the corporation, it was reduced by the net profit from the first year and titled "Deficit."

15.6   COMMON STOCK

If a corporation issues only one class of stock, it is known as *common stock*, with all shares having the same rights. The ownership of a share of common stock carries with it the right to:

1. Vote in the election of directors and in the making of certain important corporate decisions
2. Participate in the corporation's profits
3. Purchase a proportionate part of future stock issues
4. Share in assets upon liquidation

15.7   PREFERRED STOCK

In order to appeal to a broader market, the corporation may also issue *preferred stock*. This class of stock does not ordinarily carry voting rights (although such rights are sometimes conferred by a special provision in the charter); however, as its name implies, this stock does take preference over common stock in several respects.

Prior claim against earnings.   The board of directors has the power to declare and distribute dividends to the stockholders. In such distributions, the claims of preferred stock are honored before those of common stock. However, the amount of dividends paid to preferred stock is usually placed on the amount paid to common stock. From an accounting viewpoint, the priority in receiving dividends constitutes the most important benefit of preferred stock.

EXAMPLE 3

Eppy Corporation has outstanding 1,000 shares of preferred stock with a preference of a $5 dividend (5 percent of $100 par value) and 3,000 shares of common stock. Net income was $20,000 and $40,000 for the first 2 years of operations. The board of directors has authorized the distribution of all profits.

	Year 1	Year 2
Net Profit	$20,000	$40,000
Dividends on Preferred		
(1,000 shares, $5 per share)	5,000	5,000
Balance to Common	$15,000	$35,000
Number of Common Shares	÷3,000	÷3,000
Common Stock Dividend per Share	$5.00	$11.67

Prior claim to assets.   If, upon liquidation of a corporation, the assets that remain after payment of all creditors are not sufficient to return the full amount of the capital contribution of preferred and common stockholders, payment must first be made to preferred stockholders. Any balance would then go to common stockholders.

Preferred stock may also carry the following benefits:

Call privilege.   The issuing company will have the right to redeem (all) the stock at a later date for a predetermined price. This call price would be in excess of the original issue price, such as 105 percent of par value.

Conversion privilege.   The stockholders, at their option, may convert preferred stock into common stock. This might be done if the corporation's common stock should become more desirable than the preferred stock because of large earnings (see Example 3).

15.8   ISSUE OF STOCK

Issue at Par

When a corporation is organized, the charter will state how many shares of common and preferred stock are authorized. Often more stock is authorized than is intended to be sold immediately. This will enable the corporation to expand in the future without applying to the state for permission to issue more shares. When stock is sold for cash and issued immediately, the entry to record the security has the usual form: Cash is debited, and the particular security is credited.

EXAMPLE 4

Carey Corporation, organized on January 1 with an authorization of 10,000 shares of common stock ($40 par), issues 8,000 shares at par for cash. The entry to record the stockholders' investment and the receipt of cash is:

Cash	320,000	
Common Stock		320,000

If, in addition, Carey Corporation issues 1,000 shares of preferred 5 percent stock ($100 par) at par, the combined entry would be:

Cash	420,000	
Preferred Stock		100,000
Common Stock		320,000

A corporation may accept property other than cash in exchange for stock. If this occurs, the assets should be recorded at fair market value, usually as determined by the board of directors of the company.

EXAMPLE 5

In exchange for 1,000 shares of $100-par common stock, Walker Corporation receives, at fair market value, machinery worth $50,000, and land and buildings worth $30,000 and $20,000, respectively. The transaction is recorded as:

Machinery	50,000	
Land	30,000	
Buildings	20,000	
Common Stock		100,000

Issue at a Premium or a Discount

The market price of stock is influenced by many factors, such as:

1. Potential earning power
2. General business conditions and other prospects
3. Financial condition and earnings record
4. Dividend record

Stock will be sold at a price above par if investors are willing to pay the excess, or premium. The premium is not profit to the corporation but rather part of the investment of the stockholders.

EXAMPLE 6

Carey Corporation issues 8,000 shares of its authorized 10,000 shares of common stock ($40 par) for $45 a share. The entry to record the transaction is:

Cash	360,000	
Common Stock		320,000
Premium on Common Stock		40,000

If the purchaser will not pay par value, the corporation may issue the stock at a price below par. The difference between par value and the lower price is called the *discount*.

EXAMPLE 7

Carey Corporation issues 1,000 shares of 5 percent preferred stock ($100 par) at 98.

Cash	98,000	
Discount on Preferred Stock	2,000	
Preferred Stock		100,000

EXAMPLE 8

Based on Examples 6 and 7, the stockholders' equity section of the balance sheet of Carey Corporation is as follows:

Paid-in Capital		
Preferred Stock, 5%, $100 par		
(1,000 shares authorized and issued)	$100,000	
Less: Discount on Preferred Stock	2,000	$ 98,000
Common Stock, $40 par		
(10,000 shares authorized, 8,000 shares issued)	$320,000	
Premium on Common Stock	40,000	360,000
Total Paid-in Capital		$458,000
Retained Earnings		22,000*
Stockholders' Equity		$480,000

* Assumed.

15.9   BOOK VALUE

The book value per share of stock is obtained by dividing the stockholders' equity amount by the number of shares outstanding. It thus represents the amount that would be distributed to each share of stock if the corporation were to be dissolved.

Individual book values for common and preferred stock are defined by separating the stockholders' equity amount into two parts and dividing each part by the corresponding number of shares. All premiums and discounts, as well as retained earnings or deficits, go to common stock only.

EXAMPLE 9

Suppose that the balance sheet reads:

Common Stock, $40 par	
(10,000 shares authorized, 8,000 shares issued)	$320,000
Retained Earnings	22,000
Stockholders' Equity	$342,000

Then we would have

$$\text{Book value} = \frac{\$342,000}{8,000 \text{ shares}} = \$42.75 \text{ per share}$$

EXAMPLE 10

For the data in Example 8, the allocation of the total equity between preferred and common stock would be

Total Equity	$480,000
Allocation to preferred stock	100,000
Balance to common stock	$380,000

and the book values would be

$$\text{Book value of preferred} = \frac{\$100,000}{1,000 \text{ shares}} = \$100 \text{ per share}$$

$$\text{Book value of common} = \frac{\$380,000}{8,000 \text{ shares}} = \$47.50 \text{ per share}$$

15.10   EARNINGS PER SHARE

To find earnings per share (EPS), take the net profit after taxes, less any preferred dividends. This will equal the earnings available for common stockholders. Divide by the number of shares of common stock outstanding to arrive at EPS:

$$\text{Earnings per share} = \frac{\text{earnings available for common stockholders}}{\text{number of shares of common stock outstanding}}$$

EXAMPLE 11

ABC Corporation, with 200,000 shares of common stock outstanding, had net income after taxes of $500,000. They declared and paid $100,000 of preferred stock dividends. What is the EPS?

$$\text{EPS} = \frac{\$400,000}{200,000} = \$2.00 \text{ EPS}$$

This figure is the dollar amount earned on behalf of each common stock shareholder. Note that this does not mean the stockholders will receive this amount in the form of a dividend. The corporation is not required to pay a dividend to common stockholders.

15.11   BOND CHARACTERISTICS

A corporation may obtain funds by selling stock or by borrowing through long-term obligations. An issue of bonds is a form of long-term debt in which the corporation agrees to pay interest periodically and to repay the principal at a stated future date.

Bond denominations are commonly multiples of $1,000. A bond issue normally has a term of 10 or 20 years, although some issues may have longer lives. The date at which a bond is to be repaid is known as the *maturity date*. In an issue of serial bonds, the maturity dates are spread in a series over the term of the issue. This relieves the corporation from the impact of total payment at one date.

15.12   FUNDING BY STOCK VERSUS FUNDING BY BONDS

The major differences between stocks and bonds may be summarized as follows:

	Stocks	Bonds
Representation	Ownership in the corporation	A debt of the corporation
Inducement to Holders	Dividends	Interest
Accounting Treatment	Dividends are a distribution of profits Stocks are equity	Interest is an expense Bonds are a long-term liability
Repayment	By selling in the market at any time	On a predetermined date

These differences give rise to alternative methods of financing, as in Examples 12 and 13 below.

EXAMPLE 12

The board of directors of a new company has decided that $1,000,000 is needed to begin operations. The controller presents three different methods of financing:

	Method 1 (Common Stock)	Method 2 (Preferred and Common Stock)	Method 3 (Bonds, Preferred and Common Stock)
Bonds, 5%	—	—	$ 500,000
Preferred stock, 6%	—	$ 500,000	250,000
Common stock, $100 par	$1,000,000	500,000	250,000
Total	$1,000,000	$1,000,000	$1,000,000

Subsequent profits before interest on bonds and before taxes are estimated at $300,000; taxes are estimated at 40 percent.

	Method 1	Method 2	Method 3
Profit	$300,000	$300,000	$300,000
Less: Interest on bonds	—	—	25,000
Net income before taxes	$300,000	$300,000	$275,000
Less: Income taxes	120,000	120,000	110,000
Net Income	$180,000	$180,000	$165,000
Less: Dividends on preferred stock	—	30,000	15,000
Common stock balance	$180,000	$150,000	$150,000
Number of common shares	÷10,000*	÷5,000†	÷2,500‡
Earnings per common share	$18	$30	$60

*$1,000,000/$100.

†$500,000/$100.

‡$250,000/$100.

For the common stockholders, Method 3 (called debt and equity financing) is clearly the best. It gives greater earnings because (1) bond interest is deducted for income tax purposes; (2) bonds are marketed at an interest rate that is lower than the dividend rate on preferred stock.

EXAMPLE 13

As the amount of profit becomes smaller, Method 1 of Example 12 becomes the best financing method. Assume that the same three methods of funding are under consideration for an anticipated net income of $60,000 before interest and taxes.

	Method 1	Method 2	Method 3
Profit	$60,000	$60,000	$60,000
Less: Interest on bonds	—	—	25,000
Net income before taxes	$60,000	$60,000	$35,000
Less: Income taxes	24,000	24,000	14,000
Net Income	$36,000	$36,000	$21,000
Less: Dividends on preferred stock	—	30,000	15,000
Common stock balance	$36,000	$ 6,000	$ 6,000
Earnings per share	$3.60	$1.20	$2.40

Summary

1. The rights to vote and to share in the profits of the company rest with the _____ .

2. The greatest disadvantage of the corporate form of business is the _____ on income.

3. The value established for stock is called _____ .

4. Shares of stock that a corporation is allowed to sell are called _____ .

5. The profit and loss of the corporation is recorded in the _____ account.

6. If a corporation issues only one class of stock, this stock is known as _____ .

7. To achieve a broader market and a more attractive issue price, preferred stock may _____ in profits beyond the specified rate.

8. The amount paid in excess of par by a purchaser of newly issued stock is called a _____ , whereas the amount paid below par is known as a _____ .

Answers: 1. stockholders; 2. tax; 3. par value; 4. authorized shares; 5. Retained Earnings; 6. common stock; 7. participate; 8. premium, discount

Solved Problems

15.1   Two separate business organizations, a partnership and a corporation, were formed on January 1, 198X.

     1. The initial investments of the partners, Blue and Gray, were $25,000 and $20,000, respectively.

     2. The Green Corporation has five stockholders, each owning 90 shares of $100-par common.

     At the end of the calendar year, the net income of each company was $15,000. (*a*) For each organization, show the proper entry to close the expense and income account. (*b*) Prepare a capital statement for the partnership and a stockholders' equity statement for the corporation, as of December 31, 198X.

(a) Partnership entry:

Corporation entry:

(b)

Partnership Capital Statement

Stockholders' Equity Statement

SOLUTION

(a) Partnership entry:

Expense and Income Summary	15,000	
Blue, Capital		7,500*
Gray, Capital		7,500*

* Profits and losses are to be divided equally if no other distribution is specified.

Corporation entry:

Expense and Income Summary	15,000	
Retained Earnings		15,000

(b)

Partnership Capital Statement

	Blue	Gray	Total
Capital, Jan. 1, 198X	$25,000	$20,000	$45,000
Add: Net Income	7,500	7,500	15,000
Capital, Dec. 31, 198X	$32,500	$27,500	$60,000

Stockholders' Equity Statement

Common Stock, $100 par	
(450 shares authorized and issued)	$45,000
Retained Earnings	15,000
Stockholders' Equity	$60,000

15.2 Redo Problem 15.1 assuming that each business suffers a loss of $18,000 in the second year of operations.

(a) Partnership entry:

Corporation entry:

(b)

Partnership Capital Statement

Stockholders' Equity Statement

SOLUTION

(a) Partnership entry:

Blue, Capital	9,000	
Gray, Capital	9,000	
Expense and Income Summary		18,000

Corporation entry:

Retained Earnings	18,000	
Expense and Income Summary		18,000

(b)

Partnership Capital Statement

	Blue	Gray	Total
Capital, Jan. 1, 198X	$32,500	$27,500	$60,000
Less: Net Loss	9,000	9,000	18,000
Capital, Dec. 31, 198X	$23,500	$18,500	$42,000

Stockholders' Equity Statement	
Common Stock, $100 par	
(450 shares authorized and issued)	$45,000
Less: Deficit*	(3,000)
Stockholders' Equity	$42,000
* Retained Earnings (Dec. 31, 198X)	$15,000
Less: Net Loss (Dec. 31, 198X)	18,000
	($3,000)

15.3 The board of directors' policy is to distribute all profits earned in a year to preferred and common stockholders. During the first 3 years of operations, the corporation earned $68,000, $180,000, and $320,000, respectively. There are outstanding 10,000 shares of 6 percent, $100-par preferred stock and 40,000 shares of common stock. Determine the amount per share applicable to common stock for each of the 3 years.

	Year 1	Year 2	Year 3

SOLUTION

	Year 1	Year 2	Year 3
Net profit (after taxes)	$68,000	$180,000	$320,000
Dividend on preferred stock	60,000	60,000	60,000
Balance to common stock	$ 8,000	$120,000	$260,000
Common dividend per share	$0.20	$3.00	$6.50

15.4 On January 1, the Greene Corporation issued for cash 5,000 shares of its authorized 10,000 shares of $10-par common stock. Three months later it was decided to issue another 5,000 shares of common stock at par and also 1,000 shares of 5 percent, $100-par preferred stock. What entries are required to record the January and April transactions?

Jan. 1			
Apr. 1			

SOLUTION

Jan. 1	Cash	50,000	
	Common Stock		50,000
Apr. 1	Cash	150,000	
	Common Stock		50,000
	Preferred Stock		100,000

15.5 In Problem 15.4, present the stockholders' equity section (*a*) as of January 31, (*b*) as of April 30.

(*a*)

(*b*)

SOLUTION

(*a*) Paid-in Capital:

Common Stock, $10 par		
(10,000 shares authorized, 5,000 shares issued)	$50,000	
Stockholders' Equity		$50,000

(*b*) Paid-in Capital:

Preferred Stock, 5%, $100 par		
(1,000 shares authorized and issued)	$100,000	
Common Stock, $10 par		
(10,000 shares authorized and issued)	100,000	
Stockholders' Equity		$200,000

15.6 Rund Corporation issues 2,000 shares of 6 percent, $50-par preferred stock at $48 and 5,000 shares of $25-par common stock at $30. (*a*) Present the entry needed to record the above information. (*b*) Present the stockholders' equity section.

(*a*)

(*b*)

SOLUTION

(*a*)

Cash	246,000	
Discount on Preferred Stock	4,000	
Preferred Stock		100,000
Common Stock		125,000
Premium on Common Stock		25,000

(b) Paid-in Capital:		
Preferred Stock, 6%, $50 par	$100,000	
Less: Discount on Preferred Stock	4,000	$ 96,000
Common Stock, $25 par	$125,000	
Add: Premium on Common Stock	25,000	150,000
Stockholders' Equity		$246,000

15.7 Boaches, Inc., receives in exchange for 3,000 shares of $100-par preferred stock and 2,000 shares of $50-par common stock the following fixed assets:

	Cost	Fair Market Value
Building	$200,000	$125,000
Land	100,000	80,000
Machinery	150,000	150,000
Equipment	60,000	45,000

Provide the entry to record the above information.

SOLUTION

Building	125,000	
Land	80,000	
Machinery	150,000	
Equipment	45,000	
Preferred Stock		300,000
Common Stock		100,000

15.8 The Tobak Corporation agrees to issue 10,000 shares of common stock in exchange for equipment valued at $250,000. Present the required journal entry if par value of the common stock is (a) $25, (b) $20, (c) $30.

(a)		
(b)		
(c)		

SOLUTION

(a)

Equipment		250,000	
	Common Stock		250,000

(b)

Equipment		250,000	
	Common Stock		200,000
	Premium on Common Stock		50,000

(c)

Equipment		250,000	
Discount on Common Stock		50,000	
	Common Stock		300,000

15.9 On January 1, P. Henry, Inc., was organized with an authorization of 5,000 shares of preferred 6 percent stock, $100 par, and 10,000 shares of $25-par common stock.

(a) Record the following transactions:

    Jan. 10 Sold half of the common stock at $28 for cash.

          15 Issued 2,000 shares of preferred and 1,000 shares of common at par in exchange for land and building with fair market values of $140,000 and $85,000, respectively.

    Mar. 6 Sold the balance of the preferred stock for cash at $105.

(b) Present the stockholders' equity section of the balance sheet as of March 6.

(a)

Jan. 10			
15			
Mar. 6			

(b)

SOLUTION

(*a*)

Jan. 10	Cash		140,000	
	Common Stock			125,000
	Premium on Common Stock			15,000
15	Land		140,000	
	Building		85,000	
	Preferred Stock			200,000
	Common Stock			25,000
Mar. 6	Cash		315,000	
	Preferred Stock			300,000
	Premium on Preferred Stock			15,000

(*b*)

Paid-in Capital:		
Preferred Stock, 6%, $100 par		
(5,000 shares authorized and issued)	$500,000	
Add: Premium on Preferred Stock	15,000	$515,000
Common Stock, $25 par		
(10,000 shares authorized, 6,000 shares issued)	$150,000	
Add: Premium on Common Stock	15,000	$165,000
Total Paid-in Capital		$680,000

15.10 Corporations A and B each have 10,000 shares of common stock outstanding. Assuming that the two stocks have the same book value, complete the following table:

	Corporation A	Corporation B
Assets	$350,000	?
Liabilities	100,000	$ 70,000
Common Stock	200,000	175,000
Retained Earnings	?	?

SOLUTION

	Corporation A	Corporation B
Assets	$350,000	$320,000‡
Liabilities	100,000	70,000
Common Stock	200,000	175,000
Retained Earnings	50,000*	75,000†

---

*Assets   = Liabilities + Stockholders' Equity

 $350,000 = $100,000 +   ($200,000 + ?)

†Because the book values of the common stock in both corporations are identical, Corporation B must have the same total for stockholders' equity: $250,000 ($175,000 + $75,000).

‡Assets = Liabilities + Stockholders' Equity

  ?   = $70,000 + $250,000

15.11 The XYZ Corporation had income before taxes of $700,000 (use a 40 percent tax rate) and paid $140,000 to the preferred stockholders. What are the earnings per share for XYZ common stockholders with 70,000 shares of common stock outstanding?

SOLUTION

Earnings before taxes	$700,000
40% tax rate	× 40%
Taxes	$280,000

Income	$700,000
Taxes	− 280,000
	$420,000
Less preferred dividends	140,000
Earnings available to	
common stockholders	$280,000

$$\text{EPS} = \frac{\$280,000}{70,000} = \underline{\underline{\$4}} \text{ per share}$$

15.12 The corporation's equity accounts appear below:

Preferred Stock, 5%, $100 par

    (5,000 shares authorized, 3,000 shares issued) $300,000

Discount on Preferred Stock   30,000

Common Stock, $50 par

    (10,000 shares authorized, 4,000 shares issued)   200,000

Premium on Common Stock   10,000

Retained Earnings (credit balance)   35,000

In order to secure additional funds, the board of directors approved the following proposals:

1. To borrow $100,000, with an 8 percent mortgage
2. To sell the remaining common stock at par
3. To issue the balance of the preferred stock in exchange for equipment valued at $185,000

Prepare (*a*) journal entries for the transactions, (*b*) the stockholders' equity section.

(*a*)   1.

       2.

       3.

(b) _____

SOLUTION

(a)

1.	Cash		100,000	
	Mortgage Payable			100,000
2.	Cash		300,000	
	Common Stock			300,000
3.	Equipment		185,000	
	Discount on Preferred Stock		15,000	
	Preferred Stock			200,000

(b)

Paid-in Capital:		
Preferred Stock, 5%, $100 par (5,000 shares authorized and issued)	$500,000	
Less: Discount on Preferred Stock	45,000	$ 455,000
Common Stock, $50 par (10,000 shares authorized and issued)	$500,000	
Add: Premium on Common Stock	10,000	510,000
Total Paid-in Capital		$ 965,000
Retained Earnings		35,000
Total Stockholders' Equity		$1,000,000

15.13 Determine the equity per share of preferred and of common stock, if the balance sheet shows:

(a)	Preferred Stock, $100 par	$200,000
	Common Stock, $25 par	100,000
	Premium on Common Stock	10,000
	Retained Earnings	40,000
(b)	Preferred Stock, $100 par	$200,000
	Premium on Preferred Stock	10,000
	Common Stock, $25 par	100,000
	Retained Earnings (deficit)	(40,000)

(a)

Preferred Stock	Common Stock

(b)

Preferred Stock	Common Stock

SOLUTION

(a)

Preferred Stock		Common Stock	
$200,000	To preferred stock	$100,000	Common stock
		10,000	Premium
$100.00	Per share	40,000	Retained earnings
		$150,000	To common stock
		$37.50*	Per share

*$150,000 ÷ 4,000 shares. The number of shares outstanding is determined by dividing the value of the stock, $100,000, by its par value, $25.

(b)

Preferred Stock		Common Stock	
$200,000	To preferred stock	$100,000	Common stock
		10,000*	Premium
$100.00	Per share	(40,000)	Deficit
		$70,000	To common stock
		$17.50	Per share

*The premium on preferred stock is allocated to common stock when computing equity per share.

15.14 Three companies have the following structures:

	G Company	H Company	I Company
Bonds Payable, 5%	$1,000,000	$ 600,000	—
Preferred Stock, 6%, $100 par	—	600,000	$1,000,000
Common Stock, $100 par	1,000,000	800,000	1,000,000
Total	$2,000,000	$2,000,000	$2,000,000

Assuming a tax rate of 40 percent of income, determine the earnings per share of common stock if the net income of each company before bond interest and taxes was (a) $140,000; (b) $500,000.

(a)

	G Company	H Company	I Company

(b)

	G Company	H Company	I Company

SOLUTION

(a)

	G Company	H Company	I Company
Income	$140,000	$140,000	$140,000
Less: Bond interest	50,000	30,000	—
Income before taxes	$ 90,000	$110,000	$140,000
Less: Tax (40%)	36,000	44,000	56,000
Net income	$ 54,000	$ 66,000	$ 84,000
Less: Preferred dividend	—	36,000	60,000
To common stock	$ 54,000	$ 30,000	$ 24,000
Number of common shares	÷10,000	÷8,000	÷10,000
Earnings per share	$ 5.40	$ 3.75	$ 2.40

(b)

	G Company	H Company	I Company
Income	$500,000	$500,000	$500,000
Less: Bond interest	50,000	30,000	—
Income before taxes	$450,000	$470,000	$500,000
Less: Tax (40%)	180,000	188,000	200,000
Net income	$270,000	$282,000	$300,000
Less: Preferred dividend	—	36,000	60,000
To common stock	$270,000	$246,000	$240,000
Number of common shares	÷10,000	÷8,000	÷10,000
Earnings per share	$27.00	$30.75	$24.00

15.15 F. Saltzman Industries has 12,000 shares of common stock outstanding. The board decides to expand existing facilities at a projected cost of $3,000,000. Method 1: issue of $3,000,000 in common stock, $50 par. Method 2: issue of $1,500,000 in preferred stock, 6 percent, $100 par, and $1,500,000 in common stock, $50 par. Method 3: issue of $1,500,000 in 6 percent bonds, $750,000 in preferred stock, 6 percent, $100 par, and $750,000 in common stock, $50 par. Assuming that the net income before bond interest and taxes (40 percent) will be increased to $300,000, find the earnings per share of common stock under each method.

	Method 1	Method 2	Method 3

SOLUTION

	Method 1	Method 2	Method 3
Income	$300,000	$300,000	$300,000
Less: Bond interest	—	—	90,000
Income before taxes	$300,000	$300,000	$210,000
Less: Taxes	120,000	120,000	84,000
Net income	$180,000	$180,000	$126,000
Less: Preferred dividend	—	90,000	45,000
To common stock	$180,000	$ 90,000	$ 81,000
Number of common shares	÷72,000	÷42,000	÷27,000
Earnings per share	$2.50	$2.14	$3.00

15.16 Rework Problem 15.15 for an expected income of $180,000.

	Method 1	Method 2	Method 3

SOLUTION

	Method 1	Method 2	Method 3
Income	$180,000	$180,000	$180,000
Less: Bond interest	—	—	90,000
Income before taxes	$180,000	$180,000	$ 90,000
Less: Taxes	72,000	72,000	36,000
Net income	$108,000	$108,000	$ 54,000
Less: Preferred dividend	—	90,000	45,000
To common stock	$108,000	$ 18,000	$ 9,000
Number of common shares	÷72,000	÷42,000	÷27,000
Earnings per share	$1.50	$0.43	$0.33

Chapter 16

Fundamental Concepts

16.1 OPERATIONS WITH DECIMALS

Addition of Decimals

To add decimals, arrange the numbers to be added in a column with all decimal places underneath one another. This helps to avoid the chance of error when adding tenths, hundredths, and so on. To simplify the process, zeros may be added to the *right* of the decimal place without changing the numbers.

EXAMPLE 1

Three plant machine parts weigh 1.26, 0.00145, and 4.3452 pounds, respectively; their combined weight is:

$$
\begin{array}{r}
1.26000* \\
0.00145 \\
4.34520* \\
\hline
5.60665 \\
\hline
\end{array}
$$

---

* Zeros added to simplify the process.

Subtraction of Decimals

To subtract decimals, arrange the two numbers to be subtracted in a column with the higher number on top. Zeros should be added to the number with fewer decimal places to simplify the solution.

EXAMPLE 2

Product A has a shipping weight of 2.49 pounds, while product B weighs 1.234 pounds. What is the difference in weight?

$$
\begin{array}{r}
2.490 \\
-1.234 \\
\hline
1.256 \\
\hline
\end{array}
$$

Multiplication of Decimals

Multiplication of decimals follows the same process used for multiplication of whole numbers with the exception that in the final answer (product), the number of decimal places is equal to the total number of decimal places in the original numbers.

EXAMPLE 3

At $4.50 per ounce, what will 1.235 ounces cost?

$$
\begin{array}{r}
1.235 \longleftarrow \text{3 decimal places} \\
\times \quad 4.5 \longleftarrow \text{1 decimal places} \\
\hline
6175 \\
4940 \\
\hline
\$5.5575 \longleftarrow \text{4 decimal places}
\end{array}
$$

Division of Decimals

Division of decimals follows the same process as division of whole numbers. The decimal point in the divisor must first be eliminated, however, by moving the decimal point in both the divisor and the dividend to the right by the same number of places. Zeros are added to the dividend if needed. For the final answer, the decimal point is placed directly above the item it has been moved to in the dividend.

EXAMPLE 4

The cost of producing 3.22 pounds of Product A is $7.1162. What does one pound cost?

$$
\begin{array}{r}
\$2.21 \\
\text{Divide: } 3.22\overline{)7.1162} \\
\underline{644} \\
676 \\
\underline{644} \\
322 \\
\underline{322}
\end{array}
$$

16.2   PERCENTAGES

Percent really means "per hundred." A percentage is simply a manner of expressing the relationship between one number or amount and another in terms of hundredths. It is a convenient, widely used, acceptable method of referring to an amount in terms of another known amount. In order to work mathematically with percentages, you must first translate the percent into a decimal or a fraction.

EXAMPLE 5

To convert a percent to a decimal, simply move the decimal place in the percent two places to the left:

$$1\% = .01 \qquad 60\% = .60$$

EXAMPLE 6

To convert a percent to a fraction, place 100 under the number:

$$1\% = \frac{1}{100} \qquad 60\% = \frac{60}{100}$$

EXAMPLE 7

To convert a fraction or decimal to a percent, the easiest method is to convert the number first to a decimal and then move the decimal point two places to the right.

$$\text{For fractions:} \quad \frac{1}{100} = .01 = 1\%$$

$$\frac{60}{100} = .60 = 60\%$$

$$\text{For decimals:} \quad .01 = 1\%$$

$$.60 = 60\%$$

The relationship in percent (*rate*) of one number or amount to another may be computed by dividing the *percentage* (the amount whose relationship to a second number you want to find) by the *base* (the number you are comparing to). The formula is expressed mathematically as

$$\text{Percent (rate)} = \frac{\text{percentage}}{\text{base}}$$

EXAMPLE 8

What percent of 80 is 20?

$$\text{Percent (rate)} = \frac{20 \text{ (percentage)}}{80 \text{ (base)}} = \frac{1}{4} = .25 = 25\%$$

EXAMPLE 9

If the cost of an item is $75 and the selling price is $100, what percent of the selling price is the cost?

$$\text{Percent (rate)} = \frac{\$75 \text{ (percentage)}}{\$100 \text{ (base)}} = 75\%$$

EXAMPLE 10

Income statement analysis: Determine the percent of each of the amounts listed in the income statement below to net sales:

LAT Company
Income Statement
For Year Ended December 31, 198X

Net Sales		$10,000
Cost of Sales		4,000
Gross Profit		$ 6,000
Operating Expenses:		
Selling Expenses	$2,000	
General Expenses	1,000	
Total Operating Expenses		3,000
Net Income		$ 3,000

$$\text{Cost of Sales:} \quad \frac{4,000 \text{ (percentage)}}{10,000 \text{ (base)}} \qquad \text{Cost of Sales} = .40 \text{ or } 40\%$$

$$\text{Gross Profit:} \quad \frac{6,000 \text{ (percentage)}}{10,000 \text{ (base)}} \qquad \text{Gross Profit} = .60 \text{ or } 60\%$$

Selling Expenses: $\dfrac{2,000 \text{ (percentage)}}{10,000 \text{ (base)}}$ Selling Expense = .20 or 20%

General Expenses: $\dfrac{1,000 \text{ (percentage)}}{10,000 \text{ (base)}}$ General Expense = .10 or 10%

Total Operating Expenses: Sell. Exp. + Gen. Exp. or 20% + 10% = 30%

Net Income: $\dfrac{3,000 \text{ (percentage)}}{10,000 \text{ (base)}}$ Net Income = .30 or 30%

This would be presented as follows:

LAT Co.
Income Statement
For Year Ended, December 31, 198X

Net Sales	$10,000		100%
Cost of Sales	4,000		40%
Gross Profit		$6,000	60%
Operating Expenses:			
Selling Expenses	$ 2,000	20%	
General Expenses	1,000	10%	
Total Operating Expenses		3,000	30%
Net Income		$3,000	30%

16.3 STATISTICAL METHODS

The accountant uses information, both internal and external, as a basis from which to make decisions regarding the direction and control of the various activities of the firm. It is important that the financial manager be familiar with certain arithmetic tools that may be used to organize and summarize this data into meaningful forms once it has been accumulated.

Ratios

One of the ways in which numbers can be compared is by expressing the relationship of one number to another (or others). This is known as a *ratio*.

When two numbers are to be compared, the ratio may be found by placing one number (first term) over the other number (second term) and reducing the resulting fraction to lowest terms.

EXAMPLE 11

If there are 80 male employees and 60 female employees in a plant, what is the ratio of male to female?

$$\frac{80}{60} = \frac{4}{3} \text{ or } 4:3$$

An alternative way of expressing this relationship is to simply divide the first term by the second term. The answer will therefore always be $x:1$.

EXAMPLE 12

The total assets of Agin Company are $80,000 and their liabilities are $50,000. What is the ratio of assets to liabilities?

$$\frac{\$80,000}{50,000} = \frac{8}{5} = 1.6:1$$

Ratios are often a common means of analyzing relationships, particularly on accounting statements. One of the most common is known as the *current ratio* and represents the ratio of current assets to current liabilities. This is a measure of business liquidity because it tells how many times over the company could pay its current debts. Another common application of ratios is the ratio of owners' equity to long-term debt. These and other ratios are convenient signposts from which the directions a business is going can be determined.

EXAMPLE 13

Company A has current assets of $50,000 and current liabilities of $20,000. Their current ratio is computed as:

$$\frac{50,000}{20,000} = 2.5:1$$

This shows that the firm has $2.50 of current assets for every $1.00 it owes in current liabilities.

EXAMPLE 14

The total stockholders' equity is $64,000, while the company's liabilities are $135,000. What is the ratio of stockholders' equity to liabilities?

$$\frac{64,000}{135,000} = 0.47:1$$

Averages

A means of presenting large quantities of numbers in summary form is accomplished by the use of an average. Three measures of averages are discussed below.

1. *Mean.* The mean is the most popular and is computed for a particular list of figures by adding the figures and dividing by the number of figures in the list. The equation used to compute the mean is

$$M = \frac{S}{N}$$

where M = mean
S = sum of the figures in the list
N = number of figures in the list

EXAMPLE 15

A group of employees earn the following weekly salaries:

Salary	Number of Employees	Total Amount Earned
$ 90	2	$ 180
100	1	100
110	2	220
120	4	480
130	2	260
140	1	140
150	1	150
	13	$1,530

The mean salary is computed as follows:

$$M = \frac{S}{N} = \frac{\$1,530}{13} = \$117 \quad \text{(rounded off)}$$

2. *Median.*   The median is the number that divides a group in half. In order to calculate the median, it is first necessary to list the figures in ascending or descending order. When there is an odd number of figures, the number that separates the list into two equal groups, so that the number of figures in one group is equal to the number of figures in the other group, must be located. When there is an even number of figures, the number that is midway between the middle two items is located. The formula used in the computation of the median is

$$M = \frac{N + 1}{2}$$

where M = median

N = number of figures in the list

EXAMPLE 16

From Example 15, the median salary is computed as:

$$M = \frac{N + 1}{2} = \frac{13 + 1}{2} = 7 \quad \text{or} \quad \$120$$

because $120 is the seventh salary in the list of salaries, taking into account the number of employees who make each salary.

3. *Mode.*   The mode is the number that occurs most frequently in a series of figures.

EXAMPLE 17

In Example 15, the mode salary is $120, because it is the salary that occurs most frequently.

Index Numbers

The index number is used to compare business activities during one time period with similar activities during another time period. If the time period considered is a full year, a value of 100 percent is assigned to the base-year value of the item. Every subsequent year's value for that same item is expressed as a percentage of that base-year value.

EXAMPLE 18

Assume that the cost of food in 1977 (base year) had a value of 100, and 10 years later the value has increased to 142.6. This indicates that the value of the food increased 42.6 percent over that period of time.

EXAMPLE 19

Assume that you wish to construct an index for the number of accounting books sold in a given year. You select 1977 as the base period. In that year, the number of books sold was 6,000,000. Ten years later (in 1987), the sales were 9,000,000. Expressed as a percentage, the index number for 1987 would be 150.0. This figure is derived by dividing the increase in sales by the base period, multiplying by 100 to get the percent, and adding the percent to 100 [that is, $(3,000,000/6,000,000) \times 100 + 100 = 150$].

Summary

1. To help avoid the chance of error while adding decimals, arrange the numbers to be added with all decimal places _____ one another.

2. The relationship between one number and another in terms of hundredths is called a _____.

3. The relationship of one number to another is known as a _____.

4. A means of presenting large quantities of numbers in summary form is by the use of an
    _____ .

5. The most popular form of average is the _____ .

6. The _____ is the number that divides a group in half.

7. In the formula $M = \dfrac{N + 1}{2}$, the letter N is _____ .

8. The _____ is the number that occurs most frequently in a series of figures.

9. The method of comparing business activities during one time period with similar activities during another
    time period is accomplished by the use of _____ .

10. In computing index numbers, a value of 100 percent is assigned to the _____ year.

Answers: 1. underneath; 2. percent; 3. ratio; 4. average; 5. mean; 6. median; 7. the number of figures in the list;
8. mode; 9. index numbers; 10. base

Solved Problems

16.1   Add the following decimals:

$$11.24 + 6.535 + 9.4372 + 21.6$$

SOLUTION

$$
\begin{array}{r}
11.2400 \\
6.5350 \\
9.4372 \\
21.6000 \\
\hline
48.8122 \\
\end{array}
$$

Note: Adding zeros to the right of the decimal does not change the number.

16.2   The costs of three different fuels are (*a*) \$1.41, (*b*) \$1.4129, (*c*) \$1.4253. What would the total be if
all three were bought together?

SOLUTION

$$
\begin{array}{r}
1.4100 \\
1.4129 \\
1.4253 \\
\hline
\$4.2482 = \$4.25 \\
\end{array}
$$

16.3 The shipping department has two packages weighing 5.4 pounds and 3.891 pounds, respectively. What is their difference in weight?

SOLUTION

$$
\begin{array}{r}
5.400 \\
-3.891 \\
\hline
1.509 \text{ pounds}
\end{array}
$$

16.4 A company purchased 400 gallons of fuel at 0.4165 cent per gallon. How much did the fuel cost?

SOLUTION

$$
\begin{array}{r}
0.4165 \\
\times \quad 400 \\
\hline
166.6000 = \$166.60
\end{array}
$$

16.5 If the total cost of making 150.5 kilograms of chemicals is \$72, what is the cost of 1 kilogram?

SOLUTION

$$
150.5\overline{)72.0000} \quad 0.478 = 48\cent \text{ per kilogram}
$$

$$
\begin{array}{r}
6020 \\
\hline
11800 \\
10535 \\
\hline
12650
\end{array}
$$

16.6 Convert the following percentages to decimals: (*a*) 4%, (*b*) 14%, (*c*) 15.5%, (*d*) 126%.

SOLUTION

(*a*) .04; (*b*) .14; (*c*) .155; (*d*) 1.26

16.7 Convert the following percentages to fractions: (*a*) 4%, (*b*) 14%, (*c*) 15.5%, (*d*) 126%.

SOLUTION

(*a*) 4/100; (*b*) 14/100; (*c*) 155/1000; (*d*) 126/100

16.8 (*a*) If the cost of an item is \$82 and the selling price is \$100, what percent of the selling price is the cost? (*b*) What is the profit on sales in terms of a percent?

SOLUTION

(*a*) $\dfrac{82 \text{ (percentage)}}{100 \text{ (base)}} = 82\%$

(*b*)
$$
\begin{array}{l}
\$100 \quad \text{Selling price} \\
\underline{82} \quad \text{Cost} \\
\$\ 18 \quad \text{Profit}
\end{array}
$$

$\dfrac{18 \text{ (profit)}}{100 \text{ (sales)}} = 18\% \text{ profit}$

16.9 Determine, based on the information below:

(a) Percent of cost to sales.

(b) Percent of gross profit to sales.

(c) Percent of net profit to sales.

Income Statement

Sales Income	$25,000
Cost of Goods Sold	14,000
Gross Profit	$11,000
Operating Expenses	5,000
Net Profit	$ 6,000

SOLUTION

$$(a)\ \frac{14,000}{25,000} = 56\% \qquad (b)\ \frac{11,000}{25,000} = 44\% \qquad (c)\ \frac{6,000}{25,000} = 24\%$$

16.10 (a) The Silvergold Printing Company prints 200 sheets of hot type for every 40 sheets of cold type. What is the ratio of hot type to cold type?

(b) The total assets of G. Miller Co. is $60,000, and their liabilities total $26,000. What is the ratio of assets to liabilities?

SOLUTION

$$(a)\ \frac{200}{40} = 5:1\ \text{ratio} \qquad\qquad (b)\ \frac{60,000}{26,000} = 2.31:1$$

16.11 Below is a condensed balance sheet of the Ed Blanchard Summer Camp:

Balance Sheet

ASSETS

Current Assets	$46,500
Fixed Assets	24,000
Total Assets	$70,500

LIABILITIES

Current Liabilities	$20,000
Long-Term Liabilities	10,500
Total Liabilities	$30,500
Capital	40,000
Total Liabilities and Capital	$70,500

Determine the current ratio.

SOLUTION

$$\frac{46,500\ \text{(current assets)}}{20,000\ \text{(current liabilities)}} = 2.33:1$$

This shows that Blanchard has $2.33 of current assets for every $1.00 it owes in current liabilities.

16.12 The weekly salaries of five employees of the SCC Corp. are as follows: $88.–; $94.50; $106.20; $145.–; $192.30. What is the mean salary of this group?

SOLUTION

$$
\begin{array}{r}
88.00 \\
94.50 \\
106.20 \\
145.00 \\
192.30 \\
\hline
\$626.00 \div 5 = \$125.20 \quad \text{Mean salary}
\end{array}
$$

16.13 A glance at a company's payroll reveals the following information:

Salary	Number of Employees	Total Amount Earned
$100	4	$ 400
110	3	330
120	6	720
130	3	390
140	2	280
150	2	300
160	1	160
170	1	170
180	1	180
	23	$2,930

(a) Determine the mean salary.

(b) Determine the median salary.

(c) Determine the mode salary.

SOLUTION

(a) $2,930 \div 23 = \$127.39$

(b) $M = \dfrac{N + 1}{2} = \dfrac{23 + 1}{2} = 12$ figures down $= \$120$

(c) $120—the most repeated figure

16.14 (a) If the cost of automobiles is 148 percent of the base year, what does this indicate?

(b) In 1978, the base year, 800,000 units were sold. In 1988, 1,500,000 units were sold. What is the index number for year 1978 and year 1988?

SOLUTION

(a) This indicates that the cost of the automobile has risen 48 percent since the base year.

(b) 1978 = 100%   The base year
1988 = 187.5%   (700,000/800,000 × 100 + 100%)

Chapter 17

Pricing Merchandise

17.1 TRADE DISCOUNTS

When merchandise is offered for sale by manufacturers or wholesalers, a *list* or *catalog* price is set for each item. This represents the price that the ultimate consumer will pay for the item.

Rather than printing separate prices for each of the potential purchasers (wholesaler, retailer, consumer), the seller gives the various classes of buyers a separate discount sheet, detailing the discount offered to his or her class of purchaser. Thus, the trade discount is not a true discount but is considered to be an *adjustment of the price*.

The use of a list or catalog price also cuts down on the printing. If the seller wishes to change the price offered to the wholesaler or retailer, a revised discount schedule, using the original list or catalog price, would be sent. The list or catalog price also provides the retailer with a suggested list selling price for the item.

The price the buyer pays for the item (*net cost price*) is computed by multiplying the list or catalog price by the discount rate and then subtracting this discount from the list or catalog price.

EXAMPLE 1

A $250 (list price) television is sold to a wholesaler at a 20 percent trade discount. The cost to the wholesaler is:

Step 1		$250	List price
	×	20%	Trade discount percent
		$ 50	Trade discount
Step 2		$250	
	−	50	
		$200	Net cost price

Mathematically, this procedure may be simplified by multiplying the list or catalog price by the complement of the discount rate (the difference between the discount rate and 100 percent).

EXAMPLE 2

	$250	List price
×	80%	(100% − 20%)
	$200	Net cost price

Transportation costs (if applicable) are not subject to a trade discount and would be added to the net cost price.

EXAMPLE 3

A $250 (list price) television is sold to a wholesaler at a 20 percent trade discount. Transportation charges on the shipment total $10. The net cost price is:

		$250	List price
	×	80%	(100% − 20%)
		$200	
Add	+	10	Transportation charges
		$210	Net cost price including transportation

17.2 CHAIN DISCOUNTS

Rather than give varying increasing single discounts to different classes of purchasers, some companies use chain discounts. These have the advantage of appearing to be higher and emphasizing to the buyer the fact that she or he receives *more* than one discount.

When using chain discounts, there are two methods that may be used to compute the net cost price:

1. Determine a *single equivalent discount* and then proceed to compute the net cost price as illustrated earlier. This method is also useful for companies that wish to compare varying discount policies of competing companies.

    To compute an equivalent discount, *multiply* the complements of each of the discounts (100 percent − discount) together and *subtract* the result from 100 percent. For example, the single discount equivalent of 10 percent and 20 percent is computed as

    Step 1. $(100\% - 10\%) \times (100\% - 20\%)$
    Step 2. $0.90 \times 0.80 = 0.72$
    Step 3.   Equivalent discount $= 100\% - 72\% = 28\%$

EXAMPLE 4

A stereo set is offered to wholesalers at a list price of $600, *less* chain discounts of 25 percent and 20 percent. What is the net cost price?

1. $(100\% - 25\%) \times (100\% - 20\%)$
2. $(.75) \times (.80) = .60$
3. Equivalent Discount $= 100\% - 60\% = 40\%$
4. Discount $= \$600 \times .40 = \$240$
5. Net Cost Price $= \$600 - \$240 = \$360$

Alternative method:

1. $\$600 \times .25 = \$150$ Price × first discount percentage
2. $\$600 - \$150 = \$450$ Price minus first discount
3. $\$450 \times .20 = \$90$ Discounted price × second discount percentage
4. $\$450 - \$90 = \$360$ Discounted price minus second discount

2. The net cost price can be computed directly by *multiplying* the list price by the complement of each of the discounts in the series. It does not make any difference in what order the discounts are arranged.

EXAMPLE 5

Assume the same information as in Example 4:

1. $(100\% - 25\%) \times (100\% - 20\%)$
2. $(0.75) \times (0.80) = 0.60$
3. $\$600 \times 0.60 = \$360$

17.3 CASH DISCOUNTS

Cash discounts are an inducement offered to the buyer to encourage payment of a bill within a specified period of time. They tend to narrow the gap between the time of sale and the time of collection, which can become a source of cash-flow difficulties for the seller.

Cash discounts are referred to as *terms* and may appear on a bill as 2/10, net 30,

where   2 = the percent of the discount
         10 = number of days within which the buyer must pay in order to qualify for the discount
    net 30 = number of days at which payment must be made in full

EXAMPLE 6

An invoice of $300, dated March 6, has terms of 2/10, net 30. If payment is made on March 16, the net amount is

1. $300 × 2% = $6 discount
2. $300 − $6 = $294

If payment is made on March 17, the entire $300 is due.

Some companies offer a varied cash discount depending on when payment is made—for example, 2/10, 1/20, net 30. This means that the company offers a 2 percent discount if the buyer pays within 10 days; if he or she pays after 10 days, but within 20 days of purchase, he or she gets a 1 percent discount; the net amount is due within 30 days.

EXAMPLE 7

A $600 invoice dated April 6 has terms of 3/10, 2/15, net 30. If paid by April 16, the discount will be $18. If paid after April 16, but by April 21, the discount will be $12. The entire bill of $600 must be paid by May 6.

Although in most cases the cash discount period is computed from the "invoice" or purchase date, the date may also be computed from either the date of *receipt of the goods* (ROG) or starting with the *end of the month* (EOM).

ROG is used primarily when there is a significant gap between the date of the sale and the delivery date. This eliminates the necessity for the buyer to pay for goods before receiving them in order to get a discount.

EOM is used primarily as a convenience with traditional end-of-month billing practices followed by most companies.

EXAMPLE 8

The last date on which a discount can be taken is shown below:

	Invoice Date	Goods Received	Terms	Last Day on Which Discount Can Be Taken
Invoice $500	Oct. 3	Oct. 8	2/10, n/30 ROG	Oct. 18
Invoice $700	Oct. 3	Oct. 8	2/10, n/30 EOM	Nov. 10*

*10 days after the end of month (EOM).

Trade and Cash Discounts

When both trade and cash discounts are offered, the cash discount is computed *after* the trade discount has been taken.

EXAMPLE 9

An invoice of $300, dated March 17 with a trade discount of 30 percent and terms 2/10, n/30, was paid on March 20. The amount of the payment is computed as

$$
\begin{array}{ll}
\$300 & \text{List price} \\
\times\ 70\% & (100\% - 30\%) \\
\hline
\$210 & \text{Net cost} \\
\times\ 2\% & \text{Cash discount percent} \\
\hline
\$4.20 & \text{Cash discount}
\end{array}
$$

$$\$210 - \$4.20 = \$205.80 = \text{amount of payment}$$

17.4   MARKUP

In order to make a profit, each company must sell its products for more than they cost. The difference between cost and selling price is referred to as *markup*.

EXAMPLE 10

A washing machine selling for $300 costs the seller $200. The markup is $100.

Percent Markup

Markup is generally expressed in terms of a percent:

$$\text{Percent} = \frac{\text{percentage}}{\text{base}}$$

where   percent = markup percent

        percentage = markup

           base = selling price or cost

17.5   SELLING PRICE AS A BASE: COMPUTING PERCENT MARKUP

EXAMPLE 11

A book selling for $8 cost the seller $6. What is the percent markup based on selling price?

$$\text{Percent} = \frac{\$2}{\$8} \quad (\$8 - \$6)$$

Percent markup = 25%

Computing Cost

In order to use the percent markup to compute either the cost or the selling price, the selling price formula must be reexamined in terms of percents. It should be noted that the base is 100 percent.

EXAMPLE 12

A book selling for $8 has a markup percent of 25 percent. What is the cost?

$$25\% = \frac{x}{8}$$

$$x = 25\% \times \$8$$

$$= \$2 \text{ (markup)} \quad \text{Cost} = \$8 - \$2 = \$6$$

Computing Selling Price

EXAMPLE 13

A book has a markup percent of $2, which is 25 percent of the selling price. What is the selling price?

$$25\% = \frac{\$2}{x}$$

$$25\%x = \$2$$

$$0.25x = \$2$$

$$x = \$8$$

17.6   COST AS A BASE

When cost is used as a base for markup percent, it is sometimes referred to as a *markon*. It has the advantage of expressing clearly the fact that the price increase is *directly* added on to its base (cost).

Computing Percent Markup

$$\text{Percent markup} = \frac{\$ \text{ markup}}{\text{cost}}$$

EXAMPLE 14

A record album that sells for $6 cost $4. What is the percent markup based on cost?

$$\text{Percent markup} = \frac{\$2}{\$4} \quad (\$6 - \$4)$$

$$= 50\%$$

EXAMPLE 15   Computing the Cost

If an item selling for $72 has a 20 percent markup on cost, what is the cost?

$$\text{Selling price} = \text{cost} + \text{markup}$$

$$\$72 \quad\quad = 100\% + 20\%$$

$$\$72 \quad\quad = 120\%$$

$$\$72 \div 1.20 = \text{Cost}$$

$$\$60 \quad\quad = \text{Cost}$$

Computing Selling Price

In order to compute the selling price from either the cost or the markup, you once again must look at the formula for selling price from the point of view of percents. The cost (base) is 100 percent.

EXAMPLE 16

If a sweater that costs $10 has a markup of 30 percent on cost, what is the selling price?

$$\text{Selling price} = \text{cost} + \$ \text{ markup}$$

$$= \$10 + (0.30)(\$10)$$

$$= \$10 + \$3$$

$$= \$13$$

17.7 MARKDOWNS

Once the price of an item has been established, there is no guarantee that this will represent the ultimate selling price. Downward adjustments of the selling price are often necessary to induce customers to buy. These are referred to as *markdowns*. The seller, in effect, is forced, because of perhaps overstocking or too high a selling price, to abandon the original price. Markdowns take the form of *direct price reductions*.

EXAMPLE 17

A suit listing for $150 was marked down 30 percent. What is the new selling price?

$$\$150 \times 30\% = \$45 \text{ markdown}$$

$$\$150 - \$45 = \$105 \text{ selling price}$$

17.8 TURNOVER—RATIOS FOR INVENTORY

The firm's investment in inventory also has a direct effect on its working capital. If there is excess inventory, it means that funds are tied up in inventory that could be used more profitably elsewhere. Also, additional costs are being incurred for storage, insurance, and property taxes, not to mention the danger of a price decline and obsolescence of goods.

Whenever any consideration is given to pricing and profit planning, it is important to consider the *merchandise inventory turnover*. This is the number of times the average inventory is sold during a year. The turnover shows how quickly the inventory is moving. Assuming that the company maintains a reasonable inventory for its type of business, a high turnover rate (such as for a grocery store) indicates that only a relatively small profit need be added to the price of each item to maintain a high profit overall. Turnover is also a good indication of the amount of working capital that needs to be tied up at one time in inventory.

Merchandise inventory turnover can be computed from the cost of goods sold section of the income statement. It should be noted, however, that the turnover is an *annual* rate and should not be computed from interim statements.

$$\text{Merchandise inventory turnover} = \frac{\text{cost of goods sold}}{\text{average merchandise inventory*}}$$

---

* Beginning inventory + ending inventory
  2

EXAMPLE 18

Cost of Goods Sold:		
Merchandise Inventory, Jan. 1	$10,000	
Net Purchases	85,000	
Merchandise Available for Sale	$95,000	
Merchandise Inventory, Dec. 31	20,000	
Cost of Goods Sold		$75,000

$$\text{Merchandise Inventory Turnover} = \frac{\$75,000}{15,000^*} = 5$$

_____

$$* \frac{\$10,000 \text{ (beg.)} + \$20,000 \text{ (end)}}{2}$$

In a retail business, such as a department store, turnover may effectively be computed either by departments or by classes of items. This can be accomplished by using the following turnover formula, which will yield approximately the same turnover rate as above:

$$\text{Merchandise inventory turnover} = \frac{\text{sales in units}}{\text{average inventory in units}^*}$$

_____

$$* \frac{\text{Beginning inventory} + \text{ending inventory}}{2}$$

EXAMPLE 19

Rosedale Speciality Shop sells dresses in four colors, red, blue, white, and pink, all of which sell for the same price. What is the turnover for each color as computed from the data below? What, if any, problems does the turnover analysis reveal?

	Sales in Units	Beginning Inventory	End Inventory
Red	600	75	125
Blue	800	140	120
White	300	210	190
Pink	900	200	150

$$\text{Red turnover} = \frac{600}{100} = 6$$

$$\text{Blue turnover} = \frac{800}{130} = 6.15$$

$$\text{White turnover} = \frac{300}{200} = 1.5$$

$$\text{Pink turnover} = \frac{900}{175} = 5.14$$

The white dress should be eliminated because of the low rate of turnover.

NUMBER OF DAYS' SALES IN INVENTORY

The relationship between inventory and cost of goods sold can also be expressed as the number of days' sales in inventory. In this ratio, the inventory at the end of the year is divided by the average daily cost of goods sold. The latter figure is determined by dividing the cost of goods sold by 365. The number of days' sales in inventory provides a rough measure of the length of time required to buy, sell, and then replace the inventory.

EXAMPLE 20

The Baker Company
Turnover of Inventory

Cost of Goods Sold	$750,000
Merchandise Inventory:	
Beginning of Year	$ 84,200
End of Year	130,100
Total	$214,300
Average	$107,150
Turnover of Inventory	7.0*

* 750,000 ÷ 107,150

The average daily cost of goods sold is $750,000 ÷ 365 = $2,055.

The Baker Company
Number of Days' Sales in Inventory

	198X
Inventory at End of Year	$130,100
Average Daily Cost of Goods Sold	2,055*
Number of Days' Sales in Inventory	63.3

* 750,000 ÷ 365

Summary

1. An adjustment of the retail price is known as a _____ .

2. A substitute for varying increasing sinngle discounts to different classes of purchases is referred to as a _____ .

3. An inducement offered to the buyer to encourage payment of his or her bill within a specific period of time is called a _____ .

4. Cash discounts are referred to as _____ .

5. The "2" in 2/10, n/30 is the _____ .

6. The abbreviation ROG stands for _____ .

7. The difference between cost and selling price is referred to as _____ .

8. When cost is used as a base for markup percent, it is sometimes known as _____ .

9. Downward adjustments of the selling price are often necessary to induce customers to buy and are referred to as _____ .

10. In order to give consideration to pricing and profit planning, it is important to consider the _____ .

Answers: 1. trade discount; 2. chain discount; 3. cash discount; 4. terms; 5. percent discount; 6. receipt of goods; 7. markup; 8. markon; 9. markdowns; 10. merchandise inventory turnover

Solved Problems

17.1 Equipment of $400 is sold to a retailer at a 25 percent trade discount. What is the retailer's cost?

SOLUTION

$400	List price	$400	
× 25%	Trade discount	− 100	
$100	Trade discount	$300	Net cost

17.2 If transportation of $20 were added to the above purchase, what would the net cost be?

SOLUTION

$$
\begin{array}{ll}
\$300 & \\
+\ \ 20 & \text{Transportation} \\
\hline
\$320 &
\end{array}
$$

Transportation costs are added to the net cost of the item and are not subject to trade discounts.

17.3 Determine the single equivalent discount in each of the following examples: (a) 20%, 5%; (b) 25%, 10%.

SOLUTION

(a) 24% (100% − 20%) × (100% − 5%) = 80% × 95% = 76%
        100% − 76% = 24%

(b) 32.5% (100% − 25%) × (100% − 10%) = 75% × 90% = 67.5%
        100% − 67.5% = 32.5%

17.4 Laura Edelstein bought $800 of supplies for her company, less chain discounts of 30 percent and 20 percent. (a) What is the single equivalent discount? (b) What is the net cost to the company?

SOLUTION

(a) (100% − 30%) × (100% − 20%) = 70% × 80% = 56%
      Single equivalent discount = 44% (100% − 56%)

(b) $800 × 44% = $352
      Net cost = $448 ($800 − $352)

17.5 Company A gives terms of 20 percent discounts on all items purchased. Company B gives chain discounts of 15 percent and 10 percent. If J. Snyder bought $500 of supplies, how much would he save by dealing with Company B rather than with Company A?

SOLUTION

Company A	Company B
$500 \times 20\% = \$100$ discount	$(100\% - 15\%) \times (100\% - 10\%)$
	$85\% \times 90\% = 76.5\%$
	$500 \times 23.5\% = \$117.50$ discount

$$
\begin{array}{rl}
\$117.50 & \text{Company B} \\
- \quad 100.00 & \text{Company A} \\
\hline
\$ \ 17.50 & \text{Savings}
\end{array}
$$

17.6   Determine the last day allowable for a company to take advantage of the full discount.

	Term	Date of Order	Date of Delivery
(a)	2/10, n/30	June 4	June 8
(b)	2/10, 1/15, n/30	June 4	June 8
(c)	2/10, n/30, ROG	June 4	June 8
(d)	2/10, n/30, EOM	June 4	June 8

SOLUTION

(a)   June 14

(b)   June 14 (full); June 19 (partial discount)

(c)   June 18

(d)   July 10

17.7   Determine the amount to be paid under the following different situations:

	Amount	Date of Purchase	Goods Received	Terms	Date of Payment Made
(a)	$600	Apr. 4	Apr. 11	2/10, n/30	Apr. 10
(b)	$700	May 1	May 14	2/10, n/30, ROG	May 23
(c)	$800	June 6	June 12	2/10, 1/20, n/30	June 25
(d)	$900	July 20	July 24	2/10, n/30, EOM	Aug. 9

SOLUTION

(a) $588

(b) $686   Date of receipt determines discount period.

(c) $792   1 percent discount allowed. Paid after 10 days (2 percent) but before 20 days.

(d) $882   10 days after end of month is allowed for discount taking.

17.8   What amount will be paid to the seller if goods bought on Sept. 6 for $500, terms 2/10, 1/15, n/30 were paid on (a) Sept. 10, (b) Sept. 20, (c) Sept. 30?

SOLUTION

(a) $490 ($500 less 2%); (b) $495 ($500 less 1%); (c) $500 (no discount).

17.9 Lester Washington bought equipment for his plant on October 17 for $3,000, subject to terms 2/10, n/30, EOM. What amount will he pay if his payment is made on (*a*) October 24, (*b*) October 31, (*c*) November 6, (*d*) November 10?

SOLUTION

(*a*) $2940 ($3,000 − $60); (*b*) $2940; (*c*) $2940; (*d*) $2940.

Mr. Washington has 10 days after the end of the month to take advantage of the discount.

17.10 H. Dryer bought $900 of goods for his company on March 5, subject to a 25 percent trade discount, bearing terms 2/10, 1/20, n/30. If the invoice was paid on March 11, how much was his payment?

SOLUTION

$$\begin{array}{ll} \$900 & \text{List price} \\ \underline{25\%} & \text{Trade discount} \\ \$225 & \text{Discount} \end{array}$$

$$\begin{array}{ll} \$900 - \$225 = \$675.00 & \\ \underline{13.50} & (\$675 - 2\% \text{ discount}) \\ \$661.50 & \text{Net payment} \end{array}$$

17.11 (*a*) Jankowich Corporation sells its $4 pens for $6. What is their percent markup?
     (*b*) Stationary selling for $10 has a markup of 25 percent. What is the cost?

SOLUTION

(*a*)
$$\text{Percent} = \frac{(\$6 - \$4)}{6} = \frac{2}{6} = 33\tfrac{1}{3}\%$$

(*b*)
$$25\% = \frac{x}{10}$$

$$x = 25\% \times \$10$$
$$x = \$2.50 \text{ profit}$$
$$\$10 - \$2.50 = \$7.50 \text{ cost}$$

17.12 Textbooks yield a profit of $3, which represents 20 percent of the selling price. What is the selling price?

SOLUTION

$$20\% = \frac{\$3}{x}$$

$$20\% x = \$3$$

$$x = \$15$$

17.13 Supplies selling for $25 per box have a markup on cost (markon) of 25 percent. What is the cost of one box?

SOLUTION

$$\text{Selling price} = \text{cost} + \text{profit}$$
$$\$25 \quad\quad = 100\% + 25\%$$
$$\$25 \quad\quad = 125\%$$
$$\$25 \div 1.25 = \$20 \quad \text{cost}$$

17.14 A necklace that costs $24 is marked up 25 percent on cost. What is the selling price?

SOLUTION

$$\text{Selling price} = \text{cost} + \text{profit}$$
$$= \$24 + 25\%$$
$$= \$24 + \$6$$
$$= \$30$$

17.15 Given the following information, determine the merchandise inventory turnover.

Cost of Goods Sold:		
Merchandise Inventory, Jan. 1	$22,000	
Purchases (net)	73,000	
Available for Sale	$95,000	
Merchandise Inventory, Dec. 31	34,000	
Cost of Goods Sold		$61,000

SOLUTION

The formula is:

$$\text{Inventory turnover} = \frac{\text{cost of goods sold}}{\text{average inventory*}}$$

$$\text{Turnover} = \frac{61,000}{28,000} = 2.2$$

$$*\frac{\$22,000 + \$34,000}{2}$$

17.16 The Walzck Company has a division that sells three unrelated products. Determine from the information below the turnover for each product. If one product had to be dropped, which would it be? Why?

Product	Sales in Units	Inventory (beginning)	Inventory (end)
A	700	50	150
B	800	180	140
C	800	500	550

SOLUTION

Product A $\dfrac{700}{100*} = 7$

Product B $\dfrac{800}{160*} = 5$

Product C $\dfrac{800}{525*} = 1.5$

---

*Average of beginning and ending inventory.

Product C should be eliminated because it has a very low turnover rate.

17.17 From the selected information below, determine:

(a) Turnover of inventory

(b) Average daily cost of goods sold

(c) Number of days' sales in inventory

Cost of Goods Sold	$800,000
Inventory (beginning)	104,000
Inventory (ending)	96,000

SOLUTION

(a) $\dfrac{800,000 \quad \text{(cost of goods sold)}}{100,000 \quad \text{(average inventory)}} = 8$

(b) $\$800,000 \div 365 \text{ days} = \$2,192$

(c) $\$96,000 \div \$2,192 = 43.8 \text{ days' sales in inventory}$

Examination IV

1. Compute the following:

   (a) 78.4 + 9.23 + 806.1235

   (b) 160.2 − 58.34

   (c) 107.7 × 15.12

   (d) 246.7 ÷ 1.92

2. Convert $7\frac{1}{4}$, $21\frac{1}{8}$, and $\frac{1}{5}$ (a) to decimals and (b) to percents.

3. Based on the information below, determine

   (a) The mean salary

   (b) The median salary

   (c) The mode salary

Number of Employees	Salary	Total
1	$100	$ 100
3	110	330
5	120	600
4	130	520
2	140	280
2	150	300
1	160	160
1	170	170
1	180	180
20		$2,640

4. Equipment bought for $3,200 on April 21, terms 2/10, n/30, was subject to chain discounts of 20 percent and 10 percent. It was paid for on April 30. What was the net cost of the equipment?

5. Determine the amount to be paid in each transaction below.

	Amount	Invoice Date	Receipt of Goods	Terms	Date of Payment
(a)	$600	June 16	June 19	2/10, n/30, ROG	June 27
(b)	$700	Aug. 15	Aug. 15	2/10, n/30, EOM	Sept. 10
(c)	$800	Aug. 19	Aug. 21	2/10, n/30, EOM	Sept. 12

6. (a) Ink selling for $10 a case cost $8. What is the percent markup based on (1) selling price and (2) cost?

   (b) If an item has a 30 percent markup on cost and sells for $260, what is the cost?

298

7. A partial income statement is reproduced below. Determine

(*a*)   Turnover rate

(*b*)   Average daily cost of goods sold

(*c*)   Number of days' sales in inventory

Cost of Goods Sold:		
Inventory (January)	$ 80,000	
Net Purchases	160,000	
Available for Sale	$240,000	
Inventory (December)	40,000	
Cost of Goods Sold		$200,000

Answers to Examination IV

1. (*a*)
```
   78.4000
    9.2300
  806.1235
  893.7535
```
(*b*)
```
   160.20
 -  58.34
   101.86
```
(*c*)
```
    107.7
    15.12
    2154
    1077
    5385
    1077
  1628.424
```
(*d*)
```
              12.8
  1.92)246.700
       192
       547
       384
      1630
      1536
       940
       768
```

2. (*a*)   7.25; 21.125; .20
  (*b*)   725%; 2112.5%; 20%

3. (*a*) $132 ($2640 ÷ 20)
  (*b*) $130 (20 ÷ 2) The 10th and 11th employees down. The middle number (as many numbers above as below).
  (*c*) $120—the most frequent number.

4. $3,200

```
    28%    (single equivalent discount)
  $ 896
```

```
  $3,200
  -  896
  $2,304
```

```
  $2,304
     2%    Discount
   46.08
```

```
  2,304.00
  -  46.08
  2,257.92    Net cost
```

5. (*a*) $588; (*b*) $686; (*c*) $800—no discount allowed

6. (*a*)   (1) $\frac{2}{10}$ = 20%
          (2) $\frac{2}{8}$ = 25%

  (*b*) $260 = cost + 30%
        $260 = 130%
        $200 = cost

7. (*a*) $\dfrac{200,000}{60,000}$ = 3.3
  (*b*) $200,000 ÷ 365 = $548 − average daily cost of goods sold
  (*c*) $40,000 ÷ 548 = 73 days' sales in inventory

Glossary of Bookkeeping and Accounting Terms

Account.   A record of the increases and decreases of transactions summarized in an accounting form.

Account numbers.   Numbers assigned to accounts according to the chart of accounts.

Accountant.   An individual who classifies and summarizes business transactions and interprets their effects on the business.

Accounting.   The process of analyzing, classifying, recording, summarizing, and interpreting business transactions.

Accounts Payable.   A liability account used by the business to keep a record of amounts due to creditors.

Accounts receivable.   Amount that is to be collected from customers.

Accrual basis.   An accounting system in which revenue is recognized only when earned, and expense is recognized only when incurred.

Additional paid-in capital.   Amounts paid in beyond the par value of stock.

Adjusting entries.   Journal entries made at the end of an accounting period in order that the accounts will reflect the correct balance in the financial statements.

Articles of copartnership.   The written agreement among the partners that contains provisions on the formation, capital contribution, profit and loss distribution, admission, and withdrawal of partners.

Articles of incorporation.   A charter submitted to the state by individuals wishing to form a corporation and containing significant information about the proposed business.

Assets.   Properties owned that have monetary value.

Authorized shares.   Shares of stock that a corporation is permitted to issue (sell) under its articles of incorporation.

Average.   A means of presenting large quantities of numbers in summary form.

Balance sheet.   A statement that shows the assets, liabilities, and capital of a business entity at a specific date. Also known as the statement of financial position.

Bank reconciliation.   A statement that reconciles the difference between the bank's balance and the balance of a company's books.

Bank service charge.   A monthly charge made by the bank for keeping a depositor's checking account in operation.

Bank statement.   A periodic statement sent by the bank to its customers that presents the current balances of the cash account and provides a detailed list of all the payments made and all receipts received for a certain period of time.

Blank endorsement.   Consists of only the name of the endorser on the back of the check.

Board of directors.   Elected by the stockholders within the framework of the articles of incorporation, the board's duties include appointing corporate officers, determining company policies, and distributing profits.

Bonds.   A form of long-term debt in which the corporation agrees to pay interest periodically and to repay the principal at a stated future date.

Book value per share.   The amount that would be distributed to each share of stock if a corporation were to be dissolved.

Bookkeeper.   An individual who earns a living by recording the financial activities of a business and who is concerned with the techniques involving the recording of transactions.

Call privilege.   Gives an issuing stock company the right to redeem stock at a later date for a predetermined price.

Cancelled checks.   Checks that have been paid by the bank during the month and returned to the depositor.

Capital.   What an individual or business is worth. Also known as owners' equity.

Capital Stock.   The account that shows the par value of the stock issued by the corporation.

Cash disbursements journal.   A special journal used to record transactions involving cash payments.

Cash receipts journal.   A special journal used to record transactions involving cash receipts.

Certified check.   A check whose payment has been guaranteed by the bank.

Chart of accounts.   A listing of the accounts by title and numerical designation.

Check.   A written document directing the firm's bank to pay a specific amount of money to an individual.

Checking account.   An account with a bank that allows the depositor to make payments to others from his or her bank balance.

Closing entry.   An entry made at the end of a fiscal period in order to make the balance of a temporary account equal to zero.

Closing the ledger.   A process of transferring balances of income and expense accounts through the summary account to the capital account.

Combined cash journal.   The journal with which all cash transactions are recorded.

Common stock.   That part of the capital stock that does not have special preferences or rights.

Computer.   A group of interconnected electronic machines capable of processing data.

Computer hardware.   A term that refers to the actual physical components that make up an installation.

Computer programs.   A set of instructions developed by a programmer that tells the computer what to do, how to do it, and in what sequence it should be done.

Computer software.   The collection of programs and supplementary materials used by personnel to give the computer its instructions.

Controlling account.   The account in the general ledger that summarizes the balances of a subsidiary ledger.

Conversion privilege.   Given stockholders the option to convert preferred stock into common stock.

Corporation.   A business organized by law and viewed as an entity separate from its owners and creditors.

Cost of goods sold.   Inventory at the beginning of a fiscal period plus net purchases, less inventory at the end of the fiscal period. Also known as cost of sales.

Credit.   An amount entered on the right side of an account. Abbreviation is Cr.

Credit memorandum.   A receipt indicating the seller's acceptance to reduce the amount of a buyer's debt.

Current assets.   Assets that are expected to be realized in cash, sold, or consumed during the normal fiscal cycle of a business.

Current liabilities.   Debts that are due within a short period of time, usually consisting of 1 year, and which are normally paid from current assets.

Debit.   An amount entered on the left side of an account. Abbreviation is Dr.

Deposit in transit.   Cash deposited and recorded by the company, but too late to be recorded by the bank.

Deposit ticket.   A document showing the firm's name, its account number, and the amount of money deposited into the bank.

Discounted notes receivable.   A term used to describe notes receivable sold to a bank and being held liable for maturity if the maker defaults.

Dishonored check.   A check that the bank refuses to pay because the writer does not have sufficient funds in his or her checking account.

Dishonored note.   A note that the maker fails to pay at the time of maturity.

Double-entry accounting.   An almost universal system that produces equal debit and credit entries for every transaction.

Draft.   An order by the seller to the buyer stating that the buyer must pay a certain amount of money to a third party.

Drawing.   The taking of cash or goods out of a business by the owner for personal use. Also known as a withdrawal.

Earnings statement.   A stub attached to an employee's payroll check that provides the employee with a record of the amount earned and a detailed list of deductions.

Employee.   An individual who works for compensation for an employer.

EOM.   Term used to denote the end of the month.

Endorsement.   The placing of a signature on the back of a check that is to be deposited or cashed.

Endorsement in full.   A type of endorsement that states that the check can be cashed or transferred only on the order of the person named in the endorsement.

Expenses.   The decrease in capital caused by the business's revenue-producing operations.

Face of note.   The amount of a note.

Federal unemployment tax.   A tax paid by employers only. Used to supplement state unemployment benefits.

FICA taxes.   Social Security taxes collected in equal amounts from both the employee and the employer. These proceeds are paid into a fund that provides disability and old-age payments. FICA stands for Federal Insurance Contributions Act.

Fiscal period.   A period of time covered by the entire accounting cycle, usually consisting of 12 consecutive months.

Footing.   The recording in pencil of the temporary total of one side of a T account.

Goodwill.   An intangible asset that results from the expectation that the business has the ability to produce an above-average rate of earnings compared to other businesses in the same industry.

Gross pay.   The pay rate, arrives at through negotiation between the employer and the employee, at which employees are paid.

Gross profit.   Net sales minus cost of goods sold.

Imprest system.   A fund established for a fixed petty cash amount and periodically reimbursed by a single check for amounts expended.

Income statement.   A summary of the revenue, expenses, and net income of a business entity for a specific period of time. Also known as profit and loss statement.

Index number.   Used to compare business activities during one time period with a similar activity during another time period.

Interest.   Money paid for the use or borrowing of money.

Interest-bearing note.   A note in which the maker has agreed to pay the face of the note with interest.

Interest rate.   A percentage of the principal that is paid for the use of money borrowed.

Journal.   The book of original entry for accounting data. It is the book in which the accountant originally records business transactions.

Journalizing.   A process of recording business transactions in the journal.

Ledger.   The complete set of accounts for a business entity. It is used to classify and summarize transactions and to prepare data for financial statements.

Liabilities.   Amounts owed to outsiders.

Long-term liabilities.   Debts that do not have to be paid immediately but are usually paid over a long period of time, normally more than 1 year.

Loss.   The amount by which total costs exceed total income.

Maker. An individual who signs a promissory note agreeing to make payment.

Markdown. Downward adjustments of the selling price. Used to induce customers to buy.

Markon. The percent increase in selling price, when cost is used as a base for markup percent.

Markup. The difference between cost and selling price.

Maturity date. The date a note is to be paid.

Maturity value. The face of the note plus interest accrued until the due date.

Mean. The most popular method of averaging a group of values. It is accomplished by adding up the values and dividing their sum by the number of values given.

Median. The number that divides a group in half.

Merchandise inventory. Represents the value of goods on hand, either at the beginning or end of the accounting period.

Merchandise inventory turnover. The number of times the average inventory is sold during a year. This ratio shows how quickly the inventory is moving.

MICR. Term standing for Magnetic Ink Character Recognition. These are numerical characters that can be read by both computers and individuals.

Mode. The number that occurs most frequently in a series of figures.

Net income. The increase in capital resulting from profitable operations of the business. It is the excess of revenue over expenses for the accounting period.

Net purchases. All purchases less returns and purchase discounts.

Net sales. Total amount of sales minus returns and sales discounts.

Opening entry. An entry made at the time a business is organized to record the assets, liabilities, and capital of the new firm.

Outstanding checks. Checks issued by the depositor but not yet presented to the bank for payment.

Outstanding stock. The number of shares authorized, issued, and in the hands of stockholders.

Par value. An arbitrary amount assigned to each share of capital stock of a given class. It has no correlation to the market value or selling price of the stock.

Partnership. An association of two or more persons to carry on as co-owners of a business for profit.

Payee. The individual that is to receive money from a negotiable instrument.

Payroll accounting. Accounting for payments of wages, salaries, and related payroll taxes.

Payroll earnings card. A card that shows payroll data and yearly cumulative earnings, as well as deductions, for each employee.

Payroll register. A specially designed form used at the close of each payroll period to summarize and compute the payroll for the period.

Payroll tax expense account. An account used for recording the employer's matching portion of the FICA tax and the federal and state unemployment tax.

Percent. The relationship between one number and another in terms of hundredths.

Post-closing trial balance. A trial balance made after the closing entries are completed. Only balance sheet items—that is, assets, liabilities, and capital—will appear on this statement.

Posting. The process of transferring information from the journal to the ledger for the purpose of summarizing.

Preferred stock. A class of corporate stock that carries certain privileges and rights not given to other shares.

Prepaid expenses. Current assets that represent expenses that have already been paid out, though were not yet consumed during the current period.

Present value. The face amount of the note plus accrued interest.

Proprietorship. A business owned by one person.

Purchase discount. A cash discount allowed for prompt payment of an invoice.

Purchase invoice. The source document prepared by the seller listing the items shipped, their cost, and the method of shipment.

Purchase Returns. An account used by the buyer to record the reduction granted by the seller for the return of merchandise.

Ratio. The relationship of two or more numbers to each other.

Real accounts. All balance sheet items—that is, assets, liabilities and capital—having balances that will be carried forward from one period to another.

Restrictive endorsement. A type of endorsement that limits the receiver of the check as to the use she or he can make of the funds collected.

Retained earnings. The accumulated earnings arising from profitable operations of the business.

Revenue. The increase in capital resulting from the delivery of goods or rendering of services by business.

ROG. Business term that stands for receipt of goods.

Running balance. The balance of an account after the recording of each transaction.

Salary. Business term used to refer to the compensation for administrative and managerial personnel.

Sales discount. A reduction from the original price, granted by the seller to the buyer.

Schedule of accounts payable. A detailed list of the amounts owed to each creditor.

Schedule of accounts receivable. A detailed list of the amount due from each customer.

Share of stock. Represents a unit of the stockholders' interest in the business.

Special journal. The book of original entry in which the accountant records specified types of transactions.

State unemployment taxes. Taxes to be paid only by employers, with rates and amounts differing among each state.

Stockholders. The owners of the business.

Subscribed shares. Shares that a buyer has contracted to purchase at a specific price on a certain date.

Subsidiary ledger. A group of accounts representing individual subdivisions of a controlling account.

T account. A form of ledger account that shows only the account title and the debit and credit sides.

Temporary accounts. Consist of revenue, expense, and drawing accounts that will have a zero balance at the end of the fiscal year.

Time clock. A clock that stamps an employee's time card to provide a printed record of when the employee arrives for work and departs for the day.

Trade discounts. This is not a true discount but an adjustment of the price. With it, a business can adjust a price at which it is willing to bill goods without changing the list price in a catalog.

Transaction. An event recorded in the accounting records that can be expressed in terms of money.

Treasury stock. Stock representing shares that have been issued and later reacquired by the corporation.

Trial balance. A two-column schedule that compares the total of all debit balances with the total of all credit balances.

Uniform Partnership Act. A law used to resolve all contested matters among partners of a partnership.

Unissued shares.   Authorized shares that have not been offered for sale.

Unlimited liability.   The right of creditors to claim any and all assets of a debtor in satisfaction of claims held against the business of the debtor.

Withholding Exemption Certificate.   Known as Form W-4, it specifies the number of exemptions claimed by each employee, allowing the employer to withhold some of the employee's money for income taxes and FICA taxes.

Worksheet.   An informal accounting statement that summarizes the trial balance and other information necessary to prepare financial statements.

Index